care at the end of the world

care at the end of the world

DREAMING OF INFRASTRUCTURE IN CRIP-OF-COLOR WRITING

jina b. kim

DUKE UNIVERSITY PRESS ⦂ *Durham and London* ⦂ 2025

Designed by Dave Rainey

Typeset in Arno Pro by Westchester Publishing Services

Library of Congress Cataloging-in-Publication Data
Names: Kim, Jina B. author
Title: Care at the end of the world : dreaming of infrastructure in crip-of-color writing / Jina B. Kim.
Description: Durham : Duke University Press, 2025. | Includes bibliographical references and index.
Identifiers: LCCN 2024033256 (print)
LCCN 2024033257 (ebook)
ISBN 9781478031710 paperback
ISBN 9781478028482 hardcover
ISBN 9781478060697 ebook
Subjects: LCSH: People with disabilities—Care | Sociology of disability | People with disabilities in literature | American literature—African American authors—History and criticism | American literature—Women authors—History and criticism | Queer theory
Classification: LCC HV1568 .K56 2025 (print) | LCC HV1568 (ebook) | DDC 362.4—dc23/eng/20250122
LC record available at HTTPS://lccn.loc.gov/2024033256
LC ebook record available at HTTPS://lccn.loc.gov/2024033257

Cover art by Tommi Parrish

Publication of this book is supported by Duke University Press's Scholars of Color First Book Fund.

TO LAUREN, WHO TAUGHT ME HOW TO DREAM

Contents

Acknowledgments

my honeyed kin
honeyed light
beneath the sky
    —Cameron Awkward-Rich, "Cento between the Ending and the End"

Somehow, the word *acknowledgment* doesn't feel like enough. When I consider all that made this book and my life possible, I think, "At the end of the world, let there be you" (from Danez Smith, "acknowledgments").[1] I look at my cat, Edie, curled up on my desk by the window, where she has kept me company since I began this project in 2013. I thumb through the book *Dirt and Desire: Reconstructing Southern Women's Writing, 1930–1990*, written by my first dissertation chair, Patsy Yaeger. Her words made me realize that scholarship could be beautiful. I reflect on my deep attachments to all the places that held this work, and me, as I wrote it: Georgia, Michigan, and now, Western Massachusetts. And in my mind's eye, I see my best friend Lauren, who is the home I return to always.

Care at the End of the World has benefited, too, from the support of many individuals, scholarly networks, institutions, and organizations. The Career Enhancement Fellowship from the Institute for Citizens and Scholars provided me with the financial support necessary to complete this project. Brown University's Center for the Study of Race and Ethnicity in America gave me invaluable community and scholarly feedback during the depths of COVID lockdown. I am grateful for the resources and financial support provided by my home institution, Smith College, via the Picker Fellowship and the Provost's Office. Following graduate school, the Consortium for Faculty Diversity postdoctoral fellowship gave me necessary time and space to further grow my work. Thank you to *Social Text* and *Multi-Ethnic Literatures of the United States* for publishing versions of what would become chapters 1 and 3. My endless gratitude goes to my devoted editor, Elizabeth Ault, who lovingly guided this project from beginning to end, and who also managed to make the process fun. A genuine thanks, also, to Benjamin Kossak, James Moore, and all the hardworking people at Duke University Press.

I want to extend my gratitude to the many interlocutors who provided invaluable commentary on this project at different stages. Thank you to my Institute for Citizens and Scholars fellowship mentor, Grace Kyungwon Hong, for carefully reading all of my chapters, buoying me with confidence, and providing vital feedback. This project is better because of her. Thank you to my developmental editor, Craig Willse, whose incredible insights helped me wrangle the project into shape. My appreciation goes out to my wonderful research assistant, Lily Sendroff, who provided invaluable help with citations. Deep gratitude to everyone who attended my Center for the Study of Race and Ethnicity in America chapter workshop: Leon Hilton, Stéphanie Larrieux, Kevin Quashie, Tricia Rose, Britt Rusert, and my fellow fellows. Thank you to the Alliance to Advance Liberal Arts Colleges gathering on queer- and trans-of-color critique for nourishing my spirit, and all the lovely comrades who organized and participated: Jih-Fei Cheng, Treva Ellison, Freda Fair, Paolo Flores Chico, Vivian Huang, Ren-yo Hwang, Elías Elena Krell, Rushaan Kumar, Ianna Hawkins Owen, Dora Silva Santana, Kyla Wazana Tompkins, Nishant Upadhyay, and Anna Martine Whitehead. Thank you to all of my writing group companions in the struggle: Sony Corañez Bolton, Verushka Gray, Ren-yo Hwang, Kei Kaimana, Dori Midnight (who called me a pomodoro top, a name that I cherish), Caitlin Pollock, and Stephanie Rosen. Thank you to the Midwest feminist disability studies summer retreats that allowed me to write prolifically, be on the beach, *and* have quality time with friends Juliann Anesi, Ally Day, Lezlie Frye, Akemi Nishida, Sami Schalk, and Jesse Waggoner. Going even further back in time, thank you to my beloved Writing for Publication classmates at the University of Michigan, who are also some of my dearest friends—Cass Adair and Tiffany Ball. Expertly taught by the one and only Sidonie Smith, that class planted the seeds of ideas that would, ten years later, grow into this book.

I cherish the many conference spaces, panels, lectures, symposia, and colloquia where I was able to share and further nourish this work. Thank you to friends and conference audiences at the Society for Disability Studies, the National Women's Studies Association, the American Studies Association, the Association for Asian American Studies, and the Modern Language Association. Your interest in my ideas gave me encouragement at crucial moments and helped me feel like I wasn't writing into a giant void. My genuine gratitude to everyone who invited me to share this work with audiences at University of Wisconsin–Madison, St. Mary's College of Maryland, Hampshire College, University of Massachusetts Amherst, Barnard Center for Research on Women, Brown University, Cal State Long Beach, University of Utah, the Center for LGBTQ Studies at CUNY Graduate Center, University of Colorado Boulder, University of Minnesota, Tufts University, Northwestern University, and the bell hooks Center at Berea College.

This project began during my graduate work at the University of Michigan–Ann Arbor, where I was blessed to have a vibrant network of mentors. Sidonie Smith is a model of ethical and loving feminist mentorship, and she gave me crucial guidance during an uncertain and painful time. Although my time in graduate school was marked by the untimely passing of Patsy Yaeger, my first dissertation chair, I have nonetheless been shaped by her words, kindness, and unorthodox ways. My sincere appreciation also goes out to Petra Kuppers, who lovingly folded me into disability culture and studies at the University of Michigan, and who continues to champion my work to this day. Thank you to Michael Awkward, Amy Sara Carroll, Maria Cotera, Matthew Countryman, Dean Hubbs, Victor Mendoza, Scotti Parrish, Tobin Siebers, and Ruby Tapia for sharing your knowledge and time with me. Before graduate school, there was Agnes Scott College, and I want to give heartfelt appreciation to my early mentors during my years in Atlanta and Decatur: Anne Beidler, Christine Cozzens, Rosemarie Garland-Thomson, and Willie Tolliver. One of my early mentors, Cindy Wu, gives me necessary guidance to this day and remains my model for ethical and honest engagement in this profession.

After leaving Michigan, I was lucky enough to land in the Five College Consortium. I first came to the Valley through a Consortium for Faculty Diversity postdoctoral fellowship at Mount Holyoke College in the Program for Critical Social Thought (now the Department of Critical Race and Political Economy). I have endless appreciation for my time with my Mount Holyoke colleagues: Nigel Alderman, Jonathan Ashby, Kimberly Juanita Brown, David Hernandez, Andrea Lawlor, Ana Soltero Lopez, Jacquelyne Luce, Amy Rodgers, Vanessa Rosa, Kate Singer, and Wesley Yu. I want to extend a special thanks to Iyko Day, who brought me to the Valley and offered invaluable mentorship.

Smith College has been the ideal place to teach, research, and write about feminist and queer literary studies. Thank you to my colleagues in the Program for the Study of Women, Gender, and Sexuality: Kelly Anderson, Lisa Armstrong, Carrie Baker, Payal Banerjee, Ginetta Candelario, Jennifer DeClue,

Ana Del Conde, Randi Garcia, Ambreen Hai, Vange Heiliger, Efadul Huq, Mehammed Mack, Andrea Moore, Liz Pryor, Loretta Ross, and Traci-Ann Wint. Thank you to my colleagues in the English department: Nancy Bradbury, Floyd Cheung, Arda Collins, Craig Davis, Michael Gorra, Tess Grogan, Lily Gurton-Wachter, Ambreen Hai, Yona Harvey, Gillian Kendall, Sara London, Art Middleton, Naomi Miller, Richard Millington, Ruth Ozeki, Melissa Parrish, Doug Patey, Cornelia Pearsall, Torlief Persson, Andrea Stone, and Michael Thurston. Outside of my departments, I am grateful to Jen Blackburn, Alex Callender, Anaiis Cisco, Matt Donovan, Susanna Ferguson, Matthew Ghazarian, Amanda Golden, Jennifer Guglielmo, Michelle Joffroy, Becca Keyel, Daphne Lamothe, Jen Malkowski, Christen Mucher, Anna Mwaba, Sara Newland, Sam Ng, Erin Pineda, Javier Puente, Laura Rauscher, Meridith Richter, Heather Rosenfeld, Kevin Rozario, EJ Seibert, and Jeanette Wintjen. Thank you to Lorraine Hedger and Jen Roberts for being incredible program administrators and assisting me in bringing visitors to campus. My endless appreciation goes out to my brilliant students across the Five Colleges who have taught me so much. Outside of Smith, I'd like to extend my gratitude to Samuel Ace, Kiran Asher, Cameron Awkward-Rich, Laura Briggs, Michelle Hardesty, Moon-kie Jung, Miliann Kang, Katrina Karkazis, Susana Loza, Asha Nadkarni, Sonny Nordmarken, Pooja Rangan, Jordy Rosenberg, Sarah Stefana Smith, Angie Willey, and Caroline Yang. Even though rural New England can be a cold (and flavor-free) place to be, you make life here feel possible.

My favorite part of this profession is getting to hang out, gossip, and make meaningful connections with fabulous scholars in feminist, queer, ethnic, disability, and literary studies. Thank you to the donut shops, karaoke bars, balconies, patios, hotel lobbies, and dance floors that facilitated and held our communion. Thank you, also, to the many virtual spaces that enabled safe gathering in the wake of COVID. Though I will inevitably (and not out of malice) forget some names, here are at least some of my beloved scholarly comrades and interlocutors: Aren Aizura, Juliann Anesi, Daphna Atias, Aimee Bahng, Rabia Belt, Liat Ben-Moshe, Lydia X. Z. Brown, Pam Butler, Karisa Butler-Wall, Umayyah Cable, Maria Elena Cepeda, Mel Chen, Brian Chung, Eli Clare, Jessica Cowing, Theodora Danyelevich, Ally Day, Jimmy Draper, Treva Ellison, Chris Eng, Nirmala Erevelles, Paul Farber, Laura Fugikawa, Jack Gieseking, David Green Jr., Alexis Pauline Gumbs, Eva Hageman, Aimi Hamraie, Kelsey Henry, Anna Hinton, Ai Binh Ho, Mingwei Huang, Emily Hue, Shereen Inayatulla, Douglas Ishii, Lisa Jong, Alison Kafer, Ronak Kapadia, Jenny Kelly, Tala Khanmalek,

Kareem Khubchandani, Mimi Khúc, Anthony Kim, Amy King, Josh Kupetz, Jenny Kwak, Marisol LeBròn, Summer Kim Lee, Katie Lennard, Crystal Yin Lie, Joan Lubin, Caleb Luna, M. Shadee Malaklou, Hil Malatino, Anita Mannur, Laura Mauldin, James McMaster, Annie Menzel, Angel Miles, Julie Avril Minich, Christine Mok, Amber Jamilla Musser, Akemi Nishida, Allison Page, Aly Patsavas, Margaret Price, Rachel Afi Quinn, Ivan Ramos, Lavelle Ridley, J. T. Roane, Liz Rodrigues, Juana María Rodríguez, Ellen Samuels, Mejdulene Shomali, J. Logan Smilges, Alyson Spurgas, Thea Quiray Tagle, Lou Tam, Kyla Tompkins, Vivian Truong, Jeanne Vaccaro, Lee Ann Wang, Elizabeth Williams, Samuel Yates, Hailee Yoshizaki-Gibbons, and Sunhay You. This constellation of names maps my scholarly coordinates, too: feminist disability studies, feminist- and queer-of-color critique, and contemporary ethnic American literary studies. More broadly, this list reflects my shared commitments to the (feminist, queer, and crip) radical imagination and all of those who labor in service of it.

Thank you to my network of friends who inhabit both academic and creative worlds, who operate entirely outside of academia, and who help me keep it real. From my time in Atlanta, Ann Arbor, Detroit, Greenfield, New York, and Northampton, I want to offer my deepest appreciation to Lisa Adang, Sophia Awad, Cameron Awkward-Rich, Ari Banias, Diana Becerra, Britt Billmeyer-Finn, Al Bland, Pia Blumenthal, Abbie Boggs, Katie Brewer Ball, Leo Cesareo, Franny Choi, Aubrey Longley Cook, Maxe Crandall, Billy Cuddy, Jared Dawson, the Flowers and Cunniffe families, Giselle Guillen-Martinez, Natassja Gunasena, Emil Heiple, Andre Keichian, Rachel Keller, Andrew Keller-Bradshaw, Taylor Zarkades King, Mike Kolassa, Heather Kuhn, Andrew Leland, Francis Lo, Jen Lorang, Mateo Medina, Dori Midnight, Elliot Montague, Coco Montellano, Beyon Wren Moor, Lex NonScripta, Voula O'Grady, Caitlin O'Neill, Tommi Parrish, Leah Lakshmi Piepzna-Samarasinha, Mara Poliak, Vick Quezada, Dre Rawlings, Annie Ricotta, Shelley Salant, Andrea Schmid, Jae Southerland, Erin Stokesbury, Zoe Tuck, Teal Van Dyck, Drew Watts, Rachel Weber, Autumn Wetli, Esther Witte, Phoebe Woerner, and Luke Woodward. You help me remember that the world is bigger than academia. Thank you for the poetry readings, barn dance parties, two-step nights, Aries Ragers, cookbook clubs, summer swims, candlepin bowling, reality TV binge sessions, and gossip.

Throughout my journey, there has been a core group of friends who have offered me key forms of support, love, and home space. They have witnessed all sides of me and, in return, have offered me safety and understanding. I name this list as both record of friendship and prayer for continued communion: Cass Adair, Tiffany Ball, Meghanne Barker, Sony Corañez Bolton, Marie Buck, Candice Haddad, Lenny Hanson, Amanda Healy, Leon Hilton, Ren-yo Hwang, Kei Kaimana, Jayson Keery, Stephanie Rosen, Sami Schalk, Allie Seekely, Jesse Waggoner, Brian Whitener, and Cookie Woolner. I am grateful for all the video calls, advice sessions, heart-to-heart talks, guest couches and beds, moving help, and pep talks. Y'all are my lifeline.

Thank you to the places, people, and practices that help keep me balanced and whole. My therapist and my comedy advice podcasts. My hairstylist, Sheri, who understands my love of gossip. The delicious food I eat when I leave Western Massachusetts. Controversially, social media. Decorating my house in the style of colorful maximalism. Long scenic drives while eating snacks. All my colleagues and comrades who fight in service of a liberated Palestine. The first spring flowers.

I am lucky to have family that extends beyond blood or biological relation. To the Dolla Club: Rahul Desai, my birthday twin and chosen brother, your ability to gently roast me is unmatched. You keep me honest and help me laugh at myself. Elizabeth Yates, the college roommate and long-term bestie of my dreams, I live for your sweetness, humor, and ability to find a good deal. Nova Terata, you're a gem and a true weirdo, and I always appreciate your hospitality. Alec Watts, you've been making me cackle for over twenty years. Wendy Sung: sometimes, when I doubt my decision to go to grad school, I remember that it's the reason I met you. Thanks for always taking care of the restaurant reservations and for being my hungriest friend. With you, I have the most fun. Lezlie Frye, my disability comrade and deep soul-friend, I am nourished by your wisdom. You are one of the brightest stars in my sky. Britt Rusert, you and Lucy have made Western Massachusetts home for me. Here's to many more years in deep companionship. To Lisa (Hae Ran) Kim, my actual mom, thank you for loving me fiercely in the ways you know how. You are my first champion, and the reason I do this work. To my cats, Edie and Percy, and my part-time poodle Minnie: you are illiterate and therefore don't judge me for my writing. Thank you for offering love and cuddles beyond the human realm. To Ryan Stratton, my partner and l.o.m.l., you are the life-giving love that I never thought I could have. Thank you for your kindness, patience, and generosity of spirit. You are my safest place to land.

Most of all, thank you to Lauren Macdonald. You taught me that friendship doesn't end with death—our love lives on and imprints on everything I touch. This book is my testimony to you.

What is it like to be stuck, night and day, dreaming of infrastructure?
——Patricia Yaeger, "Introduction: Dreaming of Infrastructure"

I am dreaming like my life depends on it. Because it does.
——Leah Lakshmi Piepzna-Samarasinha, "Cripping the Apocalypse"

When my best friend was diagnosed with stage 4 brain cancer in October 2018, I found myself consumed by dreaming. More than any romantic partner, she was the person to whom I had anchored my life, the one who first modeled for me the art of queer-of-color survival. With her diagnosis, I both dreamed of and mourned the future we would never share. My dreams contended with the lived reality of her illness, too, and with the structures coordinating her medical care: the waiting room, the rehabilitation hospital, the social worker, the insurance labyrinth siphoning her time and energy, her accumulating medical costs. They contended with the troubling dynamic emerging between her and her primary caregiver / long-term romantic partner, who increasingly isolated her from other sources of care and support. And my dreams contended with her repeated insistence that her cancer made her a burden to others and because of this, she should be grateful for any crumb of support she received.

I wanted so much more for her. In my grief, I found myself dreaming of other, more expansive arrangements of care that would render her less vulnerable to social isolation and abuse. I found myself dreaming of a robust and free healthcare system that does not harvest sickness for profit, does not treat sick and disabled people as burdens, and honors the inherent value of disabled lives. I found myself dreaming of care networks that would make nourishment and pleasure possible even in the midst of her illness. At the end of her life, I found myself dreaming of infrastructure.

I know, however, that as a disabled Korean American woman, this kind of dreaming is not allowed. At the very least, it is not expected. As the disability justice writer-activist Leah Lakshmi Piepnza-Samarasinha observes, "Sick and disabled and neurodivergent folks aren't supposed to dream, especially if we are queer and Black or brown—we're just supposed to be grateful the 'normals' let us live. But I am the product of some wild disabled Black and brown queer revolutionary dreaming, and I am dedicated to dreaming more sick and disabled queer brown femme dreams."[1] Other writer-activists in the disability justice movement, such as Shayda Kafai and Talila "T. L." Lewis, have similarly affirmed the centrality of dreamwork to projects of radical disability liberation.[2] These writers situate disability politics within the long tradition of freedom dreaming, what Robin D. G. Kelley defines as the imaginative practice of "[producing] a vision that enables us to see beyond our immediate ordeals."[3] This, too, is unexpected, because disability is so often seen as antithetical to freedom. In the popular imagination, we are bound: bedbound, housebound, wheelchair-bound. This narrative of boundedness further takes hold in many revolutionary and ethnic American political imaginaries, which have implicitly centered able-bodiedness in their visions of freedom.[4] Here, disability is equivalent to dependency, failure, and neediness—something to avoid in the pursuit of liberatory futures.

This is a book about the dreamwork that disabled, feminist, and/or queer-of-color writers do to envision alternate infrastructural arrangements in a world and nation that has refused to support us. First and foremost, it asks, how can disability justice politics and aesthetics provide imaginative blueprints for navigating contemporary crises of care? While disability has often been cast outside the scope of racial justice and political liberation, this book demonstrates how contemporary ethnic American writers such as Jesmyn Ward, Karen Tei Yamashita, Samuel Delany, and Aurora Levins Morales bring disability and dependency to the forefront of their literary freedom dreaming. In their writing, freedom does not take the shape of the unfettered or (self-)possessive individual, nor does it hinge on the achievement of independence. Instead, it emerges from the recuperation of dependency, the cultivation of radical *inter*dependency, and the recognition of the numerous support systems on which survival depends.

This refusal of support has assumed many forms, and I focus here on the eviscerated US welfare state, which includes social assistance programs such as

Medicaid and Supplemental Security Income (ssi). My anchoring event is the passage of the 1996 Personal Responsibility and Work Opportunity Reconciliation Act (PRWORA), a piece of legislation known as major welfare reform. By ending the federal entitlement to aid, alongside other significant restrictions, PRWORA weakened an already shoddy support system for assisting low-income and/or single mothers, and it did so through the language of family, work ethic, and independence. This rhetorical framework persists in the present day: over twenty years after Bill Clinton pledged to "end welfare as we know it," the mythical threat of state dependents continues to animate the national imagination. Organized around figures such as the welfare queen, the undocumented or noncitizen immigrant, and the disabled nonworker, this myth conjures up the specter of needy populations, implicitly racialized and feminized, draining the American public of its hard-earned resources. This narrative crucially has shaped not only contemporary US public policy but also, as I argue here, the writing of women and queers of color who fought, theorized, and dreamed under the long shadow of Reagan.

Looking to feminist disability and feminist-of-color theories of interdependency, *Care at the End of the World* demonstrates how contemporary ethnic American writers recuperate the maligned condition of dependency. They do so through their imaginative engagements with civic infrastructure: education, sanitation, transportation, and health/care. By drawing readerly attention to these networks, such texts emphasize our contingency on human and material infrastructures alike—the pipes, wires, roads, and labor networks that coordinate contemporary life yet so often go unnoticed. They thus invite, in the words of the performance scholar Shannon Jackson, "an acknowledgment of the interdependent systems of support that sustain human beings."[5] For scholars of feminist disability studies, interdependency suggests a condition of shared dependence, an ecology of contingent relations, in which dependency can be understood in terms of its mutualistic, symbiotic properties. Rather than being a parasitic relationship abused by certain types of people, here dependency becomes legible as a value-free relationship articulated across all subjects and the support systems in which they are embedded. Public infrastructure, in my project's archive, thus becomes a key figure for articulating a counterdiscourse of dependency—one that documents the disabling violence of state neglect while foregrounding a public ethics of care.

By deriving a disability politics and aesthetics of interdependency from the supporting operations of literary infrastructures, this book develops what I term a *crip-of-color critique* from the underexamined intersection of antiracist, anticapitalist, and feminist disability analysis. In this way, it enables the exploration of a "crip affinity," as disability scholar Lezlie Frye puts it, between disability politics and the targeted populations of welfare reform.[6] At once a coalitional practice, critical methodology, and epistemological project, a crip-of-color critique demonstrates how theories and narratives of disability authored by women and queers of color can intervene in state-authored myths of resource parasitism. Through examining state narratives of stigmatized dependency, the crip-of-color framework highlights the centrality of ableism to contemporary regimes of austerity and racialized state violence, while simultaneously underscoring the function of the state as an instrument of mass disablement.

However, it doesn't stop there. In addition to naming the ableist ideologies key to welfare reform, this book highlights the alternate structures of support envisioned by women and queer writers of color in the face of infrastructural divestment. In so doing, it centers the "ruptural possibilities," to borrow Roderick A. Ferguson's formulation, engendered by minority literary expression that enable and call forth other modes of knowing.[7] As Lisa Lowe has argued, minority literary and cultural expression often exists in a dialectical relation to official state narratives, insofar as such literatures can register the shape of dominant culture while simultaneously offering other ways of imagining and inhabiting the world. As such, minority literary production functions as "the site of more than critical negation of the U.S. nation; it is a site that shifts and marks alternatives to the national terrain by occupying other spaces, imagining different narratives and critical historiographies, and enacting practices that give rise to new forms of subjectivity and new ways of questioning the government of human life by the national state."[8] Following Lowe, each of the following chapters examines ethnic American literary and cultural engagements with infrastructure: infrastructural divestment (chapter 1), sanitation (chapter 2), transportation (chapter 3), and health/care (chapter 4). I consider how these infrastructural narratives generate new perspectives on and pathways around the punitive logics of public resource distribution, which weaponize the charge of dependency to argue that some people deserve less than others. *Care at the End of the World* demonstrates how feminist, disabled, and/or queer writers of color, rather than distancing themselves from this charge, craft rival systems of thought that take up dependency beyond the singular register of pathology.

This introduction proceeds in five parts. First, I begin by describing the US infrastructural landscape against which this book takes shape. Then, I explain the concept of infrastructural violence, tethering this term to political economies of care work. Shifting to the imaginative work of rupture, the third section offers an infrastructural reading of the 1981 anthology *This Bridge Called My Back*, demonstrating how the writers in this book refuse existing arrangements of support to dream of more and better. Following this, I explain in greater detail the crip-of-color methodology I develop and employ throughout. I conclude by returning to the concept of infrastructural freedom dreaming, a practice that not only destigmatizes dependency but also envisions it as a site of aesthetic possibility and political transformation.

Infrastructure and the US Welfare State

In examining fictional accounts of infrastructure, *Care at the End of the World* forwards a theory of disability analysis attuned to the networks of resource distribution and circulation that maximize life chances for some while disabling others. Rather than framing the US nation-state as a haven of protection for disabled people, it addresses the debilitating effects of state-sanctioned racialized resource deprivation—what I term *infrastructural violence*—that constitute the primary context for the literary dreams examined here. While early disability scholarship often aligned itself with the 1990 Americans with Disabilities Act (ADA), crediting the legislation's passage for the emergence of the field, my emphasis on infrastructural violence instead furthers a disability framework that decenters the ameliorating function of legislation and policy.

Toward this end, Lezlie Frye and Samuel Bagenstos have pointed out how the passage of the ADA colluded with the conservative logics of welfare reform, insofar as some supporters posed the legislation as vital to weaning disabled citizens off public assistance and sending them into the workforce.[9] Examining the denigration of dependency deployed by white disability rights advocates, which served to distance them from implicitly racialized welfare recipients, Frye writes that the "lost opportunities for coalition remain glaring."[10] My focus on infrastructural violence and welfare reform, then, aims to resuscitate some of these coalitional opportunities, which were set adrift in the late 1980s and early 1990s. Following scholars like Frye, I ask, how might disability studies shift if antiwelfare and austerity policies occupied a focal point of analysis?[11]

Care at the End of the World therefore builds on disability studies interventions forged by scholars such as Lezlie Frye, Nirmala Erevelles, Jasbir Puar, Akemi Nishida, and Liat Ben-Moshe, all of whom forgo the rights-based, individualistic accounts of disability favored by first-wave disability scholars in order to highlight bio/necropolitical accounts of racialized disablement and debilitation.[12] My theory of disability, then, might be more accurately described as an analytic of dis-/enablement, in which I ask, who is supported by infrastructure? Who is disabled by it? And which racialized and gendered subjects, through the exploitation of their unseen and unvalued labor, become the living infrastructure for others' fantasies of independence? It is impossible, my book asserts, to understand US infrastructure without understanding disability.

In its most literal sense, *infrastructure* refers to the built networks that enable cities and regions to function: the roads, electric wires, sewers, and fiber-optic cables that allow for the circulation of people, goods, and ideas. The term also refers to public services and institutions, such as schools, hospitals, and welfare offices, which often travel under the term *soft infrastructure*. Finally, taking a cue from AbdouMaliq Simone's concept of "people as infrastructure," I also use the term to describe the support labor of care, service, and maintenance disproportionately performed by women and people of color, as well as the more informal networks that distribute resources in the absence of state assistance.[13]

By centering support labor in my understanding of infrastructure, my book builds on ongoing conversations in feminist-of-color, Marxist feminist, and disability justice circles around the often-devalued status of care work. The practice of care, or what disability scholar Akemi Nishida defines as "the energy and time we spend in intention to contribute to others' well-being," opens up a complex definitional universe that carries multiple contradictory functions.[14] For disability scholars and activists, *care* names what we do to ensure the life force of our disabled comrades and friends; it is the necessary labor we expend to assert the value of disabled lives in a world that insists otherwise. However, *care* has also been the word applied to systems of state control, such as the incarceration of disabled people in psychiatric wards, institutions, and prisons under the pretense of protection—a practice and ideology Liat Ben-Moshe terms "carceral ableism."[15] Marxist feminists favor the term *social reproduction*, described by Tithi Bhattacharya as the "tremendous amount of familial as well as communitarian work that goes on to sustain and reproduce the worker, or more specifically, her labor power."[16] Rather than seeing domestic tasks (childcare, cleaning, cooking) as a set of practices natural or innate to women, social reproduction theory understands such tasks as necessary forms of labor. Social reproduction names the work that makes survival—of the worker, of capitalism—possible. It also names a site of uneven labor extraction, a means of positioning some as the ones who always give support and some as the ones who always take.

The conceptual entanglements of infrastructure and care work came to the fore in recent political debates, when the Biden administration released plans for a bipartisan infrastructure bill in early 2021.[17] This bill included a proposed $400 billion for at-home care for the elderly and disabled, which caused Republicans (and some Democrats) to bristle at the thought of including care under infrastructure's semantic umbrella. Others saw the term as a means of validating and honoring the labor of support, with Senator Kirsten Gillibrand of New York tweeting, "Paid leave is infrastructure. Child care is infrastructure. Caregiving is infrastructure."[18] Rather than attempting to resolve the contradictory nature of care work or debating what "counts" as infrastructure, my book takes up all of these registers of meaning. It focuses particularly on the relationship between literary representations of infrastructure—in its hard, soft, and living formats—and the US welfare state, which is also at once an infrastructural form.

In their critiques of contemporary antiwelfare policy, many feminist scholars have turned to the passage of the 1935 Social Security Act to examine the welfare state's origins.[19] A cornerstone of Franklin Delano Roosevelt's Second New Deal, this omnibus bill established a social welfare safety net encompassing programs such as Aid to Dependent Children (ADC), unemployment insurance, and old-age insurance. Zooming outward, it also represented and enacted a form of state-managed capitalism in which governments assumed some level of social responsibility for populations in need, thereby managing the crisis of social reproduction generated by the Great Depression and mass unemployment. As such, the Social Security Act aimed to provide a system of state assistance for elderly people, people with disabilities, nonworking populations, single mothers, and other vulnerable classes.

However, the act came with a set of vital exclusions: occupational groups such as agricultural laborers, private domestic workers, and government employees were barred from accessing benefits. Such exemptions disproportionately impacted working women, Black workers, and other workers of color, thereby creating a state support system bifurcated along lines of race and gender. Further, as scholars such as Gwendolyn Mink and Dorothy Roberts have argued, welfare has historically reinforced the nuclear family form through mechanisms of surveillance and control, such as the enforcement of "man-in-the-house" and "suitable home" rules for ADC recipients.[20] Following this, while *Care at the End of the World* condemns welfare reform and its attendant logics of austerity, it also recognizes that systems of state care are themselves violent and punishing and therefore cannot constitute the horizons of our political imagination.

The ADC program, later the central target of 1996 welfare reform, emblematizes the regressive moralism and white supremacy underlying the US welfare state. With the program's creation, mothers' pensions became policy at the federal level. However, many states claimed discretion to disperse benefits based on standards of moral fitness and suitability, which they assumed Black women and other women of color inherently could not meet. Eventually, in part due to welfare policy shifts and urban migration, women of color did gain access to ADC in disproportionate numbers. By the 1950s, the single and/or Black mother had become the imagined face of the program, a change in public perception aided by increasing political attacks on welfare. Such assaults on welfare access were mobilized using the seemingly race-neutral language of dependency, which condemned women for their reliance on government rather than a husband. This dependency on state assistance, while once seen as understandable for white widowed women, became reframed as a source of familial harm and individual pathology when associated with women of color.[21]

With the emergence of globalization and the exportation of US production abroad in the 1970s, the meaning of *dependency* was made to signify anew.[22] Business and political elites, who now relied less on a domestic workforce, increasingly cast social welfare spending as wasteful and detrimental to economic growth, decrying "big government" and the gains of social movements. Further, the enforcement of Global North economic development policies on formerly colonized nations, such as structural adjustment programs, drove new waves of immigration to the United States comprising people who could no longer afford to live in their home countries. These migratory classes, figured disproportionately in the national imagination as Mexican/Latinx, were similarly cast as underserving drains on public resources. Meanwhile, in 1974, the creation of a new federal supplemental security program significantly raised Social Security benefits for elderly, blind, and disabled people, which seemingly intensified the perceived distinctions between the deserving (e.g., elderly and disabled) and undeserving (e.g., single-mother) poor. However, the emergence of SSI as a disability program soon led to controversy, as the program's critics raised the specter of disability fraud.[23] The program became the target of many of the same allegations lobbed at welfare and its recipients. Noncitizen recipients of SSI were particularly vulnerable to these accusations, as they were targeted by the pervasive nativist myth that immigrants come to the United States to take advantage of its social programs.

Though single-issue identity politics may have partitioned these subjects—single mothers, working immigrants, and disabled nonworkers—into separate categories, the maneuvers of austerity politics linked them under the banner of pathological dependency. Following the signing of PRWORA in 1996, these US fictions of dependency helped underpin the large-scale decimation of the welfare state. PRWORA constituted a multipronged attack on the nation's perceived drains: racialized motherhood and families, poor single mothers, disabled people, and immigrants. With PRWORA, the Aid to Families with Dependent Children (AFDC), formerly the Aid to Dependent Children (ADC), program became Temporary Assistance for Needy Families (TANF), transitioning from an open-ended entitlement program to a block grant replete with time limits and stringent work requirements. For children, the parameters for claiming disability and SSI tightened. For noncitizen immigrants, access to federal, state, and local public services, including SSI and food stamps, was restricted. Finally, to enforce the "proper" dependency represented by the nuclear family, the newly minted law discouraged single-parent households and children born out of wedlock, declaring both that "marriage is the foundation of a successful society" and that "out-of-wedlock pregnancy and reduction in out-of-wedlock births are very important Government interests."[24]

PRWORA thus marked a watershed moment in the ongoing divestment from US welfare and infrastructural support, occupying the epicenter of a constellation of policy shifts spanning the late twentieth and early twenty-first centuries. Given the immense material and cultural impacts of antidependency discourse on the US infrastructural landscape, impacts disproportionately borne by multiply marginalized populations, I identify 1996 US welfare reform as my periodizing event. PRWORA perpetuated and worsened the manifold crises of care making up the terrain on which this book unfolds, "shortening [welfare] recipients' lives by nearly six months," as Felicia Kornbluh and Gwendolyn Mink write.[25] It is therefore the anchoring example, though by no means the only example, of what I term *infrastructural violence.*

Infrastructural Violence and Political Economies of Care

While many of the conversations around state-sanctioned violence have focused rightfully on carceral systems and police brutality, the term *infrastructural violence* aims, in the words of Cathy Cohen, to "expand where we look for victims of and resisters to state violence"—beyond and in addition to confrontations with police.[26] My usage of *infrastructural violence* offers a variation on Omar Jabary Salamanca's deployment of the term, which he employs to describe Israel's absolute control over Gazan utilities and fuel, capturing the inscription of colonial violence in the "tiniest details of daily life."[27] Drawing from concepts such as "organized abandonment" (Gilmore), "administrative violence" (Spade), and "debility" (Puar), this book mobilizes infrastructural violence to name the dis-/enabling effects of degraded state infrastructures, the US welfare state, and pro-austerity policies.[28] These effects emerge from the punitive operations of welfare administration as well as the manufactured neglect of social programs and public institutions: the defunding of school lunches, the militarization of public schools in underresourced neighborhoods, right-wing attacks on Medicaid, and a profit-driven health/care system.

Yet, far from describing just the debilitating aspects of state neglect, infrastructural violence also describes the attendant production of *enablement* for highly resourced populations through welfare reform and other forms of safety net retraction, which further fortify white supremacy, the heteropatriarchal nuclear family, and class stratification. For instance, in chapter 1, I describe how Sapphire's novel *Push* (1996) and Jesmyn Ward's novel *Salvage the Bones* (2011) generate forms of infrastructural literacy that foreground the structural production of racialized disablement via actively harmful systems of education, welfare, and heath/care. These works further link racialized disablement to the simultaneous creation of white enablement through exploitative workfare programs (*Push*) and land theft (*Salvage*). Though literary scholars have often emphasized infrastructure's downright "boring" nature, noting how it often occupies the background of collective attention, I find that it emerges, again and again, as a key site through which women and queer-of-color writers grapple with the intensifying resource deprivation of a postwelfare United States.[29]

As I note throughout the book, one primary function of infrastructural violence is the privatization of care—that is, the ongoing enclosure of resources such as healthcare, childcare, housing, education, transit, and food. Such enclosures wear away at infrastructures of disabled survival while disabling low-income and racialized people en masse. Indeed, to be disabled is often to be hyperaware of existing care systems and the many ways they fall short. It is also to be particularly brutalized by these shortcomings. The privatization of care, then, constitutes one of the most fundamental elements of disability oppression.

Returning to social reproduction theory, Nancy Fraser places this privatizing drive at the heart of contemporary care crises, or what she describes as the increasing inability to perform the work of care in an unforgiving context of both reduced state support and eviscerated labor protections. Fraser locates the root of such crises in a socially reproductive contradiction inherent to capitalist accumulation: capitalism depends on socially reproductive labor in order to sustain itself, and yet, the increasing pressures generated by capitalist demands deplete all reserves available to do the work of social reproduction. In our era of global financialized capitalism, those who can afford to outsource care labor do so, thus creating a "dualized organization of social reproduction, commodified for those who can pay for it, privatized for those who cannot."[30] Transnational and feminist-of-color scholars including Chandra Mohanty and Evelyn Nakano Glenn have demonstrated how this dualized organization fortifies racial and class hierarchies across domestic and global scales, and further, how these care crises are unevenly distributed across race and class.[31] In dualized care arrangements, elite families extract domestic and support labor from low-income racialized and/or immigrant women, depleting their workers' personal and familial well-being.

Following this, my analyses of infrastructural violence—as both an uneven system of resource distribution and a figure of literary representation—foreground the political economies of racial-gendered care work generated through policies and practices of safety net divestment. And so, while scholars like Ruth Wilson Gilmore highlight the "prison fix" as a key response to "organized abandonment," or what she defines as the purposeful dismantling of the welfare state, this book focuses on care crises under racial capitalism as its chief terrain of struggle.[32] In this way, I offer a crip expansion of feminist- and queer-of-color perspectives on historical materialist critique, which have broadly sought to address the limitations of Marxist analysis in relation to white supremacy, heteropatriarchy, heterosexism, and sex work.[33]

Roderick Ferguson in particular has identified how Marx's own naturalization of heteropatriarchy—as the proper order of social life—effectively rendered the "heteronormative subject the goal" of both liberal and revolutionary projects.[34] As a result, these ostensibly antiestablishment projects often conspired with the "normative investments of nation-states and capital," a reproduction of heteronormative ideals that Ferguson's queer-of-color framework sought to disrupt.[35] Akin to queer-of-color critique, the crip-of-color framework argues that these "normative investments" are also fundamentally shaped by ableist ideas around disability and dependency, in which those deemed too needy of care are paradoxically deemed the least deserving of it.

As Julie Avril Minich, James Kyung-Jin Lee, and the Harriet Tubman Collective have observed, such ideas have shaped leftist political imaginaries, which at times have defined political work and social change in ways that reproduce the capitalist state's devaluation of care, dependency, and disability.[36] For instance, Leah Lakshmi Piepzna-Samarasinha's 2018 book *Care Work: Dreaming Disability Justice* has detailed the tendency to elevate certain forms of activist labor (marches, speeches) over others (emotional support, food preparation, organizing and logistics). In response, the crip-of-color framework registers and refuses the ableist ideals undergirding the simultaneous retraction of (state) care and forcible extraction of care work from racialized and immigrant women. In so doing, it denaturalizes the particular calculus of need and support enforced by the nation-state and global capitalism and envisions more just distributions of caring labor.

Toward this end, *Care at the End of the World* highlights the support imaginaries generated within feminist-, queer-, and crip-of-color literature as vital sites through which struggles around care are waged, emphasizing the ideological and narrative elements of infrastructural violence. To put it simply, the writers I examine offer different stories around care: how we define it, how it works, and who works it. Even as disabled, racialized, and feminized people have borne the brunt of care crises, we have also, out of necessity, spent ample time reimagining what care means. In addition to naming an identity and a movement, then, disability also names a practice of reinventing care.

Consider, for example, Audre Lorde's 1988 essay "A Burst of Light: Living with Cancer," which contains the famous quote "Caring for myself is not self-indulgence, it is self-preservation, and that is an act of political warfare."[37] Written after Lorde's breast cancer had spread to her liver, "A Burst of Light" offers a radical theory of self-care incubated in Black queer feminist disabled experience, one that refuses the hierarchies of life-value upheld by a racist, profit-driven healthcare system. In addition to asserting the worth of her own Black queer disabled life, Lorde articulates this assertion against the backdrop of the Reagan administration, whose evisceration of state care provides key context for Lorde's cancer journaling. In one of the first entries penned after her liver cancer diagnosis, dated February 9, 1984, Lorde reflects on the retraction of welfare and public housing, positioning these processes adjacent to her own health struggles:

> So. No doubt about where we are in the world's story. It has just cost $32,000 to complete a government-commissioned study that purports to show there is no rampant hunger in the U.S.A. I wonder if they realize *rampant* means *aggressive.*
>
> So. The starving old women who used to sit in broken-down rooming houses waiting for a welfare check now lie under park benches and eat out of garbage bins. "I only eat fruit," she mumbled, rummaging through the refuse bin behind Gristede's supermarket, while her gnarled Black hands carefully cut away the rotted parts of a cantaloupe with a plastic Burger King knife.[38]

Akin to the figures of welfare queen, the noncitizen immigrant, and the disabled nonworker, the ideological arm of infrastructural violence is captured by the "government-commissioned study." It indexes state-authored narratives of care that justify routing resources away from Black, elderly, poor, and disabled communities—that is, the "starving old women" who cut fruit with "gnarled Black hands." Lorde's journal entry grants form and urgency to the state's particular metric of care distribution, highlighting a paradox key to my formulation of infrastructural violence: that systems of state care are brutal, punishing, and not enough, and still, their evisceration by the capitalist state is similarly brutal, punishing, and not enough.

In response to the narrative weapons of the state, Lorde's essay engages in a crip-of-color practice of redefining and rerouting care work toward alternate political ends—that is, toward the (Black, queer, disabled) self and toward the communities in which Lorde was embedded. For instance, she begins "A Burst of Light" with a sumptuous dinner shared by the Black and brown lesbian group Sapphire Sapphos, describing all the dishes one by one: "There was sweet potato pie, rice and red beans, black beans and rice . . . spinach noodles with clam sauce, five-bean salad, fish salad, and other salads of different combinations."[39]

Her recollection of this feast, which lingers on each pleasurable detail, models a more lateral and collective arrangement of care work, one in which queer Black and brown women are the recipients of nourishment rather than the ones always coerced to give. Against the meager options offered by the United States, "A Burst of Light" dreams of alternate infrastructural arrangements that can honor the sacredness of Black, queer, and disabled lives. In the following pages, I further outline what these rival arrangements might look like.

"I Have Dreamed of a Bridge . . .": Envisioning Rival Infrastructures of Care

As decrying "dependency" in the 1970s and 1980s became a viable discursive strategy for liberals and conservatives to further privatize care, there emerged another set of fictions in which dependency enabled other ways of knowing, living in, and surviving an increasingly hostile world. The 1981 anthology *This Bridge Called My Back: Writings by Radical Women of Color*, coedited by Chicana lesbian feminists Cherríe Moraga and Gloria Anzaldúa, put forth a revolutionary vision of interdependency furthered by the infrastructural motif of the bridge. This vision refused the instrumentalization of women and queers of color as bridges "[to be] walked over."[40] In the face of infrastructural violence, it articulated instead a vision of reciprocal support for those most targeted by state divestment and racialized dispossession.

I begin this analysis with *Bridge* because it both models and presages the rival infrastructures of care envisioned by the literary texts in this study. While *Bridge* was published long before the Bay Area activist performance group Sins Invalid coined the term *disability justice*, the anthology's radical feminist-of-color platform addressed the interrelations between multiple axes of difference, of which disability was unquestionably a part.[41] Take, for instance, Moraga and Anzaldúa's articulation of "El Mundo Zurdo," or "the left-handed world," inhabited by "the colored, the queer, the poor, the female, the physically challenged."[42] This vision expressed the necessity of coalitional politics in order to address the "many-headed demon of oppression."[43] In the vein of "El Mundo Zurdo," *Care at the End of the World* continues *Bridge*'s project of solidarity building across categories of difference. One of my central interventions, then, is bridging the adjacent intellectual fields of disability studies and feminist-/queer-of-color critique through the axis of dependency, demonstrating how they can be—and already have been—in generative dialogue. It is through "blood and spirit connections with these groups," Moraga and Anzaldua write, that we might "brew and forge a revolution."[44]

Throughout the anthology, contributors draw on the bridge metaphor to describe the exploitation of women and queers of color in single-issue ethnic nationalist and feminist movements, which often depended on the unremunerated labor extracted from multiply marginalized members. In the prefatory text "The Bridge Poem," the Black lesbian poet Kate Rushin renounces this role, stating, "I've had enough / I'm sick of seeing and touching / Both sides of things / Sick of being the damn bridge for everybody."[45] Similarly, Audre Lorde's canonical "The Master's Tools Will Never Dismantle the Master's House," anthologized in *Bridge*, foregrounds this support labor and names what it makes possible. In this paper, she asks white academic feminists, "What do you do with the fact that the women who clean your houses and tend your children while you attend conferences on feminist theory are, for the most part, poor and third world women?"[46] This characterization of Black and brown women as bridges and support structures offers a powerful counterpoint to myths like the welfare queen and the noncitizen migrant mother, which framed women of color as primary symbols of state dependency. Rushin and Lorde suggest that, in fact, so much more depends on the disregarded care work of women of color, including but not limited to the functioning of political movements and academic institutions.

Rather than serving as bridges toward other ends, the contributors of *Bridge* express the queer desire to redirect the labor of support toward each other. In her preface to the 1981 edition, Moraga details this infrastructural vision, writing, "Literally, for two years now, I have dreamed of a bridge."[47] In her dream, women who "contradict each other" come together to form an intimate textual coalition. Here, they can "make faith a reality and . . . bring all of our selves to bear down hard on that reality."[48] Through the metaphor of the bridge, Moraga dreams of care, intimacy, and freedom for women and queers of color during a time of accelerated resource deprivation. At times, her dream is made manifest: she recalls receiving "encouragement and identification" from "five Latina sisters" while speaking on a panel about racism in San Francisco.[49] Later, Moraga and her companions "buy burritos y cerveza from 'La Cumbre' and talk [their] heads off into the night, crying from the impact of such a reunion."[50] Her dream of the bridge thus furthers an understanding of liberation for women and queers of color that can emerge only through the mutual, loving practice of support. "For the women in this book," she writes, "I will lay my body down for that vision."[51]

Moraga's infrastructural freedom dreaming, which emphasizes dependency between feminist and queer-of-color comrades, further resonates with a feminist disability ethos that emphasizes the value of care work as well as the transformative potential of interdependency. "Interdependency," writes disability and transformative justice activist Mia Mingus, "is both 'you and I' and 'we.' It is solidarity, in the best sense of the word. . . . Because the truth is: we need each other."[52] As Rosemarie Garland-Thomson and other feminist disability scholars have argued, disability presents the self-sufficient, autonomous individual as a mere fiction, forcing us to contend with the very real needs of our bodyminds.[53] Rather than denying our embodied and enminded limitations, a feminist disability perspective insists we learn to accommodate them, foregrounding the support systems that make life more possible. "Our bodies need care," writes Garland-Thomson. "We all need assistance to live."[54] Dependency, in this context, is not evidence of failure; instead, it names a social bond vital to individual and collective well-being. Interdependency describes the webs and networks that emerge through these bonds, as well as a set of practices that honors bodily limitations and vulnerabilities.

Care at the End of the World identifies interdependency as a primary node of alignment between disability and feminist-/queer-of-color politics. This work continues, too, with essays such as Cathy Cohen's "Punks, Bulldaggers, and Welfare Queens: The Radical Potential of Queer Politics?," in which Cohen envisions a politics where "one's relation to power, and not some homogenized identity, is privileged in determining one's political comrades."[55] This book takes seriously Grace Kyungwon Hong and Roderick Ferguson's call, issued in the 2011 anthology *Strange Affinities*, to develop relational, coalitional, and cross-categorical analytics that can assess how "particular populations are rendered vulnerable to processes of death and devaluation over and against other populations" in the afterlives of the civil rights movement and decolonization.[56] Following this, I foreground the dominant discourse of dependency as a chief rhetorical instrument justifying racialized death and disablement following the abolition of legal racial discrimination.

By highlighting interdependency as a link between adjacent intellectual fields, I draw on a feminist-of-color tradition that privileges not sameness in identity as a basis for political solidarity, but rather a "common context of political struggle," to use Chandra Talpade Mohanty's oft-cited phrase.[57] To further elaborate on this potential affinity, I return once again to the work of Audre Lorde, who has in the past two decades been reclaimed as a queer disabled ancestor by a new generation of scholars and activists.[58] In the "Master's Tools" paper, delivered at the *Second Sex* conference soon after her breast cancer treatment, Lorde prefaces her condemnation of third world labor exploitation with a radical theory of interdependence. Critiquing feminist discussions of "nurturance" that fail to consider "lesbian consciousness" and "the consciousness of third world women," Lorde speaks to the "mutuality between women," "systems of shared support," and "interdependence" that offer alternate models for nurturance beyond the reproduction of the white heterosexual nuclear family.[59]

For Lorde, interdependency constitutes an alternate infrastructure of care for those women "forged in the crucibles of difference," the occupants of El Mundo Zurdo.[60] She writes, "Interdependency between women is the only way to the freedom which allows the 'I' to 'be,' not in order to be used, but in order to be creative."[61] In this passage, interdependence becomes legible as a liberatory ideal and practice, one that nourishes lives that were, as Lorde once famously wrote, "never meant to survive."[62] As she makes clear, this practice of interdependency must not only account for difference (along the lines of race, sexuality, ability, and class) but also honor such differences as vital sources of political creativity and change making. What Lorde terms "the interdependence of mutual (non-dominant) differences" is the condition of possibility for "true visions of our future," a vision of unqualified support that "[defines] and [seeks] a world in which we can all flourish."[63] Learning how to support and "make common cause" with those living "outside the structures" is the primary way to not only survive an otherwise unlivable world but also imagine viable ways out of it.[64]

Paired with her critique of white academic feminists delivered later in the paper, in which she underscores the childcare labor performed by "poor and third world women" that makes conference participation possible, Lorde furthers a theory of interdependency that also takes into account the political economy of racial-gendered care work.[65] This element feels crucial, as it demands a more in-depth analysis of the interdependency concept. At times, in disability writing, *interdependency* can function as a kind of vague utopian cure-all for an ableist world, a move that all too often evacuates the power dynamics and fraught histories shaping social relations of care. Or, as Leah Lakshmi Piepzna-Samarasinha so aptly puts it, "Interdependence Is Not Some Giant Living in the Hillside Coming Down to Visit the Townspeople."[66] For Lorde, then, *interdependency* carries multiple meanings—it can describe a web of reciprocal support between those who exist at the intersection of multiple oppressions, or a system of exploitation fueled by the disregarded, devalued care labor of Black and brown women, among other possibilities.

Following Lorde, *Care at the End of the World* considers the question of interdependence vis-à-vis political economies of care throughout the chapters, mapping the different ways that women- and queer-of-color writers have explored the relationships between care work, state divestment, and freedom dreaming. For instance, in chapter 3, I take up Octavia Butler's novel *Parable of the Sower* (1993) alongside Karen Tei Yamashita's novel *Tropic of Orange* (1997) in order to delve further into the exploitative version of interdependence, linking it to the dependency myth of the undocumented migrant worker. Chapter 2 turns to Samuel Delany's novel *Through the Valley of the Nest of Spiders* (2012) to examine a vision of mutual reciprocity, exploring the possibilities of queer eroticism that the novel derives from care work. Lorde's distinction between ecologies of interdependence, as well as her recognition of the maintenance labor often performed by racialized women, therefore provides a key touchstone for this project's analysis of dependency and support.

While "The Master's Tools" does not make explicit mention of disability, the essay's politicized focus on care and dependency is nonetheless aligned with a feminist disability ethos, demonstrating how disability politics can be present even in the absence of straightforward representation. Lorde's emphasis on the racialized divisions and dimensions of care labor further calls to mind recent disability justice interventions, such as Leah Lakshmi Piepzna-Samarasinha's *Care Work: Dreaming Disability Justice* and Akemi Nishida's *Just Care: Messy Entanglements of Disability, Dependency, and Desire*, both of which contextualize disability justice theories of care within longer histories of labor extraction from Black, brown, and Indigenous femmes.[67] In the following pages, I will explain more fully my methodological approach of disability as an analytic lens, in which disability functions less as a category of identity—a descriptor of what someone is—and more as a reading practice and framework for understanding the US landscape of infrastructural violence.

Crip-of-Color Critique as Methodology

This book models an analytic I term a *crip-of-color critique*, which considers how disability politics and aesthetics can offer useful interventions into anti-welfare narratives about who deserves care. It examines how the language of disability helps enable the ongoing evisceration of public resources, as well as the necessity of a radical disability ethos in overturning the operative logics of racialized resource deprivation. In this way, I address a seeming contradiction in the role of disability within racial capitalism, in which disability operates as both archive and evidence of state-sanctioned violence and a key political practice through which we might refuse the continued proliferation of that violence. Rather than seeking to resolve this tension, I embrace disability as a multivalent site of meaning, one that serves multiple and sometimes opposing functions: a testament to the "violence of social/economic conditions of capitalism," a joyful source of freedom dreaming, and finally, a lens for making sense of a postwelfare United States.[68]

Disability scholars such as Carrie Sandahl and Robert McRuer have termed this form of analysis *cripping*, a reading practice analogous to queering that "[spins] mainstream representation or practices to reveal able-bodied assumptions and exclusionary effects."[69] To be clear, cripping does not necessitate looking for diagnostic evidence of disability in a text, nor does it prioritize the positive representation of identifiably disabled characters. Instead, it uses disability as a lens to read across literary and cultural works, through which the critic pays attention to how the text engages the "able-bodied assumptions" organizing the world. Indeed, cripping can explain how a text furthers a critical disability ethos even if no disabled characters are present at all.

Following this, while some of my analyses—the fourth chapter in particular—center the testimony and embodied experiences of disabled queer people of color, other chapters highlight the structuring presence of a disability ethics, aesthetics, and politics even as disabled representation and authorship seem to be absent. A crip-of-color critique, then, does not privilege a highly specialized subject position—the disabled queer person of color. Rather, it names an analytic for understanding US infrastructural arrangements that disable some while enabling others. In so doing, it follows the analytic strategies forged by Cohen in "Punks, Bulldaggers, and Welfare Queens," in which queerness functions less as a category of identity—naming what someone *is*—and more as a framework for assessing (and condemning) state surveillance, punishment, and control of Black women's sexualities. Not limited in scope to the disabled subject, a crip-of-color critique similarly foregrounds disability as an organizing principle of state investment and abandonment. To return to my earlier assertion, it is impossible to understand US infrastructure without understanding disability.

A crip-of-color critique also shows how disability as methodology might further expand the scope of disability critique beyond its once single-issue focus, as demonstrated by Sami Schalk and Julie Avril Minich in their scholarship.[70] In "Enabling Whom? Critical Disability Studies Now," Minich explains how a disability studies defined by its framework of analysis rather than its objects of inquiry would further connect the field to questions of race, power, and redistribution. For Minich, disability as methodology "involves scrutinizing not bodily or mental impairments but the social norms that define particular attributes as impairments" and that disproportionately concentrate disability in vulnerable populations.[71] "Cripping" welfare reform, then, entails underscoring how normative ideologies around dependency, labor, care, and (re-)production undergird US regimes of resource austerity.

As a coalitional analytic linking feminist- and queer-of-color thought with disability perspectives, a crip-of-color critique attends to the coarticulation of systems of domination, recognizing ableism as one vector operating alongside and through other matrices of oppression. It thus draws from the theorizing of disability justice organizations such as Sins Invalid and activists such as Patricia Berne, Stacey Milbern Park, and Talila "T. L." Lewis, while also recognizing the specificity of disability justice as a movement-organizing framework. Patricia Berne offers a useful summary in "Disability Justice—a Working Draft," where she writes, "We cannot comprehend ableism without grasping its interrelations with heteropatriarchy, white supremacy, colonialism, and capitalism."[72] The crip-of-color framework thus envisions an explicitly intersectional disability politics attuned to regulatory regimes of power. What's more, it highlights the imaginative and cultural strategies envisioned by writers, activists, and intellectuals of color who refuse these regimes. As the chapters demonstrate, these refusals are often articulated in terms of infrastructure—as a representational strategy, category of labor, and built environmental network.

Chapter Overview

In chapter 1, I offer an overview of the US landscape of infrastructural violence and the operative logics of welfare reform. Turning to Sapphire's 1996 novel *Push* and Jesmyn Ward's 2011 novel *Salvage the Bones*, I pay particular attention to how these novels forge necessary links between welfare reform's dis-/enabling reorganization of public infrastructure and ableist narratives of Black mothering that frame so-called welfare queens as parasitic on the collective well-being. The welfare queen, I argue, functions as perhaps *the* definitive disability narrative of global financialized capitalism: she is defined as a pathological mother, a cautionary tale of state dependency that enabled the reallocation of public resources toward a global elite. Yet, rather than disavowing disability, both novels depict young Black mothers grappling with the debilitating context of infrastructural divestment, in which the basic support systems for maintaining life—public schools, hospitals, housing, social services—have become increasingly compromised. As such, both novels enable the elaboration of a critical disability politic centered around welfare queen mythology and infrastructural violence, one that identifies, contests, and overwrites the punitive aims of public resource distribution.

Chapter 2 extends the previous chapter's analysis of welfare queen mythology and state narratives of dependency by taking up dependency's counterpart: the American mythology of independence, tied to one's capacity to perform waged labor. Here, I turn to the sanitation and waste management systems of Samuel R. Delany's 2012 novel *Through the Valley of the Nest of Spiders*, which depicts a lifelong, interracial, and incestuous partnership between gay garbage workers. I argue that *Through the Valley* takes up waste management—as vocation, infrastructural figure, and non-(re-)productive sexual practice—in order to refuse the naturalized relationship between waged labor, normative kinship, and independence forged by welfare-to-work narratives. This refusal further marks a form of crip-of-color insurgency, given that it disarticulates the connections between paid employment, nuclear family making, and access to life-sustaining resources. I anchor this chapter with the concept of "refuse work," which carries multiple registers of meaning across Delany's novel: (1) the literal work of sanitation infrastructure; (2) the erotic management of human waste; (3) the intimate labors of sex and care that honor the body's needs; and (4) the refusal of an antirelational American work ethic that disavows dependency on others. Through refuse work, I demonstrate how Delany's reverent depiction of sanitation infrastructure makes imaginable a crip-queer politics of labor, insofar as it highlights the kind of work that sustains abject social collectivities in excess of welfare reform's imaginings.

While chapters 1 and 2 deal with welfare reform policy in the domestic arena, chapter 3 examines the extension of antiwelfare logics to the transnational arena of so-called free trade. Taking up the infrastructure of transportation, I look to the California freeway fictions of Octavia Butler and Karen Tei Yamashita in order to articulate the relationship of infrastructural violence to coerced migration, transnational capitalism, and the myth of the parasitic noncitizen immigrant. A long-standing emblem of social and spatial division, California's freeways emerge in Butler's 1993 novel *Parable of the Sower* and Yamashita's 1997 novel *Tropic of Orange* as multivalent sites for engaging questions of mobility, movement, and migration under the exigencies of transnational capitalism. Specifically, Butler's *Parable of the Sower* and Yamashita's *Tropic of Orange* prompt reflection on three infrastructural narratives: (1) the open road story and its fantasy of unfettered freedom; (2) global capitalism's dependence on unseen, undervalued migrant laboring networks; and (3) the alternate webs of survival dreamed into being by neurodivergent visionaries who further the disability justice principle of interdependence. I argue that both novels direct attention to California's freeway network in order to address the differential production of mobility by transit and economic infrastructures in the wake of trade deregulation, with the North American Free Trade Agreement as the nucleus event. This unequal production across the lines of race and class, in which the freedom of movement enjoyed by resourced populations is linked to the constriction of more vulnerable classes, is one of the primary ways that this chapter and this book theorizes disability.

Finally, the fourth chapter considers disability justice life-writing and poetry that navigates the health/care infrastructural landscape of the 2010s, anchored by the passage in 2010 of the Affordable Care Act (Obamacare). In so doing, chapter 4 bridges major welfare reform with the adjacent arena of health/care reform, and in particular, the state benefit programs of Medicaid, Medicare, and ssi. Looking to Leah Lakshmi Piepzna-Samarasinha's 2019 poetry and performance text collection *Tonguebreaker* and Aurora Levins Morales's 2013 essay and poetry collection *Kindling: Writings on the Body*, this chapter examines how radical queer-of-color writers negotiate the ableist bureaucracies and diagnostic gatekeeping of the medical-industrial complex while simultaneously dreaming of other configurations of care. I begin by mapping out how health/care infrastructure emerges and makes itself present in these works, shaping the form of what I call disability justice life-writing. Then, I turn to what Piepzna-Samarasinha calls "wild disability justice dreams" and elaborate on the rival care infrastructures envisioned by *Kindling* and *Tonguebreaker*. What, I ask, does care look like in the context of abandonment, apocalypse, and social isolation, when the state wants people to subsist on less and less? How do we reclaim, define, and practice care outside existing models offered by the state and the medical-industrial complex, in which care all too often exists on a continuum with control and abuse? I argue that *Kindling* and *Tonguebreaker* offer wild disability justice blueprints for health and care in an era of deprivation, in which care suggests not restoration and movement back toward the status quo—the reacquisition of a fabled norm—but rather the serious and sustained tending of a lifeworld that makes room for sickness and grief while generating real moments of joy.

The epilogue relays my own disabled, femme-of-color dreams of infrastructure and further describes my experiences with my best friend at the end of her life. I reflect on how queer-of-color and disability life-writing functioned as a kind of safety net for us during this time, offering support and recognition in a healthcare landscape that does not always view friendship as a legitimate connection. Looking to the essay "After Peter," written by gay Korean American author Alexander Chee, I examine some of the ways that queer people have acted as infrastructure for one another through sickness and death, when nothing else in the world will hold us.

Toward More and Better

This book emerges from the desire for more and better infrastructures of care—for adequate systems of support that can honor the sanctity of Black, brown, queer, feminized, and/or disabled lives. In the summer of 2019, I knew I could not separate my friend's illness from the context of a postwelfare United States, in which escalating healthcare costs and eviscerated public support systems rendered harmful care by one's romantic partner one of the few viable options in a threadbare world. I knew I could not separate it from the context of a presidential regime bent on killing sick and disabled people through its persistent attacks on Medicaid and ADA. I knew I could not separate it from the inflating numbers of the uninsured, or from the profit motives of the pharmaceutical industry. But I also knew that infrastructure did not have to look this way. And I knew this because of the blueprints left by my queer-of-color and/or disabled peers, elders, and ancestors. Now in the middle of the COVID-19 pandemic, which has underscored for so many the lived reality of state abandonment, I once again look for those dreams on the written page.

Care at the End of the World identifies disabled, feminist, and/or queer-of-color literary expression as a vital site of freedom dreaming in an era of accelerating infrastructural violence. Not frivolous or passive, dreaming envisions a different way out of the world that currently exists, and it requires very little aside from time and space. As Shayda Kafai suggests, "Perhaps the most compelling survival tool that disabled, queer, gender nonconforming, and transgender communities of color have is their dreamwork. . . . In dreaming, our communities materialize a world where, through fury and love, transformation in all its rebelliousness thrives."[73] Octavia Butler knew this when she wrote *Parable of the Sower*, which begins with the line "I had my recurring dream."[74] Recorded by Black disabled protagonist Lauren Olamina in her journal, the dream first registers a doorway, then a burning wall—a figure that encapsulates the hyperpermilitarized state of *Sower*'s California. Yet, the dream does not linger there. It tilts upward toward the stars, and toward the dream of "city lights" invoked by Lauren's mother: "Kids today have no idea what a blaze of light cities used to be—and not that long ago."[75] By calling up the memory of infrastructures past, great grids of power that seem unimaginable within *Sower*'s context of manufactured scarcity, Lauren's dream intervenes into the realities created and upheld by uneven systems of resource distribution. In the face of abandonment, she dreams and calls forth a "blaze of light," one that might illuminate other possible horizons of life.

I see infrastructural dreams like Butler's as bridges out of a turbocapitalist world that asks us to subsist on less and less. Within the lights, roads, pipes, and care networks spanning my project's archive, I locate the "desire for life between all of us" that Cherríe Moraga prophesied in her dream of a bridge.[76] Through the genres of speculative fiction (Butler, Delany, Piepzna-Samarasinha), magical realism (Yamashita), and myth (Ward), the writers in this book divine new maps from the seemingly mundane world of infrastructure, dreaming up ways of organizing life based in reciprocity and mutual support. These visions not only offer liberatory ways of knowing and inhabiting dependency but also pose dependency's recuperation as one key to liberation. Because freedom, at least in the crip-of-color imaginary, hinges on the support structures and care labor that make life more possible. This vision of freedom, as Piepzna-Samarasinha writes, means that we "massage the feet of those who make us live," including the radical Black, brown, queer, feminist, and/or disabled writers whose infrastructural dreams I recount here.[77] Together, like Moraga and Anzaldúa, we "brew and forge a revolution."[78]

Disability and Infrastructural Violence in Sapphire's *Push* and
Jesmyn Ward's *Salvage the Bones*

The Congress makes the following findings:

(1) Marriage is the foundation of a successful society.

(2) Marriage is an essential institution of a successful society which promotes the interests of children.

(3) Promotion of responsible fatherhood and motherhood is integral to successful child rearing and the well-being of children.

> —Personal Responsibility and Work Opportunity Reconciliation
> Act of 1996

I was left back when I was twelve because I had a baby for my fahver. That was in 1983. I was out of school for a year. This gonna be my second baby. My daughter got Down Sinder. She's r—d. I had got left back in the second grade, too, when I was seven, 'cause I couldn't read (and I still peed on myself).

> —Sapphire, *Push*

I want to begin, as these narratives do, with the institution of the family. Published in 1996, both of these documents grapple with the allocation of care and resources in a post-Reagan United States, and both offer competing visions of infrastructural support. The first epigraph, excerpted from the opening lines of the Personal Responsibility and Work Opportunity Reconciliation Act (PRWORA), offers an unqualified celebration of heterosexual marriage, reaffirming the private family unit as the nation's chief social safety net. While much critical discourse frames PRWORA as a tool of infrastructural divestment, I note here that this legislation functioned simultaneously as a form of investment in the nuclear family form, promoting this particular social arrangement as the primary means of distributing life-giving support. The legislation also is a vision and blueprint of infrastructure—and one that further absolves the state from accountability to its most vulnerable members.

As this chapter will argue, welfare reform's platform of "responsible" parenting was enforced, at least in part, through the anti-Black weaponization of disability and dependency. Proponents of antiwelfare policy, most famously Ronald Reagan, propagated myths of pathological Black mothering in order to justify racialized resource deprivation and the ongoing privatization of care. These myths, such as the "welfare queen," framed low-income communities—and single mothers in particular—as overly dependent and irresponsible. In response, the second epigraph cites the opening lines of *Push*, the controversial debut novel of the Black queer author and poet Sapphire. As opposed to the romance of nuclear domesticity promoted by PRWORA, *Push* registers the disabling effects of infrastructural violence wrought by US fictions of dependency. It does so from the perspective of a single Black teenage mother brutalized by state institutions. For the novel's protagonist Claireece "Precious" Jones, as well as her disabled baby daughter, the state-sanctioned infrastructures of patriarchal family and underfunded public education do not promote the "well-being of children," to cite PRWORA's formulation. Rather, they uphold nothing but cycles of trauma, abuse, and illiteracy, indexing the "national refusal," as Aliyyah Abdur-Rahman puts it, to "extend to [African Americans] ordinary resources of the state."[1]

Set nearly ten years after the passage of major welfare reform, Jesmyn Ward's 2011 novel *Salvage the Bones* maps the persistent effects of PRWORA and its anti-Black maternal mythologies into the next century. Like *Push* and PRWORA, the novel opens with a family portrait, in this case, introducing us to the African American Batiste household, who have lived and struggled for generations in the fictional Mississippi Gulf town of Bois Sauvage. *Salvage* begins with a description of a pit bull, the family dog, China, giving birth to puppies in a way that underlines her ferocity: "What China is doing is fighting, like she was born to do."[2] These paragraphs also establish the grief-soaked storyline of Mama, the Batiste matriarch, dying in childbirth: "She said she didn't want to go to the hospital. Daddy dragged her from the bed to his truck, trailing her blood, and we never saw her again."[3] *Salvage*, like *Push*, mobilizes figures of racialized maternity in order to map the purposeful failures of public support systems. Mama's undesired hospital visit, for instance, captures the medical harm inflicted by inadequate public healthcare infrastructures in exploited Black communities, which contribute to disproportionately high national rates of Black maternal death.

In response to state-sanctioned myths of familial pathology, this chapter offers a literary-cultural reframing of racialized mothering considering critical discourses of disability. It argues that Sapphire's *Push* and Ward's *Salvage the Bones* forge necessary links between welfare reform's dis-/enabling reorganization of state infrastructure and ableist narratives of Black mothering that frame so-called welfare queens as living parasitically on the collective well-being. Both *Push* and *Salvage* depict young Black mothers grappling with the disabling context of infrastructural divestment, in which the basic support systems for maintaining life—public schools, hospitals, housing, social services—have become increasingly compromised. They then tie these processes to the simultaneous production of white enablement through exploitative workfare programs (*Push*) and land theft (*Salvage*). As such, both novels enable the elaboration of a critical disability politic centered around welfare queen mythology and infrastructural violence, one that identifies, contests, and overwrites the punitive aims of public resource distribution.

I begin by establishing the relationship between the welfare queen figure and disability politics, highlighting the significance of medicalized language to antiwelfare narratives. I then demonstrate how this figure renders legible key connections between disability and Black feminist politics, linking them through the mutual engagement of crip-of-color critique. A crip-of-color critique, as this chapter will demonstrate, foregrounds the critical purchase of disability for Black feminist and feminist-of-color theories of gendered and sexual state regulation, and in turn brings considerations of racialized reproduction and state violence to the forefront of disability analysis. The next two sections examine the relationship between crip-of-color critique and literary form, or the devices and techniques enabling Sapphire and Ward to craft meaningful interventions into pathological narratives of dependency. First, I focus on *Push*'s use of the literary bildungsroman, a genre that enables Sapphire to model a form of infrastructural literacy grounded in disability consciousness. Next, I turn to *Salvage*'s use of mythology as a means of generating alternate narratives of Black maternity. I foreground how storylines of dependent subjectivity, articulated through the novel's reimagining of the welfare mother, interrupt the logic of disposability that casts racialized and disabled populations as parasitic, unproductive, and without value.

I conclude by describing the alternate care infrastructures—anchored by a disability ethos of interdependence—that both *Push* and *Salvage* articulate as a crucial part of their freedom dreaming. If, as the Marxist feminists Sophie Lewis and Kathi Weeks have argued, the family's "most fundamental feature" is that it privatizes care, then both novels attempt to envision social arrangements beyond the nuclear family form that might allow for care's collectivization.[4] In the disabling context of infrastructural violence, *Salvage* and *Push* both posit mutual, nondominant interdependency as a primary means of mothering a viable world.[5]

Cripping the Welfare Queen

Over the past several decades, the mythical figure of the welfare queen has occupied a key space in the US national imaginary. Beginning at least in the 1970s, business and political elites attacked "welfare queens" to deploy their disgust for Black women and mothers.[6] This tactic helped propel a major shift in the relationship between US state and capital during that period, from one in which the creation of the US welfare state aimed to resolve crises of capitalism, such as the Great Depression, to one in which so-called big government was framed as itself a crisis, undermining the capitalist drive for accumulation.[7]

In the 1980s, the emergence of Reaganomics signaled the advancement of a policy agenda that sought to resolve crises of capitalism by reallocating resources toward wealthy and propertied classes via "trickle-down economics" and the downsizing of welfare. Presaged by Democratic senator Daniel Patrick Moynihan's 1965 report on Black matriarchal households and popularized during Ronald Reagan's 1976 bid for the Republican presidential nomination, the welfare queen offered a story of racialized mothering that would soon become the nation's primary narrative of public dependency. Reagan's depiction of a spendthrift from Chicago's South Side who posed as a mother of fourteen to obtain state benefits inaugurated a discourse of policy reform that would breed slogans like George H. W. Bush's "cross-generational dependency," the commonly invoked "welfare as a way of life," and the Clinton administration's "end of welfare as we know it."

Indeed, Reagan's persistent narrative of the welfare mother "hit a nerve" with audiences across the campaign trail.[8] It represented a key tactic in long-standing histories of state-sanctioned assaults on racialized maternity, which range from

the destruction of kinship ties along the Black Atlantic to the punitive surveillance of state foster care practices. Famously, Daniel Patrick Moynihan's *The
Negro Family: The Case for National Action* identified "family structure," and in
particular single mother–headed households, as the "fundamental problem"
driving "the cycle of poverty and disadvantage" in African American communities.[9] Further, as the 1996 passage of major welfare reform attests, theories
around the "culture of poverty" proved attractive to US policy- and lawmakers,
who crafted official courses of action based on the perceived behavioral shortcomings of low-income Black families.[10]

According to PRWORA, the purpose of welfare reform is to "end the *dependence* of needy parents on government benefits by promoting job preparation,
work, and marriage."[11] Toward this end, this legislation imposed work requirements on welfare recipients, coercing poor mothers to accept low-paying jobs
in domestic, janitorial, or healthcare in exchange for benefits. It criminalized
parents for nonpayment of child support, further shifting the responsibility of
care from state and federal government to the private sphere. Further, through
PRWORA, the federal government empowered individual states to cut direct
aid to poor families, thereby shrinking local welfare rolls. A series of studies
published from 2013 to 2015 traced the deadly impacts of reform, finding links
between increased and earlier mortality among poor women and the enforcement of welfare-to-work programs.[12] One study in particular found that in Flor-
ida and Connecticut, new state welfare policies authorized by PRWORA reduced
the lives of recipients by .44 years.[13] Narratives of welfare dependency, anchored by ever-present mythologies of Black motherhood, thus vitally shaped
the ongoing regime of infrastructural violence whose intensification of material
and social inequality we see fully in our contemporary moment.[14]

Yet, in response to the propagation of this mythology by Reagan and others,
numerous writers, scholars, and activists claimed the welfare mother as a generative site for Black feminist and feminist-of-color thought. In Cathy Cohen's 1997
essay "Punks, Bulldaggers, and Welfare Queens: The Radical Potential of Queer
Politics?," for instance, the "non-normative and marginal" position of the welfare queen becomes one of the centers around which a radical queer politics
takes shape.[15] Additionally, Black feminist critics such as Dorothy Roberts,
Ange-Marie Hancock, Hortense Spillers, Patricia Hill Collins, Wahneema
Lubiano, and Alexis Pauline Gumbs have thoroughly outlined the gendered,
raced, classed, and queer dimensions of her narrative.[16] Gumbs, for instance,

responds to the state-sanctioned attacks on Black families and children by articulating a queer theory of Black mothering as revolutionary care praxis, a framework key to this chapter's analysis of Ward's *Salvage the Bones*.[17]

Following this rich critical legacy, I want to now foreground the ways in which discourses of inability have shaped the figure of the welfare queen and imbued her with rhetorical power. As Lezlie Frye has convincingly argued, disability emerged during this period as a "newly-wielded, indispensable tool for policing Black female sexuality, reproduction, and mothering . . . one that crucially enabled policies of welfare reform and prison expansion."[18] The welfare queen functions as perhaps *the* definitive disability narrative of late capitalism, a cautionary tale of state dependency that enabled the reallocation of public resources toward a global elite. She became legible as a public figure largely through ableist language and reasoning: the welfare queen is defined necessarily as a pathological mother, a social aberrancy to be rehabilitated through workfare programs. Through her alleged inability to mother, work, or re/produce in accordance with social norms, articulated through the charge of her dependency on state resources, she furnished a useful "cover story," to borrow Wahneema Lubiano's coinage, for global capitalism to propagate itself through the dismantling of social safety nets.[19]

Alongside the rhetorical mainstays of anti-Blackness and misogyny, the language of disability, pathology, and disease wrote the welfare queen into public legibility. According to Sanford F. Schram, the "new paternalism" of welfare reform shifted public dependency "from an economic problem to a medicalized one."[20] PRWORA in particular "helped accelerate the tendency to construct welfare dependency as an illness, thereby transforming welfare into a set of therapeutic interventions designed to cure people of a malady."[21] The Welfare Indicators Act of 1994, sponsored by Daniel Patrick Moynihan, similarly framed welfare dependency as a public health problem and suggested that the Department of Health and Human Services author annual reports to Congress on predictors of welfare dependence.[22] In other words, the dominant ideology of antiwelfare policy framed the need for public assistance *as itself* a disability, subject to state management and cure.

Further, as Alexis Pauline Gumbs has argued, the Reagan-era discourse around racialized reproduction framed Black teenage motherhood as an illness that justified the "wars on poverty and drugs that combined to situate disease and enmity in the bodies of poor women."[23] In *Erotic Welfare: Sexual Theory and Politics in the Age of Epidemic,* Linda Singer identifies how, at the beginning of the HIV/AIDS crisis, teenage and single motherhood were explicitly framed as epidemics, a characterization that later justified an uptick in punishment and surveillance of young women of color and the subsequent denial of health services.[24] The framing of Black mothers as disease vectors, Gumbs elaborates, insinuated "a threat [to] privileged populations through tax burdens, crime, and the generally [*sic*] erosion of quality of life," representing a path of infection that ostensibly moved from "oppressed" sites to privileged ones.[25]

Notably, PRWORA makes explicit use of illness in the Title I section on block grants for Temporary Assistance for Needy Families. Here, the legislation argues that "children born out-of-wedlock have a substantially higher risk of being born at a very low or moderately low birth weight," and "children born out-of-wedlock are more likely to experience low verbal cognitive attainment, as well as more child abuse, and neglect."[26] Describing them as both an epidemic and a threat, then, this framework of illness positioned poor single mothers as disabling to the nation writ large.

Given the centrality of disability to antiwelfare mythology, I view the welfare queen as a key figure for bridging disability and feminist-of-color politics, transforming them through the mutual engagement of crip-of-color critique. To briefly reprise my introduction, a crip-of-color critique demonstrates how disability politics and aesthetics can offer useful interventions into antiwelfare ideology. It registers and challenges the metaphors of illness, disability, and dependency that made welfare reform palatable to a larger audience, highlighting the centrality of ableism to antiwelfare policy. Returning to its bridging function, the crip-of-color framework further imagines coalitional possibilities between disability politics and the targeted populations of welfare reform. In so doing, it identifies possible axes of solidarity across lineages of liberatory thought, in which the ableist logic of welfare reform offers—perhaps counterintuitively—the potential for political affinity and consolidation.

Like Cohen's "Punks, Bulldaggers, and Welfare Queens," Sapphire's *Push* underscores the radical potential for "progressive transformative coalition work" between the groups most antagonized by welfare reform: racialized, low-income, and disabled populations.[27] Consider, for instance, the relationship between the protagonist, Precious, and her disabled baby daughter. In introducing her child, Precious states, "[My mother] don't love me. I wonder how she could love Little Mongo (thas my daughter). . . . What it is short for is Mongoloid Down Sinder, which is what she is; sometimes what I feel I is."[28] For scholars of disability studies, this passage may seem a strange place to locate political affinity, as it reduces the baby daughter to a diagnostic category.[29] But in naming her daughter "Little Mongo," an affectionate diminutive, Precious renders the language of diagnosis strange, redirecting it from its intended function of pathology to one of coalition and kinship. "Mongoloid Down Sinder" names what her daughter is, and also what Precious sometimes feels she is.

However, as a crip-of-color framework underscores, this unexpected affinity between Precious as welfare mother and her disabled baby daughter is not incidental. Rather, it reflects the ways in which ableist reasoning anchors antiwelfare rhetoric, casting entire categories of people as undeserving of public support. Turning to the disability scholar Michelle Jarman's argument, Precious's conceptions of her daughter—as not only *having* Down syndrome but *being* Down syndrome—mirror her assessment of her own circumscribed potential, as well as the static nature of her life circumstances.[30] As Jarman has noted, the novel's protagonist—sixteen-year-old Claireece Precious Jones—is "[haunted] by disability," as she must navigate the conjoined forces of "poverty, sexual abuse, illiteracy . . . , HIV, and having a daughter with Down syndrome."[31]

Set in 1980s Harlem, *Push* further entangles disability with the mechanisms of state violence specific to Reagan-era reform: the actively harmful public infrastructures, state agencies, and municipal services that allegedly aim to support vulnerable populations but in fact reproduce social and material harm. Reliant on public infrastructure, both Precious and Mongo are embedded in oppressive state systems—the welfare office, the public school, the psychiatric institution—that reproduce and further retrench their poverty. Just as Precious attends a school that prioritizes punishment over education, so Mongo is kept in a "r—d house" where "she lay on floor in pee clothes."[32] Through the paralleling of Precious's life experience with Mongo's, *Push* highlights the ways in which, to cite Cynthia Wu and Jennifer James, the "social, political, and cultural practices" of resource erosion work to "[keep] seemingly different groups of people in strikingly similar marginalized positions."[33] It thus demonstrates how a value system that idealizes a productive, economically independent, and able-bodied subject similarly works to empty both Precious and her disabled daughter of life worth.

Salvage the Bones, too, amplifies potential affinities between Black feminist and disability politics through its depiction of unsupported Black maternity. Published fifteen years after Sapphire's *Push*, Ward's novel centrally contends with the punishing legacies and structuring presence of state infrastructural divestment. *Salvage* documents the impoverished Batiste family in both their maintenance of everyday life and their preparations for imminent emergency. The emergency in question is Hurricane Katrina, a disaster intensified by a spectacular failure of public infrastructure—the failure of burst levees, emergency prevention, and federal assistance. As the data shows, $71 million evaporated from the budget of the Army Corps of Engineers in 2005, denying necessary improvements to the city of New Orleans's levee system.[34] Local, state, and federal emergency response systems collapsed in Katrina's wake, both unprepared and unwilling to navigate a disaster of such unprecedented scale. And while the connection to PRWORA may initially seem scant, Katrina's horrific repercussions, as many have noted, were the culmination of years of assaults on public infrastructural upkeep. "Soon after Hurricane Katrina hit the Gulf Coast," writes the educational scholar Henry Giroux, "the consequences of the long legacy of attacking big government and bleeding the social and public service sectors of the state became glaringly evident."[35] The aftermath of the storm is, in many ways, the outcome of welfare reform's deadly ideologies.

While New Orleans was the primary backdrop for this drama of state abandonment, Ward's Bois Sauvage, too, is indelibly shaped by the erosion of public services. There is the hospital, mentioned repeatedly throughout the novel, that none of the Batistes want to visit; it remains inaccessible for reasons we can only infer. There is the lone phone call from the state government, issued by a man with an "iron throat," that mandates evacuation using the language of personal responsibility: *"If you choose to stay in your home and have not evacuated by this time, we are not responsible. . . . These could be the consequences of your actions."*[36] And there is the "birth in a bare-bulb place," the title of the first chapter, which refers to both the Batiste homestead named "the Pit" as well as the work of birthing and mothering that is the novel's narrative engine. While the Batiste family cobbles together some semblance of protection against the storm, the protagonist, fifteen-year-old Esch Batiste, grapples with the knowledge of her unexpected pregnancy.

The novel begins by introducing three of Bois Sauvage's many mothers: Esch's mama, Esch, and China, the Batiste family pit bull. In the opening scene, Mama's death during childbirth functions as a framing event, a filter that all of the novel's meditations on infrastructure, mothering, and care pass through. Ward weaves memories of Mama's loving presence throughout *Salvage*; this character thus directly challenges state storylines of pernicious and disabling Black mothering. Recollecting moments when Mama laid rugs "over the [car] seat when [her children] were small and the upholstery would get so hot in the summer," and when she would catch fish with a "laugh that swooped up into the sky," Ward characterizes Mama as the indisputable anchor of the Batiste family and the primary way that her children learn about love and care.[37]

Yet, Mama's birthing crisis also indexes a salient intersection of anti-Blackness and disablement key to the novel's infrastructural critique: the prevalence of medicalized racism and obstetric violence that Black birthing people must regularly endure. As briefly mentioned in this chapter's introduction, Mama's hesitancy to seek medical attention speaks to a much larger crisis of care and active neglect disproportionately borne by places like Bois Sauvage. This lack of access to quality healthcare as the novel makes clear, also shapes her daughter's world. Esch Batiste describes the absence of reproductive support for low-income, rural Black communities when she recalls the misguided folk advice spouted by teenagers who "can't afford an abortion": "The girls say that if you're pregnant and you take a month's worth of birth control pills, it will make your period come on. Say if you drink bleach, you get sick, and it will make what will become the baby come out."[38]

While PRWORA cast poor mothers as disabling agents and public health threats to their children, Salvage highlights one actual public health crisis wrought by manufactured state neglect: the disproportionately high rates of Black maternal death and distress due to actively harmful healthcare and educational systems that cannot and will not support Black reproductive wellness. As Annie Bares notes, Mississippi state policies enacted through the "Personal Responsibility Education Program" determined "abstinence-only education as the state standard and forbid teaching that abortion ends pregnancy."[39] Such policies therefore placed responsibility on individuals to "[discover] health-related information without institutional support."[40] In Salvage, the fracturing of Black families cannot be attributed to the prevalence of matriarch-headed households, as Moynihan argued in his infamous report. Rather, the novel trains our focus on the deadly outcomes of infrastructural divestment, the repression of information about sexual health, and an anti-Black narrative context in which, as Esch puts it, "nobody wants what is inside you."[41]

In response to state mythologies that routinely blame Black mothers for economic and familial precarity, Salvage and Push instead underscore how absent and/or ailing state infrastructures erode the fabric of family and community, creating inhospitable conditions for low-income parents and children to live, provide care, or survive intact. Further, by illuminating dis-/enabling regimes of infrastructural violence, such as nonexistent reproductive healthcare, inadequate sex education, and underfunded public schools, both novels frame state institutions as actually doing the work of bad mothering, insofar as they reproduce a world incompatible with Black, low-income, and disabled life. In the following pages, I discuss how *Push* in particular mobilizes the literacy bildungsroman genre in order to offer a more granular view of racialized dis-/enablement.

Modeling Infrastructural Literacy in Sapphire's *Push*

A literacy narrative par exemple, Sapphire's *Push* is organized around Precious's gradual acquisition of reading and writing skills in spite of her subpar education. Its narrative arc details the protagonist developing new literacies from her engagement with the actively disabling public infrastructures of New York's Harlem, as well as the self-actualizing, "humane, [and] fail-safe communal infrastructures" of Each One Teach One, a community-based adult learning center led by the Black lesbian mentor Ms. Rain and attended by Precious alongside other marginalized women of color.[42] Returning to the novel's opening scene, Sapphire introduces the audience to Precious's world through the punishing logics of New York's public school system: "I was left back when I was twelve because I had a baby for my fahver. That was in 1983. I was out of school for a year. This gonna be my second baby. My daughter got Down Sinder. She's r—ded. I had got left back in the second grade too, when I was seven, 'cause I couldn't read (and I still peed on myself)."[43]

These lines document the deep connections linking family trauma and harmful state support—the perpetuation of harm by a system that cannot offer necessary interventions into clear cases of parental violence and that also worsens Precious's situation through the punishment of "[leaving] back." Precious is the product of relentless abuse to a nearly hyperbolic degree; raped and impregnated by her father, tormented daily by her mother, and warehoused by educational and social services, she encapsulates the violence of patriarchy, racism, and state divestment besieging Black urban communities in the 1970s and 1980s. Despite her clear signs of aptitude ("My grades is good") and her enthusiasm about school ("'n I really do want to learn"), she is nonetheless threatened with suspension due to her two teenage pregnancies, thereby exposing an educational ethos more committed to punishment than to care.[44] This scene further establishes the novel's amplification of infrastructure as a key narrative strategy, and accordingly, the forceful intrusion of state authority in every aspect of Precious's life. We soon observe the unwanted home visits paid by Precious's white teacher, Mrs. Lichenstein, who she describes as a "social worker teacher" and who her mother fears may cut them off from welfare.[45]

While *Push* condemns the brutality of state institutions, it is also necessary to note that the novel's adoption of the literacy bildungsroman, which imposes on its protagonist a developmental journey of progress, simultaneously underscores some of its potential limitations as a site of radical disability politics. In many ways, this genre implicitly frames Precious as a character in need of improvement, when in fact she is already a subject with knowledge prior to her acquisition of literacy. As documented by the novel's opening lines, Precious has an inherent understanding of state systems and the way they work to delimit Black lives.

Rather than dismiss the novel outright for its bildungsroman form, however, I argue that *Push* crips this genre by foregrounding the public institutions that reproduce illiteracy in vulnerable populations, therefore reformatting the form of the literacy bildungsroman to serve alternate political ends. The bildungsroman, in this context, enables a different kind of literacy that attunes both the novel's audience and protagonist to infrastructural violence. And while the literacy narrative may evoke mythical associations with progress and self-ownership, or the "easy and unfounded assumption that better literacy necessarily leads to economic development, cultural progress, and individual improvement," *Push* in fact disarticulates the simple association of education (and its correlate, hard work) with social mobility.[46]

Particularly in the context of US race relations, the acquisition of literacy has often been linked to the domestication and assimilation of Black and brown populations.[47] "Liberal ideology," Roderick Ferguson writes, "has often presented literature as a mechanism by which marginalized groups can bid for the normative positions of state and civil society."[48] Precious's acquisition of literacy, however, does not grant her such a position; at the novel's conclusion she is arguably farther from the dream of social mobility than ever before. Rather, her narrative of literacy presents reading and writing as potential but imperfect avenues of insurgency, a means of overwriting the antiwelfare discourse that decries the dependency of the city's most vulnerable, as well as challenging the prowelfare discourse that frames recipients as in need of tutelage and saving by the state.

Following this, while *Push* has frequently been read as a linear progress narrative, I contend that it functions equally as an account of antiprogress and socioeconomic stagnancy.[49] That is, though Precious gains self-confidence through her acquisition of literacy, her prospects for economic stability and security nonetheless remain foreclosed by the novel's conclusion, when she has a recent diagnosis of HIV/AIDS, a second child, and no money. The novel, then, fosters a crip-of-color politic that highlights the structural reproduction of irrationality and illiteracy in underresourced communities, thereby mapping the process of group-differentiated disablement itself. In so doing, it frames disability not as a static category of identity or "condition of being," but as a condition "of becoming," which Nirmala Erevelles has termed a "historical event."[50] Rather than regarding literacy as a transparent quality tied to reason and, by extension, humanity, Sapphire's *Push* foregrounds the material conditions of possibility for literacy itself. It illustrates how the manufactured scarcity of public services—including but not limited to public education—produces the seeming irrationality conveyed by adult illiteracy. In other words, if disability is a "historical event," then *Push* narrates how Precious comes to be "haunt[ed] . . . with disability" through the reorganization of state infrastructure marking the Reagan era.[51]

As a realist novel in the protest tradition, *Push* foregrounds the seismic economic shifts shaping US cities that have increasingly compromised public services. In *The New Urban Frontier: Gentrification in the Revanchist City*, geographer Neil Smith identifies gentrification (with New York City as primary test case) as an effect of and contributor to "the restructuring of national and urban economies in advanced capitalist countries toward services, recreation and consumption" and away from the maintenance of public infrastructure.[52] As both *The New Urban Frontier* and *Push* indicate, the interrelated forces of gentrification and infrastructural divestment share an ecological relation, as capital investment in the Upper East and Upper West Sides is inextricable from the decline of social spending in Harlem. Precious identifies this uneven landscape in her writing journal, where she records a subway trip from Harlem to these wealthy neighborhoods:

> but from our red bricks in piles
>
> of usta be buildings
>
> and windows of black

broke glass eyes.

we come to buildings bad

but not *so* bad

street cleaner

then we come to a place

of

everything is fine

big glass windows

stores

white people

fur

blue jeans

its a different city[53]

This journey enables a different kind of literacy, in which she reads the cityscape in terms of economic inequality and uneven development.

Part of Precious's journey, then, involves an increasing literacy of public infrastructural systems themselves, and the ways in which they optimize life for some while conscripting others to death and disablement. If narratives of development—like the literacy bildungsroman—have often involved the proper suturing of a subject to the nation-state, in *Push* literacy is instead deployed to expose the pernicious effects of state infrastructural systems, which produce the disabilities they devalue while upholding ideals of able-bodiedness. For instance, the novel's climactic moment—where Precious declares to her mother that she has been raped—also introduces us to New York City mayor Edward Koch, a mayor "deeply indebted to private developers for campaign contributions."[54] "I don't even think," Precious narrates, "my feets just take me back to Harlem Hospital. You know Koch wanna close it, say n— don't need no hospital all to theyself."[55] In addition to the school, the public hospital is depicted as a resource-strapped site that gives low-income Black communities the bare minimum of support. As Precious notes, the overworked nurses ("It's like they tired") treat her with contempt: "I'm a problem got to be got out they face. . . . Nurse say lots of people get out hospital wif no place to go, calm down, you not so special."[56]

By illuminating an infrastructural ecology of disablement, *Push* identifies eroding public supports as the cause of the cultural, behavioral, and familial "pathology" decried by Moynihan and PRWORA. Precious's illiteracy, domestic trauma, and unsupported pregnancies are poorly managed by inadequate social service systems, which then subsequently foreclose access to care and economic stability. In other words, infrastructure and dwindling public resources *produce* the signs of so-called pathology that then transform into the mythology of the welfare queen. The novel thus offers a reversal of the punitive discourse of public dependency that distinguishes between deserving and undeserving subjects. Ostensibly the *reason* for welfare cutbacks, here dependency is presented as the *result* of capital and state divestment: Precious and her communities are mired in municipal systems unwilling and unable to support them.

The infrastructural literacy modeled by *Push* underscores the relationships between an eviscerated welfare state and the attendant fortification of white supremacy and class stratification. The novel conveys this critique both in the subway ride and through its depiction of Precious's hypothetical stint as a home care aide, an arrangement she condemns through her journal entries. These written reflections respond to the emergence of welfare-to-work programs, which forced poor women to work in order to obtain benefits. Rather than viewing parenting as a real and necessary form of work, workfare rhetoric instead argued that single, low-income mothers needed to join the labor force in order to earn their right to state assistance.[57] Defined against the ideal of the productive, able-bodied worker, the low-income mother as alleged nonworker offered yet another stereotype steeped in ableist language, in which waged labor was presented as a cure-all for the disease of welfare dependency. "Race-laden press coverage and public discussions of Black migration, 'illegitimacy,' promiscuity and laziness," writes Premilla Nadasen, "transformed [Aid to Families with Dependent Children] from [a program] supporting the right of single mothers to stay home to one encouraging work outside the home."[58] Decried by liberals and conservatives alike, the Black mother's alleged refusal to work, furthered by the specter of disability, provided ongoing ammunition for the undoing of the welfare state. This particular line of logic demonstrates how disability, rather than signaling a *lack* of utility, rendered low-income women and mothers particularly useful to the expansion of global capitalism, which is contingent on resource privatization and racial-gendered labor exploitation.[59]

Claireece Precious Jones knows these state narratives quite well and repeats them back to her reader: "I know who I am. I know who they say I am—vampire sucking the system's blood. Ugly black grease to be wipe away, punish, kilt, changed, finded a job for."[60] Her story further illustrates the weaponization of disability against low-income, racialized women to create cheap pools of labor. Precious's disabilities, reflected through her low test scores, her "obvious intellectual limitations," sexual trauma, HIV diagnosis, and state dependency, provide validation for her social worker to funnel her into a welfare-to-work program.[61] Stolen from her social service worker's office drawer, her official state file contains medical diagnoses and standardized test data that facilitate this placement, and that enable the exploitation of her labor by the state.[62] In this way, it reproduces the diagnostic frame of disability's medical model in making sense of Precious's experiences. Her file is not a story of progress, but a declension narrative: though Precious is a "phenomenal" success at Each One Teach One, her "TABE test scores are disappointingly low. . . . She scored 2.8 on her last test."[63] It concludes with an account of Precious's health history and an indictment of her public dependency: "She has a history of sexual abuse and is HIV positive. . . . The client seems to view the social service system and its proponents as her enemies, and yet while she mentions independent living, seems to envision social services, AFDC, as taking care of her forever."[64]

After she discovers her social worker's intention to place her as a home health aide, Precious writes a journal entry detailing the exploitative economy of workfare:

> If I'm working twelve hours a day, sleeping in peoples houses like what Rhonda usta do, who will take care of Abdul? The ol white peoples had her there all day and night, "on call," they call it. But you only get pay for 8 hours (is the other 16 hours slavry?) so that's $8 \times \$3.35 = \$26.80$ dollars a day, but then you is not really getting that much cause you is working more than eight hours a day. You is working 24 hours a day and $26.80 divided by 24 is $1.12. . . . Home attendints usually work six days a week. I would only see Abdul on Sundays? When would I go to school? Why I gotta change white woman's diaper and then take money from that and go pay a baby sitter to change my baby's diaper? And what about school?[65]

Considering the diagnostic language of Precious's state file, workfare is presented as a means of rehabilitating a young Black mother's seeming profligacy. The file thus organizes the raw material of Precious's life into a narrative of cure, which replicates the medical model of disability and its attempted resolution or eradication of "impairments." The medical model, as Eunjung Kim and many others have observed, views disability as "an individual deficit or pathology to be corrected through professional interventions," with the goal of cure presented as the primary solution.[66] Akin to medical intervention, workfare is presented as a means of "curing" the welfare queen's pathology, of ostensibly making her into a productive citizen while in actuality creating a conduit for cheap domestic labor.

However, Precious's journal entry ruptures the smooth rhetorical operations of workfare initiatives. As Abdur-Rahman notes, *Push* is "structured dialogically": Precious's "autobiographical account of her life" intersects with and contests the "'official,' state-generated record of her life," represented by her "file," the "tesses," and welfare mythology.[67] In her writings, Precious identifies the paltry pay scale that works to devalue caring labor, as well as the racist and unjust economy of caregiving (e.g., her thoughts on diapering narrated above) that workfare necessitates. In her reflections on this economy, she evokes the long history of forced labor extracted from Black and racialized immigrant women for the well-being of white families, a system that deprives Black mothers of the time and resources to nurture their own children.[68] Rather than as a channel for social mobility, workfare is depicted here as a means of reproducing socioeconomic stagnancy, as well as a contemporary approximation of enslavement that redirects Black women's care work toward the reproduction of white supremacy. Within this arrangement, Precious, as a potential care worker, cannot be recognized as a disabled person in need of care herself.

As underscored by the novel's method of infrastructural literacy, the state does not provide care that actually affirms and sustains Precious; it instead extracts care work from her through workfare initiatives and falsely names that extraction as cure and progress. In Precious's self-authored narrative, however, disability does not function as a justification for labor exploitation; rather, it becomes key to the recuperation of the welfare mother as a figure of crip insurgency. Sapphire's *Push* thus renders particularly evident the relationship of disability to antiwelfare rhetoric, as well as the utility of a critical disability politic to overturning that rhetoric's operative logics.

In the following pages, I offer another meditation on crip-of-color literary form, examining how Jesmyn Ward employs mythmaking to craft alternate ideologies of care. Resonant with a radical disability ethos, Ward's rival myths of mothering both expose and interrupt the antirelational logics of welfare reform that decry dependency on others. As opposed to the rhetoric deployed by Reagan, Clinton, and others, *Salvage the Bones* suggests that a politics and aesthetics of dependency is not only possible but necessary for the survival of those populations cast as drains on the state.

Rival Myths of Mothering in Jesmyn Ward's *Salvage the Bones*

While Ward's *Salvage the Bones* does not engage explicitly with the welfare mother stereotype, it nonetheless centralizes the figure of the Black teen mother, who, according to Ward herself, "continues to loom large in the public consciousness" and provides a mythology of mothering that is "still too useful to some."[69] *Salvage the Bones*, in all of its mythic preoccupation with mothering, suggests that we need new narratives of racialized mothering to navigate an era wrought by infrastructural erosion, in which the most basic structures for sustaining life have quite literally been washed away. Yet, rather than asking the Black women and mothers buried underneath these state-sanctioned myths "to come clean," to borrow Hortense Spillers's formulation, *Salvage* instead counters myth with myth, redirecting myth's social and often sacred function to produce new systems of thought for a culture bent on punishing its most vulnerable members.[70] Resonant with the 2016 anthology *Revolutionary Mothering: Love on the Front Lines*, originally titled *This Bridge Called My Baby*, here mothering functions not as biological imperative or property relation, but as a repertoire of what the anthology's coeditor Alexis Pauline Gumbs terms "transformative bridgemaking acts."[71] This description enables us to see mothering as a kind of infrastructural labor: the practice of "creating, nurturing, affirming," and above all, "supporting" life.[72] Returning to the infrastructural hermeneutic of crip-of-color critique, I view the bridge of these "bridgemaking acts," as well as the bridge of the original *This Bridge Called My Back*, not only as metaphors but as infrastructural figures that speak to the crises of state support unfolding in Reagan's wake. Intervening into the social order reproduced by the welfare queen myth, which leveraged the specter of dependency to argue that some people deserve less than others,

Salvage the Bones instead mothers a vision of survival that encompasses *all* forms of life. As sixteen-year-old Skeetah Batiste puts it, "Everything deserve to live."[73]

This vision of survival importantly unfolds as a crip or disability ethos, as it contests the consequences of an ideology of ability while suggesting interdependency as a primary mode of survival. Erica Edwards describes the novel's ethical code as such: "Here, the weak survive, and survival articulates itself as the preservation of collectivity against singularity."[74] Similarly, Annie Bares draws on disability theory to identify the novel's "reject[ion] [of] pity or compassion as organizing principles for relationships among characters" in favor of "relationships based on an acknowledgement of mutual dependence."[75] Building on Edwards's and Bares's insights, I describe this ethos as crip because it takes bodily vulnerability as a given, approaching physical and psychological needs as simple matters of fact rather than evidence of pathology. As the disability justice activist Patricia Berne puts it, "All bodies have strengths and needs that must be met," and, following this, we must "attempt to meet each other's needs as we build toward liberation."[76] Meeting—or failing to meet—those strengths and needs is the work of infrastructure. Through its ethos of interdependency, or "the preservation of collectivity against singularity," *Salvage the Bones* furthers a crip vision of reciprocity and care, sketching out an alternate social order in which vulnerable human and nonhuman lives mutually sustain one another.[77] Drawing on the world-making properties of myth, it describes what can or even must arise in the context of state neglect.

This alternate order begins with a myth of creation: the birth in a bare-bulb place. Accordingly, the novel's chapter structure and titling conventions mimic the book of Genesis; its plot is spaced out over twelve days that each correspond to a chapter title—"The First Day," "The Second Day," and so forth. And for all of its unrelenting realism, the novel nonetheless signals its adoption of mythic structures as a means of imagining a habitable world. For instance, Esch Batiste calls on the myth of Medea, vengeful mother and sorceress, to give narrative form and meaning to her own conundrum of creation: "My stomach sizzles sickly, so I pull my book from the corner of my bed where it's smashed between the wall and my mattress. In *Mythology*, I am still reading about Medea and the quest for the Golden Fleece. Here is someone that I recognize. . . . I know her."[78] On Medea's ancient stage, Esch plays out the events of her own life, a practice that is a primary means of psychic survival.

Myths, according to Patricia Yaeger, are particularly well suited for this kind of visioning work, as they "establish long-term models for guiding behavior."[79] They require, first, mystery; second, a topos, or "an explication of cosmic shape"; third, an epistemology; and fourth, an "ethic—a set of rules or maxims about how to live within the parameters of the everyday."[80] And while myths might potentially retrench the oppressive norms of a culture, as in the case of the welfare queen, they also provide the possibility of cultural transformation.[81] The birth in a bare-bulb place thus outlines the cosmic shape of the world that the Batistes both inhabit and endure. The Pit, as Esch describes it, is the bare-bulb place, which refers both to its primary source of light—the bare bulb—and to the bare essentials of formal support and power to which the Batistes have access.

Like *Push*, the birth in a bare-bulb place entangles infrastructural violence with the phantoms of deviant mothering, layering the self-obliterating labor of giving life with the grid of electric power: "Mama had all of us in her bed, under her own bare burning bulb, so when it was time for Junior, she thought she could do the same. It didn't work that way."[82] The bulb also figures into China's own violent experience with birthing: "What China is doing is fighting, like she was born to do. Fight our shoes, fight other dogs, fight these puppies that are reaching for the outside, blind and wet. . . . It's quiet. Heavy. Feels like it should be raining, but it isn't. There are no stars, and the bare bulbs of the Pit burn."[83] This scene of birth twinned with death, of worlds both made and unmade, reformats another iconic scene of power and creation: the subterranean light installation that bookends Ralph Ellison's novel *Invisible Man* (1952). Viewing himself as part of "the great American tradition of tinkers," which include Thomas Edison and Benjamin Franklin, Ellison's protagonist famously gives life to "1,369" light bulbs powered by stolen electricity.[84] His seizing of the grid is not a purely aesthetic move but rather signifies an attempt to effect social change. As a tinker and inventor, the Invisible Man signals the need to create the world anew through the radical redirection of light and power.[85]

In *Salvage the Bones*, the burning bulb similarly draws on electricity's transformative properties. It illuminates another possible horizon for organizing social life, one that redraws the boundaries of the individual self and its claims to bodily wholeness. We see, for instance, how the birthing process both undoes and exceeds the self, transforming the bodies of Mama and China, the pit bull: "She seems to be turning herself inside out. . . . China is blooming."[86] In pregnancy, as Lily Gurton-Wachter has written, "the distinction you once knew between self and other comes undone."[87] Pregnancy, too, describes a system of interdependent relations; the fetus and the pregnant person are linked, if only temporarily, in their bids for survival. And while pregnancy and disability are not one and the same, they nonetheless both name categories of being that highlight the inherent changeability, porosity, and dynamism of bodies. "Disability," according to Rosemarie Garland-Thomson, "invites us to query what the continuity of the self might depend on if the body perpetually metamorphoses," and in so doing, it critiques the "normalizing phallic fantasies of wholeness, unity, coherence, and completeness."[88] Akin to disability activism and theory, the myth of the burning bulb takes the vulnerable, dynamic, and changeable body as a *given*, placing it at the center of the novel's alternate social order. In this way, the burning-bulb narrative demonstrates the world-making properties of dependency and vulnerability, insofar as it describes a cosmos generated *from*, rather than *despite*, embodied fragility.

The opening scene further undoes the differential worth assigned to human and nonhuman subjects, as it throws into question the hierarchies of life that value some forms of existence above others. This becomes evident in the mirroring language used to describe China and Mama Batiste, which, rather than reducing Mama to the status of animal, underscores the connection between two beings whose reproduction is similarly framed as a societal threat. Ward's use of bestial imagery further foregrounds the entanglement of race, gender, and reproduction with discourses of animality. It thereby suggests the coarticulation of "logics of race" with "logics of species," as well as the shaping impact of anti-Blackness on the "taxonomies that purport to divide human from animal," as Zakiyyah Iman Jackson so aptly puts it.[89] Rather than bidding for inclusion into the category of human, *Salvage* rejects the human-animal divide altogether, modeling instead a trans-species solidarity across and against the eugenicist logics of population control.

Animals, rather than occupying a lesser or subordinate position, coexist with their human companions in a mutual interrelation of need. "Some people," Skeetah Batiste observes, "understand that between man and dog is a relationship. . . . Equal."[90] Though *Salvage the Bones* articulates this vision of interspecies reciprocity throughout its pages, the first chapter sets the stage for this ethos of interdependence, as it highlights the all-encompassing love between Skeetah Batiste, Esch's older brother, and China, his pit bull. Waiting for China to give birth, Skeetah sleeps with her nightly in the shed, "curled around

China like a fingernail around flesh."[91] And just as China provides Skeetah with salable puppies and companionship, so Skeetah devotes himself to their survival in a world bent on their undoing: "They're going to live, and they're going to be big."[92] Rather than making appeals to self-ownership and independence, then, the novel's bare bulb sheds light on a world in which human and nonhuman life form an informal structure of support, generating an interspecies network of assistance in which the most vulnerable life-forms might (yet often do not) endure.

There is also the bare bulb itself, which as a recurring image of power and provision sketches its own mythology of mothering, survival, and creation. At its most surface level, the bare bulb signals the poverty of the Batiste household, who get by largely through the work of salvaging auto parts, wood scraps, flooring, and so forth. It also depicts, with swiftness and economy, the regime of resource deprivation that intensified Katrina's destruction. Yet the bulb signals more than just infrastructural violence; it also accompanies, again and again, the acts and figures of deviant mothering on which the novel turns. *Salvage the Bones* describes China, one of the novel's many mothers, as "burning bright," "so bright it is hard to look at her."[93] Like the bare bulb, China is fragile, vulnerable, yet in all of her vulnerability, she exudes a paradoxical kind of power. When Manny, Esch's romantic interest, suggests to Skeetah that China, as a recent mother, is too weak to fight, Skeetah replies, "You serious? That's when they come into they strength. They got something to protect. . . . That's power. . . . To give life . . . is to know what's worth fighting for."[94] The bare bulb and China both convey a myth of mothering in which power paradoxically hinges on fragility. Both can burn so brightly only *because* of their fragility, thus remapping the terrain of what power is or can be. Mothering, then, also taps into the epistemic registers of myth—that is, mothering as a means of knowing power differently, and as a system of thought that frames seemingly expendable life as "worth fighting for."[95]

But the labor of mothering a habitable world, as *Salvage the Bones* suggests, must go beyond a myth of creation. It also requires a myth of destruction, which unmakes a world incompatible with Black life. Consider, for instance, China's fatal maiming of one of her puppies, a gruesome scene that mirrors the oft-referenced Medea myth and its enactment of vengeance. While China's killing of the "red puppy" may at first seem anathema to the life-sustaining practice of revolutionary mothering, the novel characterizes this puppy as "the fattest, the most well fed, *the bully*," a "fat mite" who is "turgid with the promise of living."[96] The language of overaccumulation and aggression suffuses the puppy's description, suggesting that his "promise of living" is stolen directly from his littermates—a stark difference from the bootstrap individualism enforced by antiwelfare narratives. China's move to kill, then, is not a bid *against* a vulnerable life, it is a bid for the survival of the collective. As a destructive mother, she authors a cautionary tale against the practice of hoarding—the dominant framework of procapitalist state infrastructures—and toward a more just distribution of resources.

Revolutionary mothering, then, not only entails the infrastructural labor of nurture and support, it also requires the obliteration of existing entities, ideologies, and structures that allow resource deprivation and family separation to continue unabated. Enter Hurricane Katrina, recast in Ward's imagination as "the mother who swept into the Gulf and slaughtered."[97] For many of us, Katrina is synonymous with slaughter, a force that dealt death along raced and classed lines. But when we come to know Katrina as *mother*, a word that signals the revolutionary work of transformation, she becomes Oya, the Yoruban goddess of storms, winds, and change. According to Luisah Teish, one of the original contributors to *This Bridge Called My Back*, Oya "brings sudden structural change in people and things. [She] does not just rearrange the furniture in the house—She knocks the building to the ground and blows away the floor tiles."[98] And so, while Katrina makes short work of the Batiste homestead, she also washes away the "yacht club, and all the white-columned homes that faced the beach, that made us feel small and dirty and poorer than ever."[99] She destroys the material emblems of a social system that reproduces poverty for families like the Batistes. Both types of property, once unequal in value, are now leveled and wiped clean, a necessary prerequisite for mothering something new altogether.

Ward's portrayal of Katrina as a mother and regenerative force of transformation may initially feel dubious, particularly given the immensity of Black death generated in her wake. The real-world Katrina did not mother anything new; rather, she rendered the infrastructural status quo painfully apparent. But Katrina, when reimagined as Oya, generates a possible future for the residents of Bois Sauvage. Notably, she spares the Batistes and their neighboring friends and family. In Ward's imaginary, she is "the murderous mother who cut us to the bone *but left us alive*. . . . She left us to learn to crawl. She left us to salvage."[100] Katrina as mythic mother thus promotes a vision of recovery for communities viewed as bad investments by the state. The final chapter, in which Katrina retreats, bears the title "Alive."

This maternal reframing feels particularly significant in light of government and mass media responses to the storm, which cast Katrina's survivors as deserving of punishment rather than support. Such responses leveraged the language of personal responsibility and disability when discussing Katrina, placing blame for disastrous consequences not on underfunded infrastructure but on "the inabilities of the unevacuated."[101] Mass media coverage framed the storm's survivors, most of whom were Black, as looters and thieves whose actions implicitly warranted negative outcomes for community and city alike.[102] This language of thievery mirrors the discursive construction of welfare mothers and so-called welfare cheats, mythical figures demonized for stealing resources that allegedly do not belong to them. This discourse helped fuel a hypermilitarized response that worsened the storm's deadly impact; several days after Katrina's landfall, the National Guard arrived in New Orleans with the authorization, as then-governor of Louisiana Kathleen Blanco put it, to shoot and kill "hoodlums."[103]

However, as *Salvage* illustrates, such mythologies masked the actual system of theft intensifying the storm's death toll, which includes the bleeding of state coffers and subsequent weakening of the levees, but also a much more longstanding history of stealing Black labor, lives, and futures. As a counterpoint to media and state narratives of personal responsibility, Ward's novel offers another myth of origin for Katrina's destruction, which begins with the Pit. The novel's first chapter recounts how Esch's maternal great-grandfather Papa Joseph owned "around fifteen acres" that "the white men he [worked] with" mined for clay "to lay the foundation for houses": "Papa Joseph let them take all the dirt they wanted until their digging had created a cliff over a dry lake in the backyard, and the small stream that had run around and down the hill had diverted and pooled into the dry lake, making it into a pond, and then Papa Joseph thought the earth would give under the water, that the pond would spread and gobble up the property and make it a swamp, so he stopped selling earth for money."[104] Ward's usage of the passive verb *let* in her portrayal of the earth selling underscores a coercive relationship between Papa Joseph and the white men, who use his land to reinforce their own wealth, and who highlight his tenuous relationship to property ownership. While the Batiste homestead may officially belong to Papa Joseph, due to his precarious economic position he must part with portions of the land until it is almost uninhabitable—a process of thievery by other means.

By the novel's eleventh chapter we learn that the gutting of the Pit renders it particularly vulnerable to flooding. Katrina's arrival realizes Papa Joseph's greatest fear, that "the pond would spread and gobble up the property." Her floodwaters "[move] under the broken trees like a creeping animal, a wide-nosed snake" with a tail growing "wider and wider, like it has eaten something greater than itself."[105] Ward's characterization of the Pit, then, casts the deadly consequences of the storm as a crisis of white theft, a relentless, intergenerational system of stealing that long predates Katrina's landfall. When we arrive at the final chapter, in which the Bois Sauvage residents sift through the posthurricane rubble to recover what remains, we see the residents not as thieves, not as looters, but as those who must salvage in bits and pieces that which has already been stolen from them. This alternate origin myth thus reverses the dominant mythology that transformed the survivors of the hurricane into criminals. In framing the residents of Bois Sauvage as survivors, and by generating myths that can mother Black survival, *Salvage the Bones* disrupts a calculus of life value that insists on the expendability of some in order to support the rest. It generates the possibility of a world in which hierarchies of life no longer hold traction, whether they are determined by race, ability, or species.

Ward's *Salvage the Bones* thus leverages myth as a narrative intervention into anti-Black frameworks of criminalization, thievery, and dependency, instead highlighting white land theft and hoarding as key elements driving Katrina's devastation. The novel fashions myths of destructive mothering in order to wipe these elements clean, thereby underscoring the necessity for mothering something altogether new. In the final pages of this chapter, I further elaborate on the motherly, creative labor of world building. Here, I detail the alternate infrastructures of care put forth by *Push* and *Salvage*—extrafamilial arrangements in which characters like Precious and Esch might survive on their own terms.

Infrastructures of Interdependency

In Sapphire's *Push*, the alternative classroom of the Each One Teach One program constitutes the novel's chief infrastructural vision of social recuperation. A community-based program designed to compensate for the shortcomings of public education and social services, Each One Teach One provides Precious with an informal support network comprising other young women of color struggling toward literacy. It thus divests from the anti-Black world reproduced through the carceral and punitive infrastructures of Precious's underfunded classroom, Mongo's state institution, and surveilling social workers.

Through its unflinching depiction of welfare offices, public schools, and hospitals, *Push* places no faith in the capacity of state agencies and institutions to generate a livable world for the so-called underclass, and it demonstrates how state care and violence can and do exist on the same continuum. At the same time, this imagined classroom once again speaks to some of the limitations of *Push*'s infrastructural freedom dreaming, as it enacts the narrative of progress so often imposed on welfare recipients—that is, the idea that they need rehabilitation. What's more, Sapphire's Each One Teach One classroom predates the now robust conversations critiquing the nonprofit industrial complex. These conversations highlight the political concessions nonprofits must make in order to secure funding and consider how organizations such as Each One Teach One might also contribute to the privatization of care.[106] As these discussions make clear, the shifting of care responsibility from the state to nonprofits, charities, and churches is yet another tactic of infrastructural divestment.

Rather than seeing these limitations as failures, however, I view them as evidence of the complicated work of infrastructural dreaming, in which proposed blueprints for liberation and care will inevitably produce more contradictions. Ms. Rain's classroom cannot compensate for the intensifying resource disparities of a Reagan-era New York City, and it potentially suggests that vulnerable populations can (and should) support themselves. It does, however, at least envision a network and ideology of care that disrupts the logics of welfare reform. The empathetic Ms. Rain leads Precious and her classmates in both their acquisition of the written word and, relatedly, the capacity to interpret and articulate their own experiences on their own terms. By encouraging the daily work of journal keeping, Ms. Rain positions the students as authors of their own experiences, thereby mirroring the book's tactic of overwriting preexisting state narratives that degrade women and queer people of color. Early on in the literacy process, Ms. Rain walks Precious, letter by letter, through the title of a book called *A Day at the Shore*. She offers encouragement with each letter and word; when Precious misrecognizes *at* as *ate*, she says, "'Good! Almost! That word is 'at.'"[107] Eventually, Precious reads the book's title in its entirety and feels waves of affirming emotion: "I want to cry. I want to laugh. I want to hug kiss Miz Rain. She make me feel good. I never readed nuffin' before."[108]

Push demonstrates how care, in addition to blunting the harsh edges of Precious's world, can also be a form of creative labor, insofar as it generates other possibilities for organizing social life. Rather than simply reproducing what exists, then, the novel frames caregiving as itself a form of political and social world making. In this way, *Push* resonates with Leah Lakshmi Piepzna-Samarasinha's disability theories of care, which posit care as "work of making the next world, the world we want, the post-Trump, post-fascist, post-apocalyptic world."[109] Like Ward's visions of destructive mothering, part of this creative process further entails the work of unmaking existing infrastructures. Ms. Rain's classroom, then, constitutes a site of dangerous knowledge production where young women of color unlearn the lessons of welfare reform: "These girlz is my friends. I been like the baby in a way 'cause I was only 16 first day I walk in. They visit at hospital when I had Abdul and take up a collection when Mama kick me out and bring stuff to 1/2way house for me—clothes, cassette player, tuna fish, and Cambull soup, and stuff. They and Ms Rain is my friends and family."[110] Rather than functioning as a bridge "[to be] walked over," the support labor provided by Ms. Rain, Precious, and her classmates operates in service of their chosen kinship network—not white folk in New York City, not workfare initiatives, and not their families of origin.[111] The women of Each One Teach One provide the necessary support networks that both state and family have denied them, routing their caring labor toward mutual survival. The novel meticulously catalogs these efforts and items, ensuring that they do not go unnoticed: "clothes, cassette player, tuna fish, and Cambull soup." What's more, *Push* does not value some of these items over others, demonstrating that Precious's needs for enjoyment (indicated by the cassette player) are key to sustaining her as a whole person, rather than just administering to her physical needs.

Further, by highlighting the sensuous pleasures of food, music, and friendship, the passage represents forms of loving exchange that reimagine care as a potential source of joy, even and especially for those for whom care functions as a site of oppression. This narrative reframe includes the presence of affirming touch: later in this scene, Precious tearfully relays the news of her HIV diagnosis to her classmates, and her friend Rita Romero responds by hugging her "like [she's] her chile."[112] In this way, Sapphire's novel offers a provisional answer to Piepzna-Samarasinha's inquiry in *Care Work: Dreaming Disability Justice*: "What does it mean to shift our ideas of access and care . . . from an individual chore, an unfortunate cost of having an unfortunate body, to a collective responsibility that's maybe even deeply joyful?"[113] Rather than depicting care work as unilaterally burdensome, or always a site of racialized oppression, *Push* envisions a queer and crip context in which care might be given and received as a practice of pleasurable connection, a counternarrative of caregiving that the next chapter explores at greater length.

To briefly elaborate on the sensuous dimensions of care highlighted by *Push*, I now turn to Audre Lorde's concept of the erotic. Lorde theorizes this concept as the often-buried "capacity for joy" shared between women that, when accessed, opens up life-sustaining possibilities for connection and freedom.[114] Described by Amber Jamilla Musser as "a space for women to form bonds with each other to repair the damage done by patriarchy and racism and to formulate ways of moving beyond those systems," Lorde's erotic might also be understood as the ethos of Ms. Rain's classroom.[115] The shaping presence of Lorde is further made explicit by a reference to the 1978 poetry collection *The Black Unicorn*: "[Ms. Rain] got us book from Audre Lorde. . . . What is a black unicorn? I don't really understand the poem but I like it."[116] Through touch, food, and music, the Each One Teach One classroom space models care that "embraces the entire body," as Sarah Chinn puts it.[117] It thereby makes imaginable multiple articulations of Black women loving other women, in ways that highlight the "overlapping terrain of the black lesbian and the black mother."[118] For instance, in hugging Precious "like [she's] her chile," Rita Romero transforms her into the beloved recipient, rather than provider, of their collective mothering efforts, a shift further underscored by Precious's observation that she's "been like the baby" of the group from day one.[119] *Push* thus establishes the Each One Teach One classroom as grounded in a Black queer (and crip) ethics of care, as evidenced by the references to Lorde and the sensuous depictions of friendship.

Much has been written about the Each One Teach One program as a site that "opens a space for sexual and familial diversity within the African American cultural context."[120] An openly lesbian poet, Ms. Rain has a commitment to teaching self-authorship that extends to overwriting the narratives of uplift promoted by the white supremacist state and by Black nationalism, both of which identify the heteropatriarchal family and nation as sites of redemption. She instead fosters a classroom community that models a nonhierarchical network of fictive kin. Here, the participants are bound not by blood ties but instead by what Chela Sandoval has termed "affinities inside of difference," a fostering of "differential consciousness" in which no single identity or ideology is prioritized.[121] Their differences and multiply marginalized experiences are, in the end, honored through an anthology collectively authored by Precious and her classmates, a multivoiced, multigenre collection titled *Life Stories* evocative of other feminist-of-color literary collections such as *This Bridge Called My Back,* *Home Girls,* and *Making Face, Making Soul / Haciendo Caras.*[122]

Rather than privileging the heterosexual nuclear family as key to social mobility, then, Precious and her classmates practice interdependent models of friendship that critique the tyranny of the family and the privatized model of caregiving ensconced therein. This critique is particularly salient considering the thematic of incest and child abuse that runs throughout *Push,* which condemns the infrastructures that protect nuclear families at the expense of other social and community relations. For Precious and her peers, family does not offer safe haven. Instead, it constitutes yet another domain of violence, one aligned with the harm and neglect of the state. In other words, while the nuclear family as political institution frames care as an individual responsibility divorced from the public sphere, the alternative classrooms of *Push* envision care as a collective practice to be shouldered by all. Notably, in Each One Teach One, the life-sustaining resources of education, food, and housing are not contingent on work ethic or access to waged labor, but given and exchanged freely as gestures toward collective survival. Here, the affective labor of teaching, mothering, and friendship is prioritized, imbued with value, and given in abundance.

Akin to Ms. Rain's classroom, *Salvage* similarly insists on an abundance of care and caring relations, in which there is more than enough to go around. The final chapter depicts the reinforcement of Esch's own support system as she navigates another form of abandonment—the unceremonious exit of her baby's father, Manny. While Esch expresses that the baby "don't have a daddy," the kind and generous Big Henry counters by insisting, "This baby got a daddy.... This baby got plenty daddies," thereby underscoring relations of care that flourish in excess of state-sanctioned kinship forms.[123] Esch's world is rich in mommies, daddies, and caregivers, a vast and textured infrastructural network that counters the scarcity characteristic of antiwelfare initiatives. *Salvage* thus connects survival to the practice of care as a social project, and a project that emerges through the interlocking efforts of many dependent life-forms. This vision of survival, further, is pointedly not the survival of the fittest (as in those with economic, racial, and able-bodied privilege), but survival of the most vulnerable. In the Pit, the vulnerable endure, and survival is the product of mutual support and reciprocity rather than self-preservation—a vision contingent on the interdependence of beings.

The closing scene perhaps most fully articulates the novel's infrastructural vision of survival. The storm has receded, and Skeetah has begun his search for China, who was carried away by Katrina—the devouring of one mother by another. Esch's language shifts into the future tense:

> We will sit with [Skeetah] here. . . . We will sit until we are sleepy . . . until Junior falls asleep in Randall's arms, his weak neck lolling off Randall's elbow. Randall will watch Junior and Big Henry will watch me and I will watch Skeetah, and Skeetah will watch none of us. . . . He will look into the future and see her emerge into the circle of his fire . . . dull but alive, alive, alive . . . *China*. She will return. . . . She will know that I have kept watch, that I have fought. China will bark and call me sister. . . . She will know that I am a mother.[124]

Here, Ward describes a myth of China's return that can manifest only through the collective efforts of the Batiste siblings and Big Henry. This manifestation of *will*, the operative term of the future tense, assumes the form of a human chain, an infrastructural network that links bodies and futures together. Esch's usage of the future tense, a means of "willing" China back into the world, intervenes into narratives of expendability in order to insist on the survival of vulnerable populations. Her usage of *will* is a mode of production toward a social world that does not yet exist, a world in which China is written back into existence and recognizes Esch as mother.

Further, this scene does not frame *will* as a characteristic of the propertied subject, in which an individual can attain success through the sheer force of hard work. Rather, *will* functions as a form of speculative futurity that is not generational or linear but lateral, a vision of the future generated between beings connected through experiences of revolutionary mothering. Here arises the final myth of mothering, a myth in which one becomes a mother through the labor of keeping watch, of fighting, of surviving; a myth in which one is not born but becomes a mother through infrastructural labor, which can build a bridge from the ruins of Bois Sauvage to another mode of social life. This is, above all, a myth of revolutionary mothering that insists on the recuperation of dependency and the recognition of shared vulnerability as a primary mode of survival, and as a means of generating a possible future for lives that survive against all odds: "*Tomorrow*," Esch thinks, "*everything will be washed clean. What I carry in my stomach is relentless; like each unbearable day, it will dawn.*"[125]

Through their counternarratives of deviant mothering, Ward's *Salvage the Bones* and Sapphire's *Push* foreground the recuperation of dependency and the re-visioning of care as vital tactics for intervening into anti-Black ideologies of familial pathology. In this way, both works encapsulate the political and aesthetic work of a crip-of-color critique. Taken together, both *Salvage* and *Push* articulate a system of values that (1) honors the vulnerability and dependency of living creatures as well as their differing needs for support; (2) underscores the dis-/enabling brutality of infrastructural violence; (3) forges solidarity between Black feminist and disability politics; and (4) envisions alternate modes of sociality organized around care for other living beings, regardless of blood relation or similarity to the self. *Salvage* in particular extends its vision of radical care to the nonhuman realm, divesting from the hierarchies of race, ability, and species underlying uneven resource distribution. And so, while disability does haunt both novels with scenes of trauma, illness, and—in the case of *Salvage*—dismemberment, I am less interested in thinking about disability as a set of identifiable diagnoses, and more interested in proposing disability as an analytic for reading across landscapes of racialized state neglect.

Further, while a crip-of-color critique explores the political potential of interdependence, it does not frame this value as a cure-all for contemporary crises of care. Even in *Push* and *Salvage*, the community-based networks that arise in the absence of infrastructure are still not enough: Precious may gain literacy and Esch may survive the storm, but their futures nonetheless remain circumscribed by material scarcity. Following this, I want to recognize the limitations inherent in a utopian discourse of interdependence that, in highlighting networks of informal infrastructure, potentially further erodes state accountability by suggesting that vulnerable populations can and should support themselves. The work of reclaiming dependency, to quote Akemi Nishida, will always be "messy," complicated, and never straightforward, especially in a world anathema to justice-based systems of care.[126]

The next chapter expands on the re-visioning of care and care work as a source of sensuous and pleasurable connection, particularly for those most often viewed as the least deserving of it. Just as Sapphire's *Push* drew on Lorde's erotic by way of queer friendship, so Samuel Delany's 2012 novel *Through the Valley of the Nest of Spiders* explores the joyful, deviant, and insurgent possibilities of interdependency through its sensual depictions of waste management. Both novels, then, highlight pleasure as a key element within a crip and Black queer ethics of care, framing it as a "measure of freedom," as adrienne maree brown puts it.[127] Further, while *Push* and *Salvage* generate rival myths of Black maternity to intervene into state storylines of familial pathology, *Through the*

Valley instead leans into the pathological charge of deviant kinship and eroticism, mining the transgressive potential of kinky crip-queer sex in order to flout the disciplinary politics of respectability and inclusion. In *Through the Valley*'s sanitation utopia, the often-eroticized pleasures of interdependency become legible as acts of insurgency, insofar as they generate possibilities for giving, receiving, and imagining care beyond state-sanctioned kinship forms.

Samuel Delany's Crip-Queer Ethics and Erotics of Waste Management

Alongside dependency, waste has long featured in antiwelfare discourses as a primary means of justifying infrastructural violence. According to proponents of reform, welfare-dependent families represented the seemingly intractable problem of government excess, or the expenditure of public resources on unproductive segments of the US population. For instance, in a 1951 debate in Congress on the Aid to Dependent Children program, Representative Burr Harrison of Virginia critiqued the "inefficiency, the waste, and the fraud in the public-welfare program," raising the specter of "shameless cheats," "chiselers," and "extravagant, ineffective, and socialistic administration."[1] As suggested by Harrison's commentary, the trope of waste demonstrates contempt for the ever-expanding category of the undeserving poor, a group distinguished from "the man who by honest toil pays the taxes."[2] This trope, as Gay Hawkins observes, functions as an instrument of censure: "Waste is at the heart of so many moral economies that it's difficult to find any sense in which it isn't bad. To be unproductive or to excessively expend is a sign of poor discipline and irresponsible conduct."[3] Waste's disciplinary function, too, extends to the denial of joy for welfare recipients, whose spending habits and choices have frequently been subject to public scrutiny.

It is through this moralizing, antiwaste, and antiwelfare paradigm that I approach the sanitation infrastructural utopia envisioned by Samuel Delany in his 2012 novel, *Through the Valley of the Nest of Spiders*. Delany's pleasure-centric novel details the lifelong gay partnership and incestuous family structure shared by Eric Jeffers (the novel's white, blond, and conventionally attractive protagonist), his mixed-race partner Morgan "Shit" Haskell, and Shit's white father Dynamite. Sanitation workers by trade, the three characters make their living by carting garbage away from the Dump, a Black gay (and, as I argue, disabled) separatist community characterized as much by its disdain of Reagan-era social policies as by its joyful commitment to piss play, perverse pleasures, and public sex.

This chapter argues that in its flagrant refusal of sexual propriety, governing kinship paradigms, and restraint of all kinds, *Through the Valley* imagines waste management as a set of insurgent crip-of-color strategies that reject state-authored narratives dictating the proper distribution of care and pleasure. According to Ronak Kapadia and J. T. Roane, insurgency describes fugitive practices and forms of consciousness that "thwart the political authority of an occupying power" (Kapadia) and "render other possibilities for configuring living, being, and collectivity" outside of government mandates (Roane).[4] Regarding the political authority of the US nation-state, welfare reform's twin pillars of (waged) work and (nuclear) family were framed as central to cutting the fat of government extravagance and enforced via welfare-to-work and marriage promotion policies. For instance, in a set of remarks accompanying the passage of the Personal Responsibility and Work Opportunity Reconciliation Act (PRWORA), then-president Bill Clinton pledged to move poor families "from welfare to independence," repeatedly invoking work as a cure-all for poverty. He states, "From now on our nation's answer to this great social challenge will no longer be a never-ending cycle of welfare; it will be the dignity, the power, and the ethic of work."[5] Clinton's commentary foregrounds one tenet of the American work ethos, which positions work as the main prerequisite for access to life-sustaining resources. Implied here, too, is the belief that those who do not participate in paid labor do not deserve state care. As a crip-of-color critique highlights, this welfare-to-work ethos has far greater impacts on those who have been structurally and historically denied gainful employment, or for those disabled people who, at the level of definition, have been cast outside of productivity itself.

Following this, I examine how Delany's *Through the Valley of the Nest of Spiders* takes up waste management—as vocation, infrastructural figure, and sexual practice—in order to refuse the naturalized relationship between work, normative kinship, and independence forged by welfare reform. This refusal marks a form of crip-of-color insurgency in that it disarticulates the well-worn connections between paid employment, nuclear family making, and access to affirming care.

In this way, I extend the previous chapter's analysis of welfare queen mythology and state narratives of dependency by taking up dependency's counterpart: the American mythology of independence, which is often tied to one's capacity to perform waged work. Independence, as Clinton's remarks make clear, offers a powerful ideological tool for furthering state austerity measures, as it was (and continues to be) weaponized against vulnerable populations to create cheap and disposable pools of labor. The weaponization of independence thus frames welfare reform as not simply an economics or policy issue, but also a discursive formation, one that relies heavily on narrative and mythmaking. As such, literature and culture— particularly that produced by and about welfare reform's targeted populations— functions as a key site of rupture for austerity's ideological operations.

The anchoring concept of this chapter, then, is *refuse work*, which carries multiple registers of meaning in *Through the Valley*: (1) the literal work of sanitation infrastructure; (2) the erotic management of human waste; (3) the intimate labors of sex and care that honor the body's needs; and (4) the refusal of an antirelational American work ethic that disavows dependency on others. Indeed, those who perform the infrastructural work of care and sanitation, who administer to and support the lived realities of disabled bodies, are often dismissed due to cultural anxieties around human waste and lack of bodily control. *Through the Valley*, however, not only celebrates these forms of labor, it frames such practices as an engine of queer and disabled world making, the informal infrastructure on which arrangements adverse to the nuclear family take shape. What's more, the novel depicts care work as a vital source of erotic, emotional, and communal joy. This narrative strategy refuses not only dominant understandings of care as "an individual chore," but also the belief systems that police the enjoyment of pleasure for nonworking populations.[6] Through the concept of refuse work, I demonstrate how Delany's reverent portrayal of sanitation and care infrastructures makes imaginable an insurgent crip-queer politics of labor insofar as it highlights the kind of work that sustains abject social collectivities in excess of welfare reform's imaginings.

I begin by making the case for waste and its management as a point of solidarity linking Black, queer, and disability politics, demonstrating how *Through the Valley* renders this connection legible. In the following pages, I linger on one particularly salient site of crip-of-color affinity: abjection. I then pivot to the novel's reverent depictions of sanitation infrastructure, exploring how the ever-present theme of waste management—which includes the sexual management of bodily fluids—offers vital interventions into the repressive work ethic propagated by antiwelfare policy. This ethic not only ties one's dignity and independence to the ability to labor but also promotes the idea that work should look a particular way. For the queer, often racialized, and often disabled residents of the Dump, dignity and independence do not register as ideals or even shared values. The community instead centers the joy, long-term sustenance, and conviviality of those deemed disposable by state policies and, as such, invests in robust civic and erotic infrastructures that support their well-being.

Finally, I demonstrate how the intimate labor of waste management enables the emergence of relational forms adverse to the nuclear family. Here, waste functions as a kind of interpersonal infrastructure upholding alternate kinship and communal arrangements, many of which are bound by a shared commitment to kinky crip-queer sex. Against the state-authored mandates of work and family, *Through the Valley* develops a utopian vision centered around abject eroticism, one that revels in the transformative dependencies and convivial networks enabled through expansive, nonnormative, and perverse enactments of bodily intimacy. It thus models for its readers an enabling infrastructural joy.

Waste Management and Crip-of-Color Critique

In a 1986 radio address delivered from his "rain-soaked mountaintop ranch," then-president Ronald Reagan prepared the ground for welfare reform legislation by mobilizing the rhetoric of government excess.[7] Critiquing the cost-effectiveness of state assistance programs, Reagan states that "the waste of money pales before the sinful waste of human potential," invoking the specter of the nonworking single mother in order to stoke anxieties around big government.[8] While *Through the Valley* begins in 2007 and highlights the historic inauguration of Barack Obama, it nonetheless grapples with the antiwelfare (and by extension, antiwaste) legacies of the Reagan administration. Reagan-era policies similarly provide the social and historical backdrop for many of Delany's other works, such as the novel *The Mad Man* (1994), the Return to Nevèrÿon series (1979–87), and the graphic novel memoir *Bread and Wine: An Erotic Tale of New York* (1999). As Michael Bucher and Simon Dickel observe, *The Mad Man* and *Bread and Wine* reflect on a "period of aggravated and sustained homelessness in the U.S.," a crisis "willfully exacerbated by the social politics of the Reagan administration," which combined "federal cutbacks to low-income housing" with the widespread deinstitutionalization of mental health patients in the "absence of effective alternative care."[9] Relatedly, *Through the Valley* responds to the homophobic and racist disposability politics enacted through the administration's purposeful mismanagement of the AIDS crisis, connecting this practice of intentional neglect to its widespread dismantling of social services.

Established by the fictional Robert Kyle Foundation, a philanthropic organization founded "the week of the announcement of the discovery of the HTLV-III virus (HIV)" in 1984, the Dump emerges from the shadow of Black and queer medical apartheid, bringing together Blackness, sexuality, and disability vis-à-vis shared experiences of government neglect.[10] HIV/AIDS is figured early on in the novel as a key intersection for race, queerness, and disability.[11] The Dump community is formed explicitly to combat the infrastructural violence characteristic of the Reagan administration, which was enacted through both safety net retraction and the administration's nonresponse to HIV/AIDS. Described early on as "like a welfare neighborhood," the Dump offers a "broad range of subsidized public services" for its Black, gay, and formerly unhoused residents.[12] The community's name, *the Dump*, further signals the novel's unconventional relationship to waste, particularly as a category used to deny government assistance to racialized, disabled, low-income, and queer communities. In contrast, the Kyle Foundation offers its collective largesse to these communities specifically; in order to gain entrance to this privately funded separatist space, "you just gotta be gay and homeless and not smoke. And black, pretty much mostly."[13] Included among its roster of services is free, nondiscriminatory healthcare offered in large part by the kink-friendly medical specialist Dr. Greene, who, for example, lauds the sexual practice of shared snot eating as a means of "bolstering each other's immune systems."[14] Here, utopia—or something like it—can emerge only from the creation of infrastructural networks supporting those most impacted by the withdrawal of public services. Support, further, does not imply only the provision of basic resources (i.e., the food, water, and medical care required at minimum to sustain life); it also extends to the proliferation of joy and pleasure so often denied welfare recipients.

Rather than disavowing waste, *Through the Valley* leans into its transgressive possibilities, leveraging the joys of hedonistic queer and disabled sex (characterized in part by snot eating, piss drinking, catheter play, and the copious consumption of "dick cheese") to flout the disciplinary (re-)productivist ethos of Reagan- and Clinton-era social reform. In this way, Delany joins other contemporary Black queer and feminist writers who have engaged the state's anti-Black enforcement of family and work values through tropes of excess. As Roderick Ferguson, Aliyyah Abdur-Rahman, and L. H. Stallings have argued, writers such as Toni Morrison and Octavia Butler have similarly employed (and transformed) the language of waste in order to critique the state's pathologization of Black kinship structures and sexuality.[15] This ranges from the "dreadful funkiness" in Morrison's 1970 novel *The Bluest Eye* to what Stallings terms the "stank matter" of Butler's 2005 novel *Fledgling*.[16] Alongside Morrison and Butler, Delany's *Through the Valley of the Nest of Spiders* mobilizes funk and stank in order to generate alternative forms of knowledge about racialized sexualities and, in this case, disability.

For the residents of the Dump and its nearby communities, waste and its management constitute key sites of pleasure and social connectivity, with much of civic life oriented around the abundant circulation of flesh and fluid. The Dump, as well as the broader municipality of Diamond Harbor surrounding it, boast extensive erotic infrastructures for the explicit accommodation of queer and frequently deviant sexual practices. There's the freestanding men's room in Dump Corners, which features a designated area for "tearoom cruising"; the Runcible Opera House and pornographic theater, which functions as a long-standing cruising zone classified as a historic site by the chamber of commerce; and the Slide, a local bar outfitted with an eighteen-foot-long urinal, piss cage, and shower area for post–piss orgy cleanup. In addition to these brick-and-mortar institutions, Kyle Foundation–funded high schools offer a progressive curriculum that supports Black queer lives and histories, featuring "evolution, women's studies, black studies, and courses in animal (and human) homosexuality."[17]

At the center of the novel's infrastructural utopia is Eric Jeffers, a white, blond, and athletic transplant from the city of Atlanta who, at the age of seventeen, relocates to the south Georgia coast to live with his mother, Barbara. Here, he meets the interracial father-son duo Dynamite Haskell, who is white, and "Shit," who is Black and biracial. They both eagerly invite him to join their garbage-hauling business. Over the course of nearly eight hundred pages, *Through the Valley* details the blissful, lifelong open relationship that unfolds between Eric and Shit, which includes a strong incestuous bond with their shared father figure Dynamite. Largely plotless, the novel is loosely structured around three periods of employment spanning 2007–77, which begins with Eric and Shit's twenty-year stint as garbagemen hauling trash to "the Bottom," then explores their decade-long job managing and maintaining the local pornographic theater, and finally concludes with their work as handymen for an upscale lesbian art colony.

While the novel speculates on emergent forms of technology (such as the development of more sophisticated flat-screen TVs and e-readers) and glosses key historical events such as "3B," it largely relegates major historical and social flash points to the background, with Eric and Shit's many sexual encounters and dalliances occupying the narrative focus. Rather than action or crisis events, then, what *Through the Valley* primarily concerns itself with is the day-to-day practice of what Eileen Boris and Rhacel Salazar Parreñas have termed "intimate labors," which encompasses sanitation work, erotic caregiving, and the slow development of partnership and community over time.[18] The novel's considerable length conveys at the level of form the temporality of sustained intimacy, which gradually accretes over the course of many social encounters. And while Eric and Shit present the reader with a study in contrasts—for instance, Shit is illiterate whereas Eric regularly studies Baruch Spinoza's *Ethics*—what ultimately binds them throughout their multidecade partnership is a shared love of and identification with all things "nasty."[19] Both characters thus develop and practice a life oriented around abjection, in which waste, perversion, and excess are not disavowed but rather framed as infrastructural materials supporting their erotic and social lives.

Like those of many other residents affiliated with the Dump community, Eric's sexuality is driven by alignment with social deviance. He is aroused by practices that resist easy incorporation into a progressive political ideology, such as rimming homeless men and being called the n-word. Part of the "porno-topic" genre explored in *The Mad Man* and *Hogg*, Delany's depictions of abject eroticism in *Through the Valley* draw on the signifying potency of transgression while also refusing the boundary-creating logic that deems certain acts taboo. As Steven Shaviro observes in his review of *The Mad Man*, Delany presents such moments of arousal as part of a "continuum with all the other aspects of life . . . rather than as some sort of rupture with them," envisioning a social world constructed around—not in spite of—the extremities of sexual expression.[20]

Pornotopia also emerges as a formal strategy in *Through the Valley* to bring sanitation infrastructure, support work, and waste management to the forefront of readerly attention. Defined by Delany as "the place where pornography occurs," where "any relationship can become sexualized in a moment," pornotopia renders everything a potential site of eros.[21] The seemingly banal category of "garbage man" surfaces in the novel as a marker of eroticism, operating as a descriptor frequently used alongside sexual acts—for instance, "without losing Dynamite's cock, Eric tried to look up, over the ridges of the garbage man's belly."[22] Similarly, the architecture of pipes and plumbing attains prominence in the novel's initial truck stop bathroom scene, in which the repetitive "hum" and "flushes" of water lend both texture and structure to the unfolding orgy.[23] The sensual language used to describe the plumbing, with its "tongues of glass" and watery "rush along the bottom," frames sanitation infrastructure itself as a site of libidinal attachment. The novel's eroticization of infrastructure and sanitation work, then, not only foregrounds the work and architecture of support, it also frames this work as sexy, exciting, and a potentially untapped source of pleasure.

Our introduction to the novel's transgressive ethic of waste management begins with Eric's initial entrance into Turpens Truck Stop. Turpens, for Eric, functions both as an erotic point of entry to the Dump and as an anchor site throughout the novel. Led to this location by the affirming gay elder Bill Bottom, Eric first encounters the self-identified "redneck" boatman Jay MacAmon, who later becomes a key figure in Eric and Shit's extended kinship network. In the hallway leading to the public john, Jay gives Eric a quick orientation to the social and sexual mores of Turpens and the Dump:

> Hey, they got a stainless steel pee trough where we can spring us a leak. . . . My partner's in there now. . . . My partner, he's a Mex—he don't talk. Spanish or English. He signs . . . ASL—good ol' 'Merican Sign Language, and from a natural born w— b—, too. We been comin' down here together every couple a' weeks for . . . well, close to fifteen years. . . . It's a nice place. We get a lot of black fellas, Injins, plain ol' redneck trash . . . like me. Truckers and boat fellas—me and Mex work the scow out to Gilead Island. [With a thick forefinger, he reached up to dig deep in a nostril, scratching inside.] Everybody gets along, tries to be sociable. Understand what I'm sayin'?[24]

Vital to Jay's description of the bathroom scene is his emphasis on interclass, interracial, and—perhaps most importantly for my argument—interabled contact as definitive elements of Dump group sexuality. The centrality of disability in this tableau extends Delany's theorization of what he terms "contact relations" in public sex and cruising zones, which he explores in the dual essay collection *Times Square Red, Times Square Blue* (1999). In it, he writes, "Given the mode of capitalism under which we live, life is at its most rewarding, productive, and pleasant when the greatest number of people understand, appreciate, and seek out interclass contact and communication conducted in a mode of good will."[25] Contact relations between people separated by social and economic difference, Delany argues, can cross boundaries of power that would otherwise calcify into animosity, violence, and further class polarization.

The practice of contact between disabled and abled queer bodies in *Through the Valley* similarly crosses and contests power boundaries, particularly as these boundaries pertain to questions of access—that is, access to the physical spaces of public sex, but also to economies of desirability writ large. In *Sex and Disability*, Anna Mollow and Robert McRuer put it frankly: "Rarely are disabled people regarded as either desiring subjects or objects of desire."[26] Frequently framed as either hyper- or desexualized, disabled people are regularly exiled from social and erotic spheres. Juana María Rodríguez has pointed out the excessive penalties for engaging in kinky and deviant sex in particular. "Racialized women and the disabled," Rodríguez writes, "have been . . . punished most viciously for seeking out the pleasures of perverse sexual license."[27] In Delany's Dump, however, the community's disabled members are key to shared erotic life, as well as to the larger social fabric. Following this, *Through the Valley* does not merely include disabled people within the realm of the social, it frames them as central to determining the Dump's communal ethics and modes of relationality. From Mex to "Big Man" Markum, a Dump resident whose catheter bag features prominently in his sexual encounters, disabled characters play a vital role in the community's shared commitment to pushing the limits of bodily intimacy and refusing cultural norms of pleasure.

In *Through the Valley*, disability becomes key to imagining the multiplicity of ways different bodies might enjoy sexual and social contact, as well as foregrounding the high value the novel attributes to the labor of care and support. As I argue throughout this chapter, Delany's novel explores waste and its management as a potent site for theorizing a crip-of-color politics and aesthetics. In this context, the novel's liberal use of slurs, racial and otherwise, might be interpreted as an extension of its meditations on racialized excess insofar as the slur furthers a register of language that inflames, provokes, and signifies in excess of dominant modes of communication. Following this, the passage's forthright description, which embraces nonexclusionary public sex while trading on slurs, sheds additional light on the novel's particular politics of solidarity. What's more, it does so in a way that moves past static, single-issue identity categories (e.g., race, gender, sexuality, ability) to not only question political emphases on symbolic change over actual material redistribution, but also highlight the limitations such an emphasis places on erotic possibility. As Eric asserts early in the novel, "But that's why I don't want nobody callin' me gay. I'd rather they called me a fuckin', cocksuckin', piss-drinkin', shit-eatin' scumbag . . . than fuckin' *gay*! At least that gets my dick hard."[28]

Akin to the crip-of-color framework, the remainder of the novel emphasizes a politics of affinity (in this case, with waste and humans deemed disposable by the state) over and above an identitarian politics grounded in sameness (of race, sexuality, and so forth), while not evacuating the importance of identity markers altogether. This position is reaffirmed by the inscription on a brass plaque marking the site of the Robert Kyle Foundation's original office, "fixed on the red bricks of the Social Service Building," which identifies the foundation as "an institution dedicated to the betterment of the lives / of black gay men and *of those of all races and creeds connected to them by elective and non-elective affinities.*"[29] In *Through the Valley*, one's commitment to the love of waste and wasted humans, and a willingness to live out this commitment in day-to-day practices, can carry more weight than one's actual embodied identity—hence, the Dump's acceptance of the white, blond Eric, and Shit's self-identified "Georgia cracker" father Dynamite.[30] However, *Through the Valley* remains attuned to waste and disposability as a field of signification and power thoroughly shaped by race, class, sexuality, and ability, categories through which waste derives much of its potency and meaning.

While Delany is often the subject of Black, queer, and queer-of-color analyses, one of the main objectives of this chapter is to bring his writing more fully into the realm of disability critique. Specifically, I aim to demonstrate how *Through the Valley* underscores the multiplicity of resonances between Black, queer, and disability politics vis-à-vis the concept of refuse work.[31] In the following pages, I elaborate on one subcategory of affinity between Black, queer, and disability politics that the Turpens bathroom scene and sanitation infrastructure make apparent: abjection.

Abjection as Crip-of-Color Affinity

Through the Valley, as well as many other of Delany's writings (e.g., the novels *Hogg* and *The Mad Man*), engages directly with the objects of disgust designated as abject in Julia Kristeva's *Powers of Horror*—what Kristeva defines as the "piece of filth, waste, or dung" that violates the fiction of a "clean and proper" body.[32] Neither subject nor object, the abject describes a stage in psychosexual development during which a not-yet-subject experiences violent splitting from the maternal body, a source from which it draws life yet must also differentiate. In this transitional moment, boundaries between self and other are rendered incoherent, generating a state of instability and ambiguity that is abjection's hallmark. Beyond this developmental stage, abjection also emerges throughout the life course, surfacing whenever "identity, system, order" are disturbed.[33] As Josh Dohmen writes, the abject encompasses all that "threatens borders, namely the border between the subject and its objects and, as such, it serves as a threat to—and reveals the fragile nature of—the narcissistic enclosure of the subject."[34] It is precisely this capacity for disorder—for disrespecting "borders, positions, rules"—that gives abjection its power.[35]

Scholars of race, sexuality, and disability have extended Kristeva's theory of abjection to encompass the segregated others of a given social body—that is, those segments of the population that ostensibly threaten the dominant order. In *Extravagant Abjection*, Darieck Scott names Blackness as "one of the go-to figures for referencing the abject," forging this connection vis-à-vis histories of domination, enslavement, and "humiliating defeat."[36] As Scott and other literary scholars have observed, Delany frequently draws on the abject as a mode of expression, which he frames as allowing a "freedom of language" within the censorious regime of "the unspeakable."[37] Scott in particular argues that Delany's use of abject eroticism, which encompasses the taboo subjects of pederasty, racial subjugation, coprophagy, and master-slave BDSM, allows him to explore racialized sexual transgression beyond the limiting registers of trauma and abuse.

The abject, then, opens up generative possibilities for pleasurable connection that might otherwise remain inaccessible to racialized and disabled subjects. In *Through the Valley*, it becomes an aesthetic mode that allows Delany to explore, in the words of Amber Jamilla Musser, "how we might acknowledge violence and still think otherwise."[38] One of these possibilities, which I explore further in the chapter's concluding pages, is the staging of erotic collectivities that refuse the disciplinary power of the white patriarchal family. As Darieck Scott discusses, the rendering of Blackness-as-abject is linked to the "break" between Blackness and family, or the "[fundamental disarticulation]" between the "black family and the State."[39] That is, abjection is produced through the perceived deviance of Blackness from normative kinship structures, a "break" that, for Scott, makes imaginable alternate formations of gender, sexuality, and caregiving.

Another of these possibilities engages the potential joys derived from bodily incoherence, incompleteness, and marginalization. After all, "abjection's pleasures," writes Musser, "emerge from the excess sensations . . . that come from the violence of objectification and social exclusion," which includes exclusion from the categories of sovereign subjectivity and self-mastery.[40] For scholars of disability, it is precisely the danger of bodily nonintegrity that has rendered disabled bodies cultural avatars of abjection. Lennard Davis, for instance, has remarked on the threat that disabled bodies seemingly pose to the temporarily able-bodied—a discomfiting reminder of a body "about to come apart at the seams."[41] In *The Rejected Body*, Wendell highlights the associations between disability and a purported lack of control, proposing that "the failure to control the body is one of the most powerful symbolic meanings of disability."[42] Here, the potential for shame and humiliation emerges from the possibility of relinquishment—of power over the embodied self and its most intimate functions. Indeed, Kristeva herself has commented on the fear experienced by nondisabled people in their encounters with disability, or what she describes as the "anxiety of seeing the very *borders of the human species* explode."[43]

For some disabled people, however, lack of bodily control is just an everyday reality—something that must be dealt with as part of disabled life. Disability often demands greater intimacy with the realities of incontinence and bodily leakiness; as disabled activist Cheryl Marie Wade "bluntly" puts it, "We [some disabled people] must have our asses cleaned after we shit and pee. Or we have others' fingers inserted into our rectums to assist shitting. Or we have tubes of plastic inserted inside us to assist peeing."[44] Rather than posing the "piece of filth, waste, or dung" as a primal site of anxiety, Wade advocates for a more open and frank discussion of bathroom assistance: "It isn't 'using the toilet,' it's having someone's hands in your private hairs so you can live in the world. It's a big booger of a deal. But it's the only deal in town."[45] Wade's reframe enables an understanding of abjection as something more quotidian, even if it is a "big booger of a deal," which allows her to turn away from shame and advocate more directly for personal care. In this way, she illuminates how disability invites other relationships with waste beyond that of denial and abdication.

In exploring the pleasurable potential of bodily porosity and social exclusion, the Turpens bathroom scene similarly offers a set of alternate orientations to waste and its management. Racialized and disabled associations with abjection—vulnerability, lack of control, and humiliation—suffuse the Turpens orgy scene and become the basis of ecstatic connection across boundaries of race, class, and ability. Here, the major players of the Dump—Shit, Dynamite, Jay MacAmon, Mex, and others—initiate a willing and eager Eric into a culture of sexual abundance marked by the uninterrupted flow of piss, semen, spit, and mucus. Welfare reform's ethic of austerity gives way in *Through the Valley* to a waste-centric ethic of sensual excess.

One of the chief ways that Delany's truck stop scene reimagines abject eroticism is through its counterintuitive depiction of humiliation. Examining the potential of "blackness-in/as-abjection," Darieck Scott theorizes how, through literary expression, the "elements of humiliation and pain" might be transformed "into a form of pleasure."[46] In the space of the public bathroom, the novel lovingly depicts erotic acts associated with degradation, such as cock sucking and piss play, framing them simultaneously as building blocks of intimacy. After Eric swallows the "[spurts] of salt urine" from Dynamite's cock, he enjoys a moment of initial closeness with Shit that presages their lifelong partnership.[47] Their "cocks [cross]," their scrotums hang together, and Eric savors the rhythm of Shit's breathing: "For all the fucking around [Eric had] done with guys he didn't usually get *this* close to them. This was really . . . nice."[48] Shit then asks Eric if he's "okay," and continues with "Good. . . . I hope he pisses in your mouth some more. Go on, try somebody else now," a comment interpretable in this context as a gesture of care.[49] The Eric/Shit exchange thus demonstrates how humiliation might serve not only as a method of domination, but simultaneously as a portal to joyful coexistence and receptivity.

All the while, the novel repeatedly documents the "floshes, flaps, flops, and fluffles" of water running through the bathroom pipes, with the atmospheric presence of sanitation infrastructure both holding and actively constructing the Dump's erotic joys.[50] Like Wade's frank discussion of toilet assistance, *Through the Valley*'s ambient depiction of pipes and sewage renders waste a part of everyday life, something that constitutes the novel's environment rather than hovering at its margins. As Timothy Griffiths has observed, "One might imagine that the research question that occupies Delany in much of his work, but particularly here, is what would happen if we put the abject at the center of the utopia?"[51] Following Griffiths, I highlight the ordinary, everyday potential of abjection produced within the Turpens orgy, which simultaneously mines the erotic charge of exclusion while resignifying the affects of humiliation and shame on which that exclusion rests. Here, the abject becomes a practice of creation in and of itself, and one that reimagines the terrain of the social insofar as it forges transgressive intimacies that operate in excess of the sovereign subject.

To further chart the forms of intersubjectivity emergent in this scene, Amber Musser's theorization of *brown jouissance* proves instructive. Defined as a "mode of being and relating" that "[revels] in fleshiness" while simultaneously accounting for the fields of power in which fleshiness circulates, brown jouissance describes a form of racialized self-making that is inherently relational, a dynamic sensuality that "prioritizes openness, vulnerability, and a willingness to ingest without necessarily choosing what one is taking in."[52] As opposed to the antisocial "phallic jouissance" theorized by Leo Bersani, which views penetration as a form of self-shattering, brown jouissance does not operate from the assumption that one "has a self to shatter."[53] Brown jouissance, then, is marked not by the desire of possession—that is, of a sovereign subject's aim to possess an objectified other—but by "an embodied hunger that takes joy and pain in this gesture of radical openness towards otherness."[54]

While Musser derives her theory specifically from sites of queer femininity, which is notably absent in the Turpens scene and in the Dump writ large, I nonetheless find a resonance in her descriptions of brown jouissance and its proximity to abjection. Particularly salient across both concepts is the "[embrace of] alterity—either one's own or that of the Other."[55] Through the seamless exchange of cum, spit, and piss, intense encounters simultaneously marked by care for and coexistence with otherness, the orgy participants enjoy forms of ecstatic exchange predicated on vulnerability, degradation, and "radical openness."[56] Rather than disavowing lack of bodily control—and thus reinforcing the myth of a rational, coherent subject—they joyfully inhabit the always incomplete state of abjection, in which bodily nonintegrity and porosity offer openings toward other configurations of communal life.

The novel's centering of abjection, which highlights pleasure, care, and conviviality derived from the partial and relational nature of selfhood, thus names one primary mode through which Black, queer, and disability politics converge around the axis of waste. In the following pages, I explore another point of convergence: the ideology of independence and its connection to waged labor. I focus in particular on the "work first" policies promoted by welfare reform, which suggest that welfare recipients need to transform themselves through the sanctifying practice of work. I examine how Delany's novel offers a set of powerful counternarratives to this ideology by highlighting forms of labor that operate in service of interdependence rather than independence, and that challenge the centrality of waged labor to the distribution of care and joy.

Refuse Work

In *Through the Valley*, the resignification of waste extends to the category of labor, which Delany presents as a continuation of (rather than separate from) the Dump's erotic life. The Turpens bathroom orgy provides Eric Jeffers with not only an entry into a new social world but also an opportunity for employment as a garbage man. As Eric navigates his way from cock to cock, Dynamite offers him a job "haulin' garbage with me and Shit."[57] The seamless transition from managing bodily waste (semen, spit, piss) to managing community waste grants further insight into the novel's politics of labor, which places the typically masculinized field of sanitation work in a continuum alongside the feminized fields of care, maintenance, and social reproduction. For Eric, garbage collection offers but one expression of a larger ethos devoted to community support. As he puts it, "I wanna be a person who does things to make other people feel better—have an easier time—like get their fuckin' garbage out of the way and off to the Bottom."[58] Much of Eric's life, then, is organized around the day-to-day rhythms of garbage collection and the labor of caring for others in the Dump.

Returning to Boris and Parreñas's formulation of "intimate labor," *Through the Valley* conjoins the often separately analyzed categories of sanitation, care, and sex work, each of which "forges interdependent relations," sustains interpersonal connections, and tends to the bodily needs of individuals and communities.[59] Delany's depictions of intimate labor thus enable me to examine how *Through the Valley* articulates a crip-queer understanding of work. This crip-queer formulation runs counter to the dominant US work ethic, which emerges prominently in state-authored justifications for workfare. The novel does so by lifting up the disregarded labor of waste management, a strategy that aligns with a feminist disability politic of care work.[60] As a method attuned to the physical realities and needs of people's lives, feminist disability analysis not only views human life as dependent on care from others but also emphasizes the material and epistemic violence generated by the culture-wide denial of such needs. This analytic enables us to see, then, the ableism inherent in the cultural disregard of sanitation insofar as this stigma is rooted in the "presence of dirt, bodies, and intimacy."[61] The cultural aversion to sanitation work is thus linked, in many ways, to the aversion to disability. Both remind us of the leaky, porous, and waste-producing capacities of the body, thereby undercutting fantasies of bodily wholeness and physical control. Waste, in the context of intimate labor, functions as a figure of condensation for cultural anxieties around bodily integrity. It also operates as shorthand for forms of work that remind us of the body's discomfiting dependency on others. By reframing the work of sanitation, then, Delany's novel not only interrogates the hierarchy of values culturally ascribed to different forms of labor but also generates another ethos of work altogether, one grounded in a crip reverence for bodily needs.

In *Picking Up: On the Streets and behind the Trucks with the Sanitation Workers of New York City*, Robin Nagle observes both the invisibility and disrespect attached to the work of waste management: "The sanitation worker is as unremarkable and as certain to arrive as the morning sun. . . . The labors of waste literally rest on the bodies of men and women who we routinely stigmatize."[62] Following this, while Eric enthusiastically accepts the position with Dynamite and Shit's business, he soon encounters resistance from other characters who represent the positions of normativity and respectability. Chief among them is his mother Barbara's Black Republican boyfriend, who bears the unsubtle name of Ronald Reagan Bodin. A businessman by trade, Bodin is astonished that his girlfriend's son wants to work as a "refuse maintenance engineer. . . . In case you ain't sure, that's a fuckin shit shoveler!"[63] For Bodin, sanitation work is antithetical to a respectable life, one marked by having a "nice house" and "nice clothes."[64] Similarly, his mother's boss, Clem Englert, who runs the Lighthouse Coffee, Egg, & Bacon diner, gently discourages Eric from garbage hauling, stating, "It's good honest work. I'm not sayin' it isn't. Still, it's not the most respectable job you could have."[65]

Despite the invisibility of waste management, sanitation nonetheless represents a prominent arena of labor struggle, particularly in a post–civil rights and postwelfare United States. The 1968 sanitation strike in Memphis, famously memorialized as the assassination site of Dr. Martin Luther King Jr., offers perhaps the most salient example of this history.[66] While the 1968 strike did lead to some labor victories, by the time of the novel's publication in 2012, workfare and other privatizing measures had thoroughly transformed the landscape of waste management. In Delany's hometown of New York City, street sanitation represents "one of the main targets of municipal austerity measures," as reflected by the title of the New York City Department of Sanitation (DSNY)'s 2009 report, *Doing More with Less*.[67] The shift from public to private sanitation work in New York, observes Natalie Benelli, was achieved by the "displacement of public service workers by cheap private sector workers and free nonemployee personnel"—namely, welfare recipients who clean the streets as a prerequisite for benefits, unhoused New Yorkers who perform sanitation labor for job-training programs, and private sweepers who work for business improvement districts.[68] Further, while unionized DSNY employees are primarily white, Black and Latinx workers comprise the majority of private sweepers, who represent an increasingly precarious laboring class that lacks basic protections. Workfare thus provided yet another means of resource reallocation toward elite interests insofar as it "[socializes] the poor to precarious and underpaid employment."[69]

As Benelli's 2010–11 ethnographic study demonstrates, the use of rehabilitative discourse in job-training programs renders evident the ongoing effects of "work first" logic, as well as workfare's remaking of sanitation labor, around the time *Through the Valley* neared publication.[70] Such workfare initiatives framed waged labor as a therapeutic intervention and cure for those suffering from welfare dependency, which, as the previous chapter discusses, was increasingly characterized as a medical problem.[71] In addition to promoting the curative properties of work, the ideological success of workfare further hinged on the unquestioned acceptance of the work ethic as a fundamental national value. This value links individual morality, dignity, and social status to one's ability and willingness to engage in employment.

Kathi Weeks identifies the persistence of this ethos in *The Problem with Work*, writing, "The social role of waged work has been so naturalized so as to seem necessary . . . [as] something that might be tinkered with but never escaped."[72] Rarely do we question the nation's "productivist values" or the ever-growing primacy of work in our lives. Rather, these features of life under capitalism are rendered inevitable, along with the troubling belief that access to life-sustaining resources (food, housing, healthcare) should be connected to waged labor.[73]

Contesting the repressive ideology of workfare, then, must begin with the refusal of the dominant work ethic. In *Through the Valley*, the refusal of work begins with the work of refuse. Here, sanitation work is explicitly linked to a politics of refusal via Shit and Dynamite's garbage service. Following the bathroom orgy, Eric exits Turpens and sees a "blue pickup" backing out of its parking place, with the words SHIT & DYNAMITE REFUSE spelled on its "sagging tailgate" in gaffer tape and black Sharpie.[74] The service's name assumes prominence on the page; both DYNAMITE and REFUSE are centered, capitalized, and separated by a full line break. Here, refuse becomes an incantation and imperative to act; it names both a category of cast-offs and a mandate of noncooperation. The novel's pointed use of *refuse* (as opposed to garbage, waste, or rubbish) therefore invokes the insurgent potential of waste management and sanitation infrastructure, particularly given that Shit and Dynamite do not seek to contain waste as much as they seek to consume it, inhabit its position, and be transformed through this inhabitation. As incestuous refuse workers who revel in sexual deviance, their orientation toward the world is one of refusal: of sexual propriety, respectability, dignity, the nuclear family, and most social norms. Most of all, Shit, Dynamite, and Eric refuse the value system that denigrates the work of sanitation, as well as the ideals of dignity and independence allegedly achieved through waged labor.

The novel's continued eroticization of sanitation infrastructure—that is, the narrative work of making waste management hot—thus articulates an antinormative ethos of work grounded in sexual humiliation and the explicit refusal of dignity. *Through the Valley*'s re-visioning of this work, then, is contingent not on its alignment with the dominant work ethic, but rather on the potential of waste management to generate another ethos of work altogether. Shit and Dynamite's invitation of employment, offered to Eric during an ecstatic exchange of bodily fluids, emerges from a mutual recognition of enjoyment in waste and all things "nasty." Their identification of Eric as a fitting employee, then, is grounded in a shared sense of erotic attachments to refuse rather than any assessment of his ability to be a so-called good worker. In this way, Shit and Dynamite articulate a value system in which work is made significant through its association with abject pleasures. They frequently fold the work of garbage hauling into their deviant sexual practices. In addition to offering Eric employment during a bathroom orgy, Dynamite issues an imperative to work while wearing on his cock a semen-filled condom gifted to Eric by an orgy participant, Al Havers. As the zipper-enclosed condom creates an "odd looking tent" in Dynamite's lap and Al's cum leaks into the surrounding denim, Dynamite states, "I mean, you guys got to remember, we got some goddam garbage to haul—as well as all this fuckin' around. It ain't *just* about bein' nasty—though, yeah . . . that's a lot of it too, I guess."[75]

One key expression of this ethos is the novel's loving depictions of sanitation and maintenance labor, and with these depictions, its recuperation of dependency. In highlighting labor that recognizes and responds to human needs, Delany's novel offers a vital counterpoint to the mandate of independence governing US work society—a mandate that has historically dismissed disabled people due to their perceived inability to perform waged labor. As Kathi Weeks observes, "That individuals should work is fundamental to the social contract; indeed, working is part of what is supposed to transform subjects into the *independent individuals* of the liberal imaginary, and for that reason, is treated as a basic obligation of citizenship."[76] However, as Eric emphatically points out, sanitation work derives its importance *from* dependency—that is, from the reliance of municipalities on the regular, effective management of waste:

> You guys are the fuckin' garbage men, Shit. I mean, suppose lightning hit the mayor of the city. It wouldn't make no major difference how things went. . . . But suppose all the garbage men upped and disappeared—Randal and Tad and you and Aim and Dynamite and Al and me . . . you couldn't even have no city here. . . . The smell and the junk would take over everything, and everybody would have to move away! Inside of a couple of months, they'd have to close this whole place up and go look for a new spot. And in the mornin', when you and Dynamite are about to get out of bed, you two roll over and plug into me and let it run, it feels so good 'cause I'm lettin' you relax for another couple of minutes, and I can go dump it in the toilet for you—and we got something to laugh at and have a good time over.[77]

Eric's awe-filled assessment of waste management, which emphasizes the crucial role that garbage workers fill for communities, disputes American myths of self-sufficiency through its personification of sanitation infrastructure. Shit, Dynamite, and other garbage workers are named and praised in a cascading polysyndeton, presenting the reader with the face of waste infrastructure—the often-invisibilized workers who tend to the basic biological needs of the collective body. The infrastructural work of waste management seamlessly blends into the work of familial care and erotic play, portraying sanitation, care, and sex as part of a larger continuum of intimate labor. Through drinking Shit and Dynamite's urine and "dumping" it in the toilet for them, a loving act framed as an extension of their garbage work, Eric presents waste management as an act of care that resonates across a number of scales.

Further, in offering Dynamite and Shit support through the sexual management of their waste, which allows both of them to "relax for another couple of minutes," Eric presents the triad's shared dependency as a collaborative source of delight. And so, while dependency is often understood as a source of shame, the novel's portrayal of waste management depicts it as sexy and joyful, and it lifts up labor that enables us to see dependency as such. This eroticization of waste management, then, is also part and parcel of a crip-of-color ethos that rejects the idealization of independence and the denigration of care work on which it stands. Not only does *Through the Valley* frame care and intimate labor as an inevitable part of life, but these labors also bring joy to the novel's characters. As Eric's loving transfer of Shit and Dynamite's piss attests, the work of caregiving is not inherently burdensome but instead a key source of pleasure.

The Disabled Nonworker

This crip-of-color work sensibility, while present in Delany's reverent assessments of waste management, emerges more prominently through his depiction of the Black, gay, and disabled character Big Man Markum. Big Man embodies the wasteful markers of disability and dependency at the heart of antiwelfare fearmongering: he does not work, or at least the novel makes no mention of his job, and he is supported entirely by his father, Joe Markum. Indeed, his nonparticipation in paid work is notable in a novel that regularly calls attention to the occupations of its characters. In the following pages, I examine the novel's depiction of Big Man as a disabled figure who lives outside of formal employment, demonstrating how this character further develops the novel's refusal of work via an explicitly crip-of-color lens.

Described as "slightly under four feet tall," Big Man has "a withered leg, [walks] with a crutch, and [wears] a permanent urine bag."[78] He is, further, a beloved figure within the Dump community: "Big Man didn't have much dick, nor did it get hard, but he was a scrappy little guy, a cut-up who delighted in foul talk. . . . He loved to get fucked and had nothing resembling a gag reflex."[79] He, Shit, and Eric regularly "[fool] around" in "the alley behind the Opera . . . or down in the Opera's tiled restroom; or, at [Big Man's] home, in the 'piss pool.'"[80] Big Man's enthusiastic penchant for "foul talk" and fellatio endears him to Dump residents, who revel in the possibilities for play that his disabled embodiment invites. Delany's portrayal of this character thus allows me to articulate a crip-queer antiwork ethos that, first, refuses waged labor as a principal arbiter of human worth, and second, imagines a rival rubric of human value grounded in one's capacity for abject eroticism, sexual generosity, and joy.

As a Black, disabled nonworker celebrated for his sexual and social skill set, Big Man provokes reflection on a system of waged work to which Black and disabled marginalization have historically been central. The institution of chattel slavery, for instance, marks one primary site of racialized dispossession through the theft of bodies and labor; its history and structuring presence is indexed in the novel through Big Man's practice of erotic slave play dominating the local white drunk Danny Turpens.[81] Additionally, at the definitional level, disability's relationship to labor has been one of exclusion. With the emergence of industrial (and postindustrial) capitalism, disability began to describe an individual's *inability* to work and produce at socially necessary rates, a definition that supported the devaluation of disabled lives.[82] This definition is further calcified by current requirements for Supplemental Security Income, which require a proven "inability to engage in substantial gainful activity," or work that brings in a certain dollar amount per month.[83] In a nation that overvalorizes productivity and waged labor, the definition of disability as the inability to work undoubtedly contributes to US culture's ableism.

The American work society, in these contexts, becomes legible as a punitive institution that produces and legitimates social hierarchies, thereby undercutting the gospel of work ethic that promotes waged labor as a democratizing force. This gospel has also animated movements for civil rights—disability rights included—which have historically focused on access to gainful employment as a liberatory strategy. As Lezlie Frye argues, the Americans with Disabilities Act in particular was framed by some advocates as a piece of legislation that "would get disabled citizens off the rolls and into the workforce so as to realize their inherent potential for productivity."[84] In contrast, *Through the Valley* generates an antiwork imaginary more resonant with radical disability visions of liberation, which envision social arrangements that decenter or eliminate waged work altogether.[85] As the disability activist and scholar Sunaura Taylor puts it, "Shouldn't [disabled people], of all groups, recognize that it is not work that would liberate us . . . but the right to not work and be proud of it?"[86]

An infrastructural utopia aligned with crip sensibilities, the Dump community demonstrates what life fulfillment might look like outside the mandate of waged labor, or "the right to not work and be proud." In the Dump, basic survival is largely disconnected from employment. The community's subsidized community services, along with its cheap cost of living, ensure that one's capacity to work does not determine one's survival. For Dump residents who do participate in the system of formal employment, *Through the Valley* notes the community's humane labor conditions, which include a minimum wage well above the national standard. As a new garbage worker, Eric makes "Kyle Chamber of Commerce minimum" wages for three months, after which he receives a "permanent salary" with "cost-of-livin' raises every eighteen months."[87] Given the Dump's extensive systems of community support—its labor protections, subsidized costs of living, and well-funded erotic institutions—residents can focus on matters other than basic survival, such as Eric's desire to "try bein' a really good person."[88]

Community members who cannot work, such as Big Man, nonetheless have access to the Dump's social and erotic largesse. What's more, they are imagined as central to generating these resources. For instance, Big Man's annual holiday parties function as a social anchor for Dump residents and are one of the few events structuring the passage of time in an otherwise temporally unstructured novel. They also constitute a key site of interabled contact and sociality for Black gay men; the initial overview of the holiday party describes attendees in wheelchairs mingling with able-bodied revelers. On entering the Markum household, sumptuous food and colorful decorations give the gathering its texture: the "Christmas tree" decorated with "stars and ringed planets and spaceships," the "greased muffin trays" with Yorkshire puddings, and the urine on tap provided by "Piss Master" Danny Turpens.[89] In so doing, the novel envisions disabled lives beyond the timeworn scripts of isolation and pity, imagining what might be possible for Black, queer, and disabled people if life fulfillment was unlinked from one's ability to labor.

This portrait of interabled revelry further suggests ways that people might be valued beyond their capacity as workers. Big Man's generosity, humor, and penchant for piss play are considered assets within Dump sociality. Near the close of the novel, *Through the Valley* once again emphasizes this value system and its long-term implications for disabled community members. Decades after his initial arrival in the Dump, an elderly Eric explains the interabled partnership of Mex Jalisco and Jay MacAmon for the dissertation student Ann Lee. After rehashing the minutes of a social group for "non-hearing gay men and women," to which Jay regularly took Mex, Ann muses, "I understand what MacAmon did for Jalisco. I'm just wondering what Mex did for him," implying that a disabled partner inherently has less to offer, or that disabled people are unable to give care.[90] In response, Eric silently thinks, "drank his piss, ate his shit, sucked his toes, fucked with any of his friends and puppies that Jay wanted him to, taught 'em to make chili, truck stop-, orgy-, and everyday-manners."[91] Eric's list highlights the worth he and other Dump residents ascribe to the intimate labors of erotic caretaking and waste management. Delany's novel offers a paean to the kinds of loving, sensual tasks and skill sets that sustain interpersonal connections over time—in this case, over the span of seventy years.

Through the Valley thus envisions a crip-queer ethos of work that supports the cultivation of interdependence, or the propagation of emotional, social, and sexual infrastructures for community well-being. Yet, instead of reproducing the American work society and the "forms of social cooperation on which accumulation depends," to borrow Kathi Weeks's phrasing, the care labor performed by Mex, Big Man, Eric, and others supports Black, queer, disabled, and/or low-income people and the life-giving connections between them.[92] *Through the Valley* regularly reframes interdependency as a vital source of sexual pleasure, accessed through abled and interabled interactions alike. The novel describes a friendly negotiation between Shit and Big Man at the start of Big Man's holiday party, regarding disability accommodations, in which the two discuss the extent to which Big Man wants to be carried around that evening. While dominant disability narratives often frame disabled people as passive recipients of care, Big Man occupies the center of these conversations, dictating, quite literally, the delivery of his own access needs. After Shit asks, "Can I carry you around a little?" Big Man deflects, reassuring him that he has "lots of places to sit."[93] However, Shit insists that he and Eric "like carryin' [Big Man]," expressing the pleasure they get from providing access.[94] Big Man responds in the affirmative while also expressing his own limits: "And I *like* [you] carryin' me! . . . But sometimes you kinda forget that I get around okay by myself."[95] Shit acquiesces and carries Big Man for a short distance, placing him down when requested. Notably, this act of caretaking arouses him: "(With one hand Shit held up his waist and with the other reached down inside his jeans. Carrying Big Man had apparently given Shit a boner)."[96] Akin to the loving transfer of urine between Shit, Dynamite, and Eric, this practice of access provision is recodified as sexy, once again demonstrating how caregiving can operate as a source of delight for everyone involved.

Yet, while these interabled relations highlight the pleasurable potential of care, *Through the Valley* also explores the structural limitations of interdependency in the Dump, as well as some of the potential abuses of power embedded within caregiving dynamics. Consider, for instance, Big Man's complicated relationship with his father, Joe Markum. A contractor and builder by trade, Joe Markum is noted for constructing "most of the seventy-five cabins in the Dump."[97] And while "not gay himself," his father is "almost as permissive with his son as Dynamite," and as such, he provides the support necessary for Big Man to live in the ways he desires. He is, further, the architect of Big Man's extensive piss orgy setup: a set of rooms in the Markum home outfitted with "rubber flooring, rubber mattress, rubber-rimmed windows and doors, rubber sheets, and drains around the raised bed."[98] And yet, their father-son relationship, though "permissive," does not exist outside of relations of power insofar as his father's position as primary caregiver grants him a considerable measure of authority over his son. That is, even while Big Man is propped up by an extensive web of support, the anchoring and overseeing of this web by his father underscores some of the messy edges of a life experienced outside of work, particularly in a world in which care for the disabled is still largely relegated to the private, familial sphere.

This dynamic emerges regularly in Big Man and Joe Markum's interactions, expressed through seemingly small gestures that mark their relationship's uneven terrain. Before "[turning] the house over" for Big Man's annual holiday party, Joe exhorts Big Man to "not make too much of a mess," asserting a quiet form of paternal discipline over his adult son.[99] And while Joe Markum says that he will return home at "seven or seven-thirty," he returns early, bringing Big Man's gathering to a premature close.[100] After Big Man's death, Shit offers additional insight into their father-son relationship. He explains to Eric why he will not attend Big Man's memorial service despite many years of sexual and social comradery, confessing, "His daddy makes me feel funny, sometimes."[101] Shit further describes how, on occasion, Joe would ignore him during his visits to the Markum household. When Eric reports Joe's absence at Big Man's funeral, along with the rest of the Markum family, Shit remarks that he "ain't surprised about that," musing that Joe likely closed up Big Man's section of the house with a fire door, never to return again.[102] Shit's perceptive comments highlight the power relations that persist even within this separatist community, leaving the more idealistic Eric awash in surprise. "When Shit was right," the novel observes, "Eric could feel lost in the confused margins of the social world."[103]

The issues with paternalism underscored by the Markum father-son dynamic are echoed—on a larger scale—by the Dump community writ large, which is overseen by the wealthy Black gay philanthropist Robert Kyle. Like Joe Markum, Kyle is permissive and progressive but nonetheless has a dominant hand in the community's operations: "Like a web whose strands reached— glittering—over the landscape, the Robert Kyle Foundation held almost everything in the county together."[104] Eventually, Kyle decides to "cut down on the money [he has] been spending on the Dump," electing to "let it become general public housing."[105] He then channels the remaining funds into another gay men's settlement in Oklahoma and converts nearby Gilead Island into a township for lesbians, where Shit and Eric eventually end up working as handymen. While Kyle's benevolence sustains a subsidized community for those most brutalized by state divestment, *Through the Valley* nonetheless underscores the limits of paternalism as support structure insofar as the Dump's continued presence hinges on the goodwill of one powerful, albeit sympathetic, man.

In examining the private sphere of family and philanthropic support, *Through the Valley* explores the kinds of infrastructural formations that might enable crip refusals of work to take place, along with the complications that might arise from such arrangements. The novel's vision of the highly subsidized Dump, as well as its treatment of the Markum family, disconnects waged work from basic survival but also works through the thorniness of how those unable to participate in waged work might survive under available systems. And so, while Delany's novel operates in a speculative mode, it remains grounded in a kind of structural realism in that its utopian longings unfold through structures of support imaginable within our current world. In this way, *Through the Valley* filters the refusal of waged labor through a crip-of-color lens in that it explores the life possibilities fostered by vibrant care webs, especially for those historically refused work, but it also demonstrates how the care supplied by those webs might still function as a mechanism of control. Delany's novel articulates a crip-queer ethos of work that throws into question the metrics by which we value different forms of labor, as well as the value we attribute to waged labor in the first place. It thus contests the governing values and assumptions put in place by welfare-to-work imperatives, as well as the kinds of social relations promoted by such imperatives. The final pages of this chapter examine how *Through the Valley*'s refusal of independence, articulated through its antinormative work ethos, further takes shape within the arena of family.

Waste as Kinship Infrastructure

In her gentle critique of Eric's chosen work, the restaurant manager Clem Englert connects respectable work to the institution of heterosexual family life: "It seems to me . . . you'd want a job where some nice young ladies might look at you and say, well, what a fine young fellow he is. He'd make a real good provider— you know, someone with prospects. A good person to start a family with. I was only wonderin' why you'd wanna work with someone livin' over with all those . . . *strange* people—in the Dump."[106] Clem's sentiments reflect the explicit connections drawn in Clinton's PRWORA commentary between work and family, which were further entrenched within antiwelfare legislation via key provisions enforcing paternal responsibility. As Kathi Weeks, Gwendolyn Mink, Patricia Hill Collins, and many other feminist scholars have noted, the work-family nexus emerged as an effect of industrial capitalism, with the nuclear, patriarchal family model encouraged in the Fordist period as a "crucial adjunct to work discipline."[107] Yet, as the first chapter discussed at length, the nuclear family has long been weaponized against racialized, queer, and otherwise deviant populations to justify the denial of state care. Indeed, alongside the institution of waged labor, the nuclear family remains one of the primary disciplinary instruments for integrating minoritarian subjects into proper citizenship. Further, as a crip-of-color framework renders evident, the institution of family promotes a curative narrative of proper development for racialized and queer subjects. In this linear trajectory, marriage and childbearing signal the subject's fitness for citizenship, as well as representing the achievement of adult autonomy and independence.

Returning to the incestuous family ties linking Eric, Shit, and their shared father Dynamite, these concluding pages examine how their perverse kinship structure furthers the novel's crip-queer politics of refusal by repudiating normative timelines of adult development. In the literature of structural anthropology, the incest taboo functions as a cultural mandate that orders and regulates marital exchange between families, creating kinship networks via a set of prohibitions. Claude Lévi-Strauss in particular views the prohibition of incest as a social rule enforcing outmarriage and the proper reproduction of culture over generations; it is "*the* intervention" to "ensure the group's existence as a group."[108] In the Freudian schema, the incest taboo emerges during the Oedipal stage as a key milestone of psychosexual formation, during which the child learns to distinguish between appropriate and prohibited objects of desire. Bringing together Sigmund Freud and Lévi-Strauss, Gayle Rubin's "The Traffic in Women" further conceptualizes the Oedipal stage as initiating the child into a regimented world of gender/sexual difference.[109] As Rubin argues, the proper resolution of the Oedipus complex prompts the young child to adopt the heterosexual imperative, thereby orienting them toward proper kinship formations.

The novel's refusal of independence and (re-)productivity thus emerges through its exploration of the incest taboo and queer restaging of the Oedipus complex, through which the novel freezes its characters in developmental time. According to Freud, prior to the child's Oedipalization—and with it, the "correct" orientation of libidinal drives—children inhabit a state of polymorphous perversity, a mode of undifferentiated pleasure-seeking in which they can derive erotic satisfaction from any part of the body.[110] Following this, the novel's refusal of developmental mandates is perhaps most readily expressed through the character of Shit, whose erotic fixation on waste suggests a permanent state of pre-Oedipal regression. Of all the novel's characters, he most fully embodies the mode of undifferentiated libido synonymous with the early phases of childhood formation. Shit, as the novel makes clear, can get turned on by anything, though he has particular sexual appetites for deviant objects and people. Dynamite recalls, "This boy been crap-crazy since he was a little thing. When he was in Pampers, he used to love to play with his own. And if you happened to leave some in the commode, soon as he could toddle around, all he wanted to do is to get in there and fuck with it."[111] This scene describes the toilet-training protocol of the anal stage, which directly precedes the phallic (Oedipal) stage. Shit, however, never emerges from this childlike mode of anal fixation: "I know this ain't nobody's idea of the best dinner table conversation in the world. But about two weeks ago . . . I went in right behind you [Dynamite] when you'd left a big hunk floatin' in the commode, and I reached in and broke me off a piece. And the same day, later, I pulled a piece of Eric's out there, too—and I ate 'em down. Both of 'em. It was sort of like magic, I was tryin' to do, so you two wouldn't ever go away and leave me."[112] For Shit, the act of eating his family members' feces—another practice of waste management at the novel's core—ritually creates a permanent bond between them. His summoning of "magic" through shit eating evokes the concept of "magical thinking," theorized by the developmental psychologist Jean Piaget. Piaget described this concept as an early childhood cognitive process in which young children believe their personal wishes affect the external world.[113] This impossible wish reaffirms Shit's childlike state and, at the same time, positions waste in *Through the Valley* as a binding material of affinity and kinship.

The resignification of waste as relational infrastructure, which connects and supports perverse kinship formations, emerges in this passage and throughout the novel. After all, erotic attachments to piss, shit, and mucus are what initially bring together Shit, Eric, and Dynamite as a family. Delany's novel thus derives from the pre-Oedipal state of polymorphous perversity forms of kinship and affinity that disrupt the dominance of the nuclear family formation and the proper directing of desire. In this way, *Through the Valley* offers a partial answer to David Eng's query in *The Feeling of Kinship*, which seeks a queer way out of Oedipal kinship mandates: "In our colorblind age of globalized capitalism, is the Oedipus complex still the guiding principle by which we can describe and measure structures of family and kinship? If not, how might we delineate a new terrain of material and psychic relations not bounded by the foundational structures of the incest taboo and the Oedipal myth, one attentive to questions of race and (homo)sexuality not withstanding the amnesias of modernity?"[114]

Through the Valley's familial imaginings "delineate a new terrain of material and psychic relations" within the disabled and seemingly pathological space of developmental delay. Following this, Shit's regressive state provides fertile ground for linking queer-of-color critiques of kinship with disability theory, as it brings queer kinship formations into the temporal orbit of nonnormative development. After all, *disability* is often the descriptor given to improper progression along developmental timelines, as indicated by the language of "slowness" and "delay." Shit therefore brings the novel's readers into the disorienting ebbs and flows of *crip time*, a term that describes the many intersections of disability with temporal regimes of regulation.[115] And certainly, while time progresses chronologically in *Through the Valley*, with the novel unfolding across the duration of Eric's adulthood, Shit's perverse predilections cast him outside of the accepted rhythms of adult life. In this way, he shares an affinity with disabled characters such as Big Man, who similarly does not conform to traditional temporal milestones.

For multiple characters, this refusal of developmental progress aligns Shit with the category of disability. For instance, in an early exchange, Barbara, Eric's well-meaning mother, informs Eric of Clem's assessment: "Clem thinks he's slow . . . r—d. 'Cause he's illiterate. She says he can't even read his name."[116] Later in the novel, in the aftermath of Dynamite's sudden death, Eric is seized with a sudden sense of shame regarding his incestuous family, and he articulates this feeling in the language of mental unwellness: "[He] felt powerless, small, and on the verge of being crazy, because he was thirty-eight and for more than a dozen years he'd been partnered with someone, now forty, who was probably psychotic, anyway, and who—until three days ago—had been fucking his own father for more than three decades."[117] Here, Shit's sexual deviancy operates doubly as a potential marker of mental disability, a category with which Eric eventually finds some affinity: "Shit and me'll probably both end up in the blackest cell in the lightless basement of some asylum."[118] Eric's partnership with Shit often situates him, too, within the space of developmental regression. For instance, their shared practice of snot eating, which brings them together and binds them in partnership, is framed multiple times as a childlike activity. The novel's repudiation of adult development, then, functions pointedly as an insurgent crip gesture against the mandate of independence.

In its depictions of developmental delay, *Through the Valley* makes space for kinship arrangements not contingent on the proper (i.e., heterosexual and exogamous) directing of libidinous drives—even as these arrangements, like the gay incestuous triad, do not lend themselves to an emancipatory politics. The Shit, Eric, and Dynamite triad names one example of a relational structure depicted in *Through the Valley* that circumvents the structure of nuclear family making. Shit's nonincorporation of the incest taboo, which leads to a long-term sexual relationship with his father, provides yet another example of his regression insofar as the irresolution of said taboo arrests him in pre-Oedipal time.

Far from exceptional, this family dynamic engages what Aliyyah Abdur-Rahman has identified as a long-standing trope of incest in contemporary African American literature, including Ralph Ellison's *Invisible Man* (1952), Toni Morrison's *The Bluest Eye* (1970), and of course, Sapphire's *Push* (1996), to name a few notable examples.[119] For Abdur-Rahman, the persistence of incest in African American women's writing in particular functions to critique "racism's profound and incessant injuries to black children and black women" as well as the state's "[vilification] of poor black families for their failure to conform to nuclear heteronormativity."[120] For Delany, however, incest is one of the many sexual taboos that *Through the Valley* engages without moralism; it names one perverse practice among many that make up the erotic fabric of Dump sociality. That is, while Sapphire's and Morrison's respective depictions of incest explore the obliterating horror of sexual violation, focusing as they do on father-daughter rape, Delany's representation instead works to convey the characters' queer attachment to an unassimilable and oftentimes unredeemable erotics of deviance.[121] In one of the many pornographic interludes featuring Shit, Eric, and Dynamite, the triad exercises the language of daddy-son play, mining the practice of incest for its unmatched erotic charge. As Eric penetrates Dynamite, Dynamite implores him to "pump that big o' fucker up your daddy's shit chute."[122] He then says to Shit, "Come on, little boy. *Suck* daddy's big ol' cracker dick!"[123]

Delany's forthright and provocative depictions of incest suggest that the novel is less interested in the trope's representational capacity to convey sexual and structural violence, and more interested in its capacity to convey a politics of radical nonassimilation. Delany's depictions of incest, pederasty, and coprophagy—which most consider unredeemable practices—thus convey the novel's insistence and desire for the abject to remain abject. Incest, then, names yet another expression of the novel's dedication to irrecuperable eroticism as a chief method of refusal. It represents one of *Through the Valley*'s many narrative strategies to refuse Black, queer, and crip assimilation into the dominant social order generally and into able-bodied nuclear heteronormativity in particular.

By unbinding its characters from the developmental script of nuclear kinship, the novel's rearticulation of the incest taboo ushers in alternate modes of queer relationality and belonging, which Elizabeth Freeman theorizes as naming not only "the longing to *be*," but also "the longing to 'be *long*,' to endure in corporeal form over time, beyond procreation."[124] That is, *Through the Valley* imagines arrangements of life outside of marriage, children, and independence that can sustain Black, queer, and/or disabled subjects over time: accessible public sex, robust social infrastructures, interabled contact zones, and a dedicated kink support network. This "longing to 'be *long*' . . . beyond procreation" further obtains in the novel's form as well as its content, as *Through the Valley*'s nearly 800 pages offer an epic treatment of a queer partnership that follows neither familial nor narrative conventions. The sizable length of the novel illustrates, through sheer scale alone, what it might look like for abject crip-queer partnership, community, and kinship to endure, and joyfully at that, across the human lifespan. Given that incest, as Abdur-Rahman has argued, "undoes the possibility of linearity and evolutionary progress in both life and narrative," Delany's depictions of incest enable considerable possibilities for literary experimentation.[125] Rather than recounting the cornerstone events that mark life's progression, then, the novel's many pornographic episodes put forth a narrative form reflective of polymorphous perversity, in which a multitude of abjected bodily pleasures, needs, and desires come together in a charged erotic tableau.

One of the primary modes of "[being] long" reimagined by the novel is the practice of intergenerational transfer, which conventionally refers to the vertical transmission of wealth and assets along lines of filiation. In Delany's novel, however, intergenerational transfer depends not on procreation and legal contract but on the recognition and active interpellation of others similarly aroused by the sexual management of waste. The novel is set into motion by such a moment of recognition: after they exchange lurid accounts of piss play with homeless Black men, the neighborhood elder Bill Bottom refers seventeen-year-old Eric to "a pretty active truck stop" that later becomes Eric's point of entry to the Dump.[126] Near the novel's conclusion, speaking to dissertation student Ann Lee, Eric explains waste as method of generational transfer: "We [Shit and Eric] like to eat up dried mucus. Our own, each other's. . . . Lots of kids do it, but most of 'em get it shamed out of them unless they sexualize it. If we'd been into havin' babies and stuff, maybe we coulda passed it on. Maybe you don't even have to pass it on genetically, though. It could just happen socially, if we'd had 'em around us more."[127]

While they do not "pass [this act] on genetically," Shit and Eric do share a moment of intergenerational recognition with a disabled character named Loop, who they witness eating snot in the balconies of the Opera. A "youngish, muscular fellow" with a visible "harelip," Loop is young enough for Shit to "be his daddy."[128] On seeing him lick his own mucus out of a "labor-hardened palm," Eric and Shit experience an electrifying moment of arousal, which leads to Eric drinking Shit's piss.[129] By mirroring Shit and Eric's keystone fetish in his comparatively youthful body, Loop suggests the endurance of this practice over time, demonstrating another way to "be long" in addition to procreation.

At the end of the novel, following multiple decades of "being long" with Shit, Eric finds himself alone, content, and reflecting on a life conducted in support of others:

> Oh, others . . . !
>
> Others help so much. Just looking. And seeing what they see, they
>
> help . . .
>
> Which is why you have to help. . . .
>
> Others.[130]

In this elliptical passage, Eric frames the world through a prism of mutual support, putting forth a model of relationality as imagined by Spinoza's *Ethics*, a book that accompanies him throughout his life. As the "tutelary spirit of the novel," Steven Shaviro argues, Spinoza imagines a "universe constituted entirely of and by its god. . . . God cannot be a being apart from the rest of the universe."[131] Or as Eric puts it, "Everybody's related to everybody and everything—even trees and mosquitos and minnows flickin' around in Runcible Creek. That's kinda reassurin,' I think."[132] In this paradigm of relationality, all beings are kin, a disarticulation of the strict organizational schema imposed by the Oedipus stage and the incest taboo.[133] And if everyone is kin to everything else, accountability to the other becomes an ethical necessity. Eric's understanding of kinship thus furthers a relational model grounded in radical interdependence, in which the unbounded distribution of support refuses the privatization of care inherent to nuclear kinship models and the stingy distributional rubric of workfare. Across Eric and Shit's lifelong partnership, the erotic and vocational practice of waste management functions doubly as a practice of queer kinship, as it foregrounds the many ways that human bodies can be vulnerable with and dependent on each other.

Against the pro-independence narratives of workfare, *Through the Valley*'s depiction of refuse work furthers a crip-of-color ethos of radical interdependence that flouts cultural norms of pleasure, productivity, and kinship. This ethos takes a number of forms throughout Delany's novel, including (1) the high value ascribed to intimate labor, which the novel grounds in a crip reverence for bodily needs; (2) the depiction of pleasure derived from acts of caregiving and access; (3) the valuing of life outside of one's capacity to perform waged labor; and (4) the lavishing of joy, pleasure, and care on those often depicted as the least deserving of it. And so, while markers of the abject frequently evoke shame, terror, and disavowal, Delany's novel instead expands abjection's terrain of signification, framing waste as the rudimentary material around which other lifeworlds might emerge. Waste and its management, then, function not only as a practice of maintenance, a way of reproducing the world we live in, but also as a relational infrastructure on which other worlds can be built: "[Eric] wanted to tell [Shit] that they were making a world, a county, a city together, and . . . it was wonderful."[134]

From the underground pipes of sanitation networks to the aboveground passages of the California freeways, the next chapter continues my exploration of infrastructural freedom dreaming in the open road narratives of Octavia

Butler and Karen Tei Yamashita. While chapters 1 and 2 examine welfare-reform policy in the domestic arena, chapter 3 explores the application of austerity logics to the transnational arena of so-called free trade. Turning to transportation infrastructure and the figure of the noncitizen or undocumented immigrant, I examine how a crip-of-color labor politics might further unfold within the context of US neocolonialism, and how Butler and Yamashita's fictional freeways lead us to other, more liberatory planes of infrastructural consciousness.

3 LINES OF TRANSIT, MIGRATION, MOBILITY

Cripping the Freeway Fictions of Karen Tei Yamashita and Octavia E. Butler

Three years prior to the passage of major welfare reform, the acclaimed science fiction author Octavia E. Butler prophesied, with terrifying precision, the cataclysmic effects of resource hyperprivatization. The 1993 novel *Parable of the Sower*, the first installment in Butler's celebrated *Parable* series, depicts a near-future Los Angeles in the throes of infrastructural collapse. For the primarily Black and brown residents of Robledo, a fictional suburb of Los Angeles, basic resources like utilities, education, fire protection, potable water, and hospitals are no longer public goods, with police and fire services commanding exorbitant fees. Yet, while the decaying infrastructures of *Parable* signal the end of a world marked by relative prosperity and security, they also incubate the creation of a new sacred order with a decidedly crip bent: "Earthseed is being born right here on Highway 101—on that portion of 101 that was once El Camino Real, the royal highway of California's Spanish past. Now it's a highway, a river of the poor. A river flooding north."[1]

So observes Lauren Oya Olamina, the Black disabled protagonist of Butler's series and creator of Earthseed, a nascent religious belief system that understands God as change.[2] The site of Lauren's revelation—the besieged California freeways, "a river of the poor"—emblematizes the conditions of desperate, disabling mobility shaping Lauren's life and the lives of her Earthseed companions.[3] Internal refugees searching for survival, the freeway pedestrians of *Sower* trace a northward journey similar to those undertaken by Black and brown communities under circumstances of structural deprivation—the Great Migration, certainly, but also the more recent migrations of Global South workers to resourced cities such as Los Angeles. The freeway scenes in *Sower* are grim, populated chiefly by dispossessed migrants stripped of security. And yet, as the container for Earthseed, a belief system that furthers the disability justice values of collective access and interdependency, Butler's freeways also signal Lauren's migratory desires to find other worlds, and with them, other ways of supporting vulnerable life. As Lauren puts it, "The Destiny of Earthseed / Is to take root among the stars."[4]

In Karen Tei Yamashita's 1997 LA-centric novel *Tropic of Orange*, the California freeway is similarly figured as a portal to other forms of infrastructural consciousness. Commuters traveling down Los Angeles's Harbor Freeway in Yamashita's *Tropic* encounter an unusual sight: a "sooty homeless man on an overpass" wielding a conductor's baton and converting traffic into minimalist symphony.[5] As the freeway's maestro, Manzanar translates the city of Los Angeles into musical composition: "Each of the maps was a layer of music, a clef, an instrument . . . a change of measure, a coda."[6] LA's hidden layers begin "with the very geology of the land," the "man-made grid of civil utilities" meshing with the "historic grid of land usage and property."[7] His freeway symphony renders audible a multilayered and multidimensional Los Angeles, turning the volume up on the "thousand natural and man-made divisions . . . patterns and connections by every conceivable definition from the distribution of wealth to race, from patterns of climate to the curious blueprint of the skies."[8] By sounding together the systems that undergird a globalizing Los Angeles—the municipal, geological, and historic grids that "ordinary persons never bother to notice"— Manzanar excavates the oft-invisible infrastructures that regulate metropolitan life and on which its residents unwittingly depend.[9] His freeway symphony thus invites readers to hear the city's underlying networks of labor, migration, and civic support that the novel itself amplifies.

A long-standing emblem of social and spatial division, California's freeways emerge in Butler's *Parable of the Sower* and Yamashita's *Tropic of Orange* as a multivalent site for engaging questions of movement and migration under the exigencies of transnational capitalism. This chapter argues that both novels direct attention to California's freeway network in order to address the differential production of mobility by transit and economic infrastructures in the wake of trade deregulation, with the North American Free Trade Agreement (NAFTA) as nucleus event. This unequal production across the lines of race and class, in which the freedom of movement enjoyed by resourced populations is linked to the constriction of more vulnerable classes, is one of the primary ways that this chapter and this book theorizes disability. It is, further, the primary example of infrastructural violence and dis-/enablement explored in this chapter. Disability scholars have long commented on the relationship between socially engineered environments and their articulation of impairment as disability, theorizing disability not as a feature contained to the individual, but as an effect produced through the encounter of nonnormative bodyminds with inaccessible spaces. In this chapter, I extend this analysis in order to address the dis-/enabling function of transit and economic infrastructures under racial capitalism, in which the illusion of independence and hypermobility for global elites produces (and is contingent on) restriction for others.[10]

Following this, I look to *Sower* and *Tropic* in order to articulate the relationship of crip-of-color critique to coerced migration and so-called free trade. In so doing, I connect my disability analysis of dependency and major welfare reform to the narratives, effects, and practices of transnational capitalist restructuring. As feminist scholars such as Grace Chang, Alejandra Marchevsky, and Jeanne Theoharis have argued, trade blocs such as NAFTA echo and extend the practices at the heart of domestic welfare reform.[11] Marchevsky and Theoharis in particular observe that "welfare reform followed from NAFTA's paradigms— removing the national fetters on work and trade while erecting higher boundaries to entitlement and state protection."[12] I argue that the California freeway as literary figure enables these women-of-color writers to grapple with the transformative effects of structural adjustment and state divestment on both local and transnational scales. Their freeway narratives, in turn, highlight potential nodes of solidarity between radical disability analysis and transnational feminist critiques of globalization.

This chapter unfolds in three parts, each of which addresses freeway infrastructure and accompanying narratives of movement, migration, and mobility: (1) the open road story and its fantasy of unfettered freedom; (2) the unseen, undervalued migrant labor networks that support global capital; and (3) the alternate webs of survival dreamed into being by the freeway visionaries Manzanar Murakami and Lauren Olamina. I begin by mapping out Butler and Yamashita's interventions into US open road mythology, a genre that often functions as an ableist tale of hypermobility. Specifically, I explore how both writers crip the road narrative by depicting the regimes of infrastructural violence wrought by unequal access to transit. In the second section, I extend my crip meditations on mobility and transit to consider how each novel foregrounds the economic infrastructures (i.e., NAFTA) prompting waves of migration to the United States. In the US public imagination, this migratory influx was understood as a threat, with recent migrants framed as opportunists looking to leech off US social programs. In response, *Sower* and *Tropic* highlight how the implementation of procapitalist economic infrastructures, such as structural adjustment programs (SAPs), force workers to uproot from their lands of origin. Rather than depicting these workers as pathologically dependent on public resources, as state-authored mythologies do, both novels emphasize the degree to which elite classes are in fact deeply dependent on racialized labor exploitation. Across Butler's *Sower* and Yamashita's *Tropic*, then, the California freeway represents a key vehicle for mapping the global imbalances of power that render certain dependencies hypervisible while erasing others.

Finally, in the concluding pages, I examine how both novels model infrastructural forms of consciousness that stress deep, sustained attention toward all that connects and supports life. They do so, I argue, through the characters of Lauren Olamina and Manzanar Murakami, both of whom experience nonnormative forms of cognition interpretable as disability. Beyond registering the existing infrastructures upholding free trade and US exceptionalism, then, Butler and Yamashita also reimagine the freeway as a conduit to other ways of sensing and feeling the world, in which crip-of-color sensibilities foster reverence for the many interdependent networks disrupting the flow of infrastructural violence. The road journeys in *Sower* and *Tropic*, then, grant us access to a world in which disabled wisdom and resourcefulness can not only intervene into the immobilizing ideologies of transnational capitalism, but also foster movement toward other ways of being in the world.

Cripping the Open Road Narrative

In his influential 1971 study *Los Angeles: The Architecture of Four Ecologies*, the architecture critic Reyner Banham depicts the freeways as the foundation of LA's urban dialect: "The language of design, architecture, and urbanism in Los Angeles is the language of movement. Mobility outweighs monumentality there to a unique degree . . . and the city will never be fully understood by those who cannot move fluently through its diffuse urban texture."[13] The freeway, as Raúl Villa observes, was vital to a discourse of developmental boosterism that gained momentum throughout the Cold War era.[14] In this "brash technocratic rhetoric," the Los Angeles freeway system represented both cultural progress and the freedom of movement.[15] From Disneyland's Autopia ride to Thomas Pynchon's 1966 novella *The Crying of Lot 49*, the California freeway in the dominant postwar LA imaginary furthered fantasies of unfettered independence.

As variations on the American open road story, both Butler's *Parable of the Sower* and Yamashita's *Tropic of Orange* draw on the kinetic energy characteristic of this genre. Yet, rather than reinforcing the autopian fantasies at the heart of such stories, which Ana Mª Manzanas and Jesús Benito argue "conflat[e] the gospel of Manifest Destiny and mobility," both novels harness the genre's dynamic movement in order to capture the migratory flows of populations newly displaced by the exigencies of global capitalism.[16] That is, while the road narrative often justifies and celebrates settler colonial impulses, which frame freedom as the right to roam and conquer, *Sower* and *Tropic* take up the freeway as an impetus to meditate on movement differently. Indeed, an excerpt from Butler's *Sower* was repurposed as one of three epigraphs for Yamashita's *Tropic*, thus signaling a shared writerly commitment to reimagining open-road narratives. In this passage and epigraph, Lauren Olamina first encounters the freeways after the sudden destruction of her hometown of Robledo:

> It's against the law in California to walk on the freeways, but the law is archaic. Everyone who walks walks on the freeways sooner or later. Freeways provide the most direct routes between cities and parts of cities. . . . Some prostitutes and peddlers of food, water, and other necessities live along the freeways in sheds or shacks or in the open air. Beggars, thieves, and murderers live here, too. . . .
>
> The freeway crowd is a heterogeneous mass—black and white, Asian and Latin, whole families are on the move with babies on backs or perched atop loads in carts, wagons, or bicycle baskets, sometimes along with an old or handicapped person. . . . Many were armed with sheathed knives, rifles, and, of course, visible holstered handguns. The occasional passing cop paid no attention. . . .
>
> People get killed on freeways all the time.[17]

This passage not only foregrounds freeway infrastructure as a vital organizing principle across both texts, it also signals each novel's re-visioning of the California freeway to serve alternate representational ends. Just as the "broad river of people walking west" repurposes the once autocentric freeway into a pedestrian route and makeshift shelter, so Butler and Yamashita repurpose the freewheeling road narrative in order to address the conditions of forced and constricted mobility for those populations most brutalized by trade deregulation, as well as the oppressive social arrangements reproduced by and through existing infrastructure.[18] Disability is explicitly named as a feature of the freeway's "heterogeneous mass," all of whom lack the (limited) security afforded by the walled-in city-states that now dot the landscape of *Sower's* dystopian California.[19] Once the domain of the wealthy and mobile, Butler's freeway is now traveled exclusively by California's most vulnerable, a river of migrants on a perilous journey up north.

In *Sower* and *Tropic*, the avowal of freeway infrastructure begins at the level of plot: both novels rely on the paper map as a structuring element, further indicating the primacy of the road narrative genre. As Butler comments in a *Callaloo* interview, maps were integral to her novel's development: "When I was writing *Parable of the Sower*, I had maps of the areas that my characters were traveling through. I went to the map store and spent a lot of money buying detailed copies of maps of different parts of California, going up to and over the Oregon border because I wasn't quite sure where my characters were going to stop."[20] Echoing Butler's process, *Sower's* Lauren Olamina similarly looks to old road maps for guidance. In one of the novel's many journal entries, Lauren writes, "I'm going to go north. My grandparents once traveled a lot by car. They left us old road maps of just about every county in the state plus several of other parts of the country. The newest of them is 40 years old, but that doesn't matter. The roads will still be there."[21] Freeway maps drive *Sower*: they enable Lauren to imagine a pathway outside of her dying community, and later in the novel, they assist her and her companions through particularly harrowing stretches of their journey.

Similar to Butler's spatially driven practice, *Tropic of Orange* began as a Lotus spreadsheet and was shaped initially by form rather than content. As Yamashita herself observes, "There was here a structure before there was a book."[22] In *Tropic*, the narrative elements of character, temporality, setting, and plot are re-visioned through the matrixlike form of the street intersection. As figure 3.1 shows, this creates an infrastructural form mirrored in the book's spatialized table of contents. *Tropic's* narrative grid interweaves seven storylines of racialized characters

HyperContexts

	Monday Summer Solstice	Tuesday Diamond Lane	Wednesday Cultural Diversity
Rafaela *Cortes*	**Midday**-Not Too Far from Mazatlán chapter 1	**Morning** -En México chapter 10	**Daylight** -The Cornfield chapter 18
Bobby Ngu	**Benefits** -Koreatown chapter 2	**Car Payment Due** -Tijuana via Singapore chapter 12	**Second Mortgage** -Chinatown chapter 15
Emi	**Weather Report** -Westside chapter 3	**NewsNow** -Hollywood South chapter 9	**Disaster Movie Week** -Hiro's Sushi chapter 20
Buzzworm	**Station ID** -Jefferson & Normandie chapter 4	**Oldies** -This Old Hood chapter 13	**LA X** -Margarita's Corner chapter 16
Manzanar *Murakami*	**Traffic Window** -Harbor Freeway chapter 5	**Rideshare** -Downtown Interchange chapter 8	**The Hour of the Trucks** -The Freeway Canyon chapter 19
Gabriel Balboa	**Coffee Break** -Downtown chapter 6	**Budgets** -Skirting Downtown chapter 14	**The Interview** -Manzanar chapter 17
Arcangel	**To Wake** -Marketplace chapter 7	**To Wash** -On the Tropic chapter 11	**To Eat** -La Cantina de Miseria y Hambre chapter 21

Fig. 3.1. Spatialized table of contents from the 1997 edition of Karen Tei Yamashita's *Tropic of Orange*.

traveling toward, away from, or around Los Angeles, who hail from different locations in the global economy. There's Manzanar Murakami, a Japanese American surgeon-turned-homeless-maestro once interned at the Manzanar camp; Gabriel Balboa, a Chicano news reporter who owns a second home in Mazatlán; Emi Sakai, a perpetually aroused Japanese American TV producer and Gabriel's girlfriend; Rafaela Cortes, Gabriel's Mazatlán housekeeper and a part-time student of globalization theory; Bobby Ngu, Rafaela's distant husband and a Chinese Singaporean expat posing as Vietnamese refugee; Arcangel, a Global South prophet and performance artist based on the border brujo Guillermo Gómez-Peña; and Buzzworm, an African American "Angel of Mercy" armed with a Walkman, a watch collection, and a progressive social agenda. This multiperspectival story plots a cross-section of multiethnic Los Angeles—its homeless population, its professional classes, its ghettoized residents, and its migrant laborers—through a dispersal of focalization. Moving between third-person narration (Rafaela Cortes, Buzzworm, Manzanar, Bobby Ngu) and first-person (Gabriel Balboa), *Tropic*'s disjunctive narrative generates numerous maps of Los Angeles, with no single perspective gaining precedence.

Over the course of a week, Yamashita's novel charts the lives of its seven characters as they navigate the warped topography produced by the hemispheric clash of Global North and South—a clash generated by a wayward orange traveling north from Mazatlán to Los Angeles. This mystical fruit carries with it the Tropic of Cancer, whose latitudinal shift drags Mexico into California. The orange's journey reimagines the multinational integration prompted by NAFTA, the defining event and nucleus of Yamashita's novel. As the orange travels up the coast, bullets bend, streets expand and contract, time stutters, and Manzanar conducts, capturing even the "endless jam of shrieking notes" produced by a massive accident on the Harbor Freeway.[23]

While this shared authorial fixation on maps, freeways, and grids might invoke the Lefebvrian concept of *abstract space*, or the bureaucratic space of capitalism founded on "the vast network of banks, business centres, and major productive entities, as also on motorways, airports, and information lattices," the California freeway instead provides a means for Butler and Yamashita to critique the uneven conditions of mobility upheld by dominant infrastructural networks.[24] That is, the freeway as literary figure enables both authors to explore how race, class, and migration status mediate relationships to movement, a differential production of mobility that also functions as a form of dis-/enablement. In so doing, they crip the open road narrative, which often relies on the rhetoric of hyper-ability as a means of signaling freedom and independence. The editors of the American Automobile Association's *Westways* magazine, for instance, described the burgeoning California freeway network as "the sinews of a supercity."[25] Further, as I have argued elsewhere, these ideologies of ability informed civic approaches to slum clearance and so-called blight, justifying intrusions into low-income and racialized neighborhoods.[26] For instance, the predominant urban planning discourses of 1940s Los Angeles, which advocated for highway construction, cast professional planners as "surgeon generals" fighting for the "physical, economic, and moral health of the metropolitan body."[27] Such medicalized narratives supported the production and reproduction of Los Angeles as a commuter's paradise—a vision of the city that protected white, moneyed, and mobile nuclear families while profiting from racialized dispossession.

Unfolding over seventy-five years after the initial wave of freeway boosterism, *Sower* takes place in a landscape indelibly shaped by this legacy. As the main form of transit for California's most dispossessed, Butler's freeways evoke histories of racialized displacement driven by urban redevelopment initiatives such as slum clearance and freeway expansion. In particular, Lauren's northward journey depicts the dis-/enabling effects of existing infrastructural arrangements, which generate race- and class-based hierarchies of mobility. Disability, in *Sower*, thus emerges as an effect of built environments engineered to reproduce raced, classed, and gendered inequities. In this way, *Sower* extends the oft-cited (and now, oft-critiqued) social model of disability, which defines disability as socially produced through the interaction of physical or cognitive impairments with inaccessible built environments.[28] This model argues that, rather than being a property contained to the individual body and best addressed by medical intervention, disability is socially created through ableist bias. It further claims that disability would no longer exist if we lived in a world designed to honor the diversity of human embodiment.

Yet, as Nirmala Erevelles has argued, the social model does not account for the historical production of disability, which is differentially distributed across categories of race and class.[29] In other words, this model does not describe how disability comes to be, or how it is disproportionately borne by underresourced populations. In *Sower*, however, the freeway functions as both instrument of and showcase for processes of racialized, gendered, and classed dis-/enablement. On the freeway, we see how disability is made. When the Robledo survivors first begin their journey, Lauren describes the immense physical stress placed on the freeway pedestrians, who are unable to eat, rest, or bathe. Soon after they depart, a "woman alongside [them]" collapses, registering the immobilizing weight of freeway travel.[30] Further, while Lauren and her fellow freeway pedestrians must navigate complete chaos on their route to attempted freedom, the rich "in some places" are "escaping by flying out in helicopters" and the "bridges that are still intact . . . are guarded either by the police or by gangs. Both groups are there to rob desperate, fleeing people of their weapons, money, food, and water—at the least."[31] In this harrowing passage, the open road story is reimagined as a tale of constricted movement, in which differential access to transit (the freeway pedestrians versus the rich in helicopters) determines one's ability to survive intact.

As these passages illustrate, Lauren's freeway exodus offers a powerful counterpoint to autopian fantasies of independence. Far from symbolizing the unfettered freedoms touted by this genre, the freeway in *Sower* signals a slowness of pace that aligns with key definitions of disablement. In *The Rejected Body*, for instance, Susan Wendell notes how an accelerated pace of life can disable those previously considered able-bodied.[32] "When the pace of life in a society increases," writes Wendell, "there is a tendency for more people to become disabled, not only because of physically damaging consequences of efforts to go faster, but also because fewer people can meet expectations of 'normal' performance."[33]

The relationship of pace to disability is registered in a number of ways across *Sower*. For instance, Lauren's disabling condition of hyperempathy, a heightened sensitivity to the physical sensations of others, was caused by her mother's use of Paracetco, an "Einstein powder" and performance-enhancing drug.[34] Further, the acceleration prompted by turbocapitalism, alongside unequal access to transit, effectively disables all of those forced to walk the freeway in Butler's California. This disablement unfolds as a form of crip temporality, in that the freeway pedestrians cannot keep up with the expectations of pace set by those in helicopters. It is further expressed in terms of sheer physical strain. One of the first things Lauren learns in her freeway journey is that "walking hurts. I've never done enough walking to learn that before, but I know it now. . . . Nothing eases the pain except rest."[35] The freeway, then, not only indicates the disablement of the racialized poor via capitalism's sped-up temporalities, it also generates a record of pain for those forced to migrate northward on foot.

In *Tropic of Orange*, Los Angeles's Harbor Freeway similarly provokes an extended meditation on the politics and aesthetics of mobility. For Manzanar Murakami, traffic offers a means to record the pulse and pace of city infrastructure and, with it, all that enables (or halts) mobility. When an explosive accident grinds the Harbor Freeway traffic to a standstill, the narrative of autopian freedom becomes a tale of immobilizing gridlock, in which "man's most consistent quest for continuing technology in all of its treaded ramifications jammed every inch of street, driveway, highway, and freeway."[36] In this chapter, Yamashita imagines the car as an impediment rather than a vehicle of physical transcendence. And insofar as the car does impart freedom, its prosthetic dimensions are highlighted by the musings of Manzanar, who on occasion imagines the commuter as a cyborgian monstrosity: "He envisioned the person within as the pulpy brain of each vehicle, and when the defenseless body emerged, for whatever reason, he often felt surprise and disgust"[37]

Like the freeway in Butler's *Sower*, Yamashita's freeway compels us to consider the historical, material, and prosthetic underpinnings of human movement and migration. In this way, it aligns with the long-standing disability studies interest in the built environment and its shaping effects on human body-minds. Just as disability theory has drawn attention to the prosthetic supports that facilitate movement through the world—even for allegedly able-bodied people—so *Tropic* imposes infrastructure onto readerly consciousness, rendering it fantastic and animate. Following this, *Tropic* often renders infrastructure monstrous—gargantuan, alive, and threatening—to the racialized low-income Angelenos it does not support. Accordingly, when the Harbor Freeway balloons due to the orange's space-warping properties, Buzzworm, described in *Tropic* as a "big black seven-foot dude, Vietnam vet" and South Central native, calls the TV producer Emi Sakai's attention to its inexplicable growth:[38]

"Can't you see it? Where we are. Harbor Freeway. It's growing. Stretched this way and that. In fact, this whole business from Pico-Union on one side to East L.A. this side and South Central over here, it's pushing out. Damn if it's not growing into everything! If it don't stop, it could be the whole enchilada."

"Kerry, what's he talking about? Do you see something?"

Kerry shook his head.

"Look, there might be some video distortion, but reality is reality. Are you all right?"

Buzzworm wondered about this reality. If they didn't see it, they didn't see it. Like the homeboy said, anyone on the ground'd know. These folks weren't on the ground. They were online or somewhere on the waves.[39]

Expanding into the neighborhoods of Pico-Union, East Los Angeles, and South Central, the 110's bizarre growth hearkens back to the destructive paths cut through low-income, racialized communities during the height of freeway expansion.[40] Buzzworm, in a previous section, summons this history through his memory of bureaucrats "[widening] the freeway" through his neighborhood.[41] In excavating this memory of displacement, Buzzworm recognizes the freeway as a system that supports the uneven topographies of Los Angeles. It can actually produce forms of spatial containment, as Buzzworm discovers when he gets "taken for a ride on the freeway": "Got to pass over the Harbor Freeway, speed over the hood like the freeway was a giant bridge. He realized you could just skip out over his house, his streets, his part of town. You never had to see it ever."[42]

Yamashita's Los Angeles emerges from layers of accumulated histories—immigration policy, de facto segregation, and urban redevelopment—that undergird the shifting urban terrain shaped by globalization. Yet, Emi and her news crew cannot sense these changes or histories. An affluent Westside TV producer invested in turning revolution into entertainment, Emi spends the novel unaware of the material world's inconveniences. Positioned "online or somewhere on the waves," she is unable to discern the palpable, "on-the-ground," and harmful effects of a freeway expanding past its limit. For hypermobile (and thus hyper-able) characters like Emi, the freeway never attains *thingness*.[43] But for Buzzworm, a figure who "[walks] the hood every day," it is menacing in its materiality.[44] In *Tropic*, then, one's awareness of infrastructure functions as a barometer of vulnerability and disability in a metropolitan ecology rutted with power asymmetries.

While these pages have examined the myth of independence ensconced within the open road narrative, I will now shift to the myths of immigrant dependency circulating in the wake of free trade. In the following pages, I demonstrate how *Tropic* and *Sower* employ freeway infrastructure to explore the root/route system of extranational labor and coerced migration, as well as the anti-immigration sentiment accompanying such changes. Building on a disability analysis of prosthetic and infrastructural support, I consider how each novel depicts the forceful extraction of labor from migrant populations, which then becomes an invisible support system for global capitalism's elite classes. Here, transit infrastructure becomes a vehicle to examine how transnational trading agreements transform so-called developing nations into substructures propping up wealthier nations.

Myths of Migrant Dependency in the Wake of NAFTA

As an interstate network spanning national and international borders, the free-ways in *Sower* and *Tropic* index the transnational shifts in trade and transit con-stituting the global reorganization of capital. In particular, they foreground the social and economic transformations both prompted by and preceding the 1994 passage of NAFTA, a major trilateral trade pact that eased regulations between Canada, the United States, and Mexico. NAFTA enforced a regime of selective and differential mobility across North American borders, accelerating cross-border transits of products, information, and capital while intensifying mili-tarization along the US-Mexico border. A "new form of colonialism," NAFTA allowed transnational corporations access to cross-border pools of labor and consumer markets, devastating local businesses and intensifying poverty.[45] Ac-cordingly, NAFTA forced the migration of working populations to the United States and Canada in search of precarious employment.

These waves of migration were then managed by a discourse of public dependency that framed the "illegal immigrant" as a drain on the public. As schol-ars like Mike Davis, Justin Akers Chacón, and Grace Kyungwon Hong have noted, the flow of goods and people across the US-Mexico border was accompa-nied by increasing anti-immigrant sentiment, which "[caused] people to blame the economic recessions not on capital re-organization and transnational cor-porate policies, but on Mexican immigrants, who were ostensibly taking Ameri-can jobs while draining the United States of its scarce social service and welfare resources."[46] Akin to the myth of the welfare queen, the subject of chapter 1, a retooled version of the illegal immigrant myth emerged in the 1990s as part of a new nativism seeking to keep immigrants, especially women and children, from the shrinking largesse of US public entitlement and social service programs. This mythology further depicted workers as migrating to the United States by choice, as opposed to being displaced by economic development programs and procapi-talist policies.

These mythologies of dependency, further, drew on long-standing able-ist rhetoric that depicts immigrants as disabling to the nation writ large. As Julie Avril Minich argues in *Accessible Citizenships*, the US nation-state is often imagined as a "whole, healthy body that must be safeguarded against pathogens and parasites," a formulation that all too often positions immigrants as exter-nal vectors of disablement.[47] Relatedly, the 1882 Act to Regulate Immigration charged a head tax of fifty cents per immigrant entering the country while excluding "the entry of idiots, lunatics, convicts, and persons likely to become a public charge."[48] In conjunction with the Chinese Exclusion Act of 1882 and the Alien Contract Labor Laws of 1885 and 1887, the Act to Regulate Immigration framed immigrants—and disabled immigrants in particular—as burdens on the national body.

Such antipathic sentiments, which reached fever pitch with the passing of California's Proposition 187, imagined racialized immigrant workers as parasitic and disabling to the nation-state. Passed in 1994, Proposition 187 (also known as the Save Our State initiative) denied undocumented migrants access to public services like healthcare, public education, and welfare, ostensibly in order to curtail "illegal" immigration. However, "the real agenda" behind Proposition 187, writes Grace Chang, "was to criminalize immigrants for presumably entering the country 'illegally' and stealing resources from 'true' United States citizens."[49] The Personal Responsibility and Work Opportunity Reconciliation Act (PRWORA), too, raised the bar for state assistance for immigrants with qualified legal status. It prohibited noncitizen immigrants with an arrival date after August 22, 1996 (the date of PRWORA's passage) from accessing Supplemental Security Income or food stamps prior to achieving citizenship, and it imposed a five-year waiting period for TANF (Temporary Assistance for Needy Families), Medicaid, and SCHIP (State Children's Health Insurance Program).

Both Butler's *Sower* and Yamashita's *Tropic* leverage the open road narrative to intervene into mythologies of immigrant workers as potential public dependents and resource thieves, mapping out a rival landscape of dependency that emphasizes global economic contingency on racialized labor exploitation. Rather than framing migrants as disabling to the nation, then, both *Sower* and *Tropic* highlight all that migrant labor enables, as well as the disabling operations of transnational trade infrastructures. In particular, Butler's *Sower* employs the freeway as a means of foregrounding the conditions of structural deprivation that drive migration. It further depicts the dependency on private employers—that is, the "company town" model—purposely generated through the privatization of life-sustaining resources.

While literary scholars have mentioned the relationship of Butler's *Parable of the Sower* to globalization and NAFTA, few have offered extended analyses of the novel's engagement with border and immigration politics, even as *Sower* centrally focuses on a multiethnic group of migrants.[50] Lauren even expresses the possibility of crossing the US border in an early conversation with her father, stating, "I heard it was easier up there . . . Oregon, Washington, Canada."[51] Moments such as these make it possible to see *Parable* as a US border studies text, even though it has rarely been taken up as such. Indeed, *Sower* makes mention of factories "just on this side of the Canada border" that mirror the maquiladoras blooming in the wake of free trade.[52] The "borderworks" factories represent one of the only employment options available to the working poor. There, workers "make things for companies in Canada or Asia" while facing debt and disablement: "They don't get paid much, so they get into debt. They get hurt or sick, too. Their drinking water's not clean and the factories are dangerous. . . . But people think they can make some cash and then quit."[53]

In interviews given around the time of *Sower*'s publication, Butler herself makes regular references to NAFTA and the "throw-away labor" created and exploited by US factories in Mexico, citing such horrific practices as source material for her novel.[54] Her comments further draw lines of commonality between Black, brown, and unhoused workers who work under conditions of mass disablement: "You know, we already have situations where, here in Southern California . . . they'll either bring in illegal aliens and work them and not pay them and forbid them to leave . . . or they'll do it with Black people who are not well enough educated . . . to get out of there, or they'll do it with homeless people who, you know, don't have anywhere to go."[55] Butler continues, "And when they're around thirty, thirty-five, they're pretty much used up if they haven't been injured or damaged in some way by the kind of work they're required to do."[56] Rather than framing anti-Blackness, immigration, disability, and poverty as separate issues, then, Butler connects these struggles via the axis of labor, articulating a coalitional politics of work that brings together antiracist, anticapitalist, and feminist disability analysis. This formulation of cross-racial solidarity offers a counterpoint to those advocates of welfare reform who "strategically linked [Black folks and nonwhite immigrants] together in public discourse," collectively constructing these groups as "freeloaders and threats to the national community."[57]

Butler's *Sower* depicts its multiethnic migrant class not as disabling parasites leeching off the largesse of other countries but instead as a "harvest of survivors" in a constant process of adaptation to nearly unlivable circumstances.[58] The "ever-flowing river of people moving north" do not take to the freeways to needlessly seek out opportunities in more resourced lands; they do so because transnational corporations and resource privatization have destroyed most of the viable ways of life in their hometowns.[59] Once a "rich, green, unwalled little city," Robledo is now a "rope, breaking, a single strand at a time," undone by theft, violence, and unlivable wages.[60] Surrounded by a world riddled with climate disasters, drought, dissipating job opportunities, and a nonexistent social safety net, Lauren is unable to imagine a future in her community, and this incites her to devise the Earthseed philosophy.

Aside from living in her "disintegrating neighborhood," Lauren names the creation and propagation of Earthseed as her only desirable prospect.[61] In order to begin this movement, she will have to "go outside" her relatively protected community.[62] Her tentative plans for escape are accelerated when desperate outsiders infiltrate her town, setting everything ablaze and killing most of its inhabitants. After the near-total devastation of her kinship networks and community support systems, she sets out to map new futures and communities, seeding new social infrastructures from the ruins of the old.

Other Earthseed converts share similar stories of dispossession, disablement, and dislocation. Zahra Moss and Harry Baiter, Lauren's first freeway companions, also survived Robledo's destruction, a crisis event precipitated by the ever-growing gap between rich and poor. Allie and Jill Gilchrist, who join later, endured a life of survival sex work, family abuse, and poverty. Emery Tanaka Solis, mother to Tori Solis, labored with her husband as a farm worker until the farm's takeover by a "big agribusiness conglomerate," a company that pays their workers in "company scrip" and ensnares them in debt.[63] The conglomerate and their exploitative labor practices further destroy Emery's kinship bonds, with her husband working until he "sickened and died" and her children taken away by the company as collateral.[64] The trauma, sickness, and family separation wrought by brutal corporate practices position exploitative companies, not migrants, as chief agents of disablement. The disabling practices and effects of resource deprivation further prompt these characters to brave the California freeway network despite its many risks. Butler's freeway thus signals both the promise and the perils of traveling toward other worlds, and of wanting a life that operates beyond the debilitating forces of global capital. As *Sower* repeatedly warns us, "People get killed on freeways all the time."[65]

By narrativizing the unbearable conditions endured by the Earthseed converts, Butler leverages the critical force of dystopia in order to depict migration under transnational capitalism as a coercive, rather than voluntary, process. As Sami Schalk has observed, the *Parable* series falls within the genre of "critical dystopia," through which authors "present a dystopian, even apocalyptic future, in order to comment on the problematic elements of the present, and to suggest that if things do not change, then such a future is possible."[66] Butler's dystopia of debt slavery, company towns, and rampant desperation comments on the future (and present-day) possibilities engendered by structural adjustment policies and trade liberalization, which have generated mass displacements on a global scale. Grace Chang and others have described the calculated nature of these dislocations, observing that the "extraction of resources by the United States and other First World nations" through SAPs coerce workers from the Global South to "migrate to follow their countries' wealth."[67] And while Butler does not explicitly portray the novel's California as a "developing" state, indebted to international financial institutions such as the World Bank, it is nonetheless subject to many of the same processes that operate under the name of structural adjustment, including the privatization of state enterprises, the cutting of wages, the deregulation of trade, and the divestment of state expenditures from social and entitlement programs (e.g., welfare reform).

In a journal entry dated November 6, 2024, Lauren documents the recent election of President Charles Morpeth Donner, who—like Ronald Reagan—has run on a platform of resource privatization and the destabilization of labor power. She writes, "Donner has a plan for putting people back to work. He hopes to get laws changed, suspend 'overly restrictive' minimum wage, environmental, and worker protection laws for those employers willing to take on homeless employees and provide them with training and adequate room and board."[68] Lauren turns her keen critical eye onto these campaign promises, predicting that the enforcement of such policies will lead to further worker exploitation, poverty, and family separation. Unsurprisingly, President Donner is "all for" the maquiladora-like factories cropping up near the Canadian border, which are "supposed to provide jobs for that northward-flowing river of people."[69] The sheer volume of migrants, "thousands of jobless for every job," enables the borderworks factories to treat their workers as disposable.[70] Sower establishes clear links between Donner's campaign platform, the disabling and extractive practices of transnational capital, and the freeway pedestrians traveling in search of work.

As the river of "California trash" flowing toward Canada makes apparent, Butler's Sower envisions a future in which the United States no longer reigns as a major economic power.[71] Instead, transnational corporations run by Canadian, Asian, and European business interests create and perpetuate profound economic dependency on private employers. The overtaking of the coastal town of Olivar by a "company called Kagimoto, Stamm, Frampton, and Company—KSF" depicts this process in detail.[72] Though Olivar, as Lauren notes, is "a lot richer than we [Robledo] are," it nonetheless cannot "protect itself from the encroaching sea, the crumbling earth, the crumbling economy, or the desperate refugees."[73]

In exchange for "security, a guaranteed food supply, jobs, and help in their battle with the Pacific," the "officials of Olivar" allow their town "to be taken over, bought out, privatized."[74] Olivar residents are "upper middle-class, white, literate," and with their purchase, KSF "gets an eager, educated work force" willing to "accept smaller salaries than their socioeconomic group is used to."[75] The smaller salaries, Lauren observes, will ensure the indebtedness of KSF's new hires, which is "an old company-town trick—get people into debt, hang on to them, and work them harder."[76] In addition to extracting labor power from Olivar residents, KSF also privatizes resources from Olivar's formerly public lands: "The company intends to dominate farming and the selling of water and solar and wind energy over much of the southwest. . . . They mean to own great water, power, and agricultural industries in an area that most people have given up on."[77] And while many people in Olivar and Robledo remain skeptical of this arrangement, many others, including Lauren's stepmother Cory, view it as an opportunity for potential security: "We could be safe in Olivar."[78]

Lauren's astute observations, which describe step-by-step the process of debt enslavement, demonstrate how private corporations leverage the promise of protection in order to manufacture worker dependency. Just as structural adjustment policies, according to Chang, "open up developing nations' economies and peoples to imperialist exploitation," so the vulnerable towns of Butler's California must hang onto any semblance of security offered by companies like KSF.[79] Butler's dystopia thus presents a future scenario in which rampant resource extraction renders even formerly protected white-collar workers vulnerable to corporate predation. In the context of structural deprivation and rampant poverty, the limited protections offered by KSF look like a life raft to the once-secure residents of Olivar, who trade their freedom and labor power for a chance at stability. Their labor becomes yet another resource taken by parasitic private interests, constituting a human infrastructural network of workers who prop up and enable further resource exploitation. Butler's depiction of Olivar as recent company town thus frames KSF and other transnational corporations, rather than the workers who sustain them, as the primary drain on collective resources. In this way, she issues a powerful corrective to narratives that pose migrant workers as burdens on the state.

Yamashita's *Tropic of Orange*, too, employs the open road story as a means of overwriting myths of migrant dependency. In addition to highlighting the social and spatial divisions imposed by extant infrastructural arrangements, *Tropic* amplifies the freeway network as a means of highlighting the unseen and unvalued infrastructures of migrant labor undergirding Los Angeles. In so doing, it illustrates how the city's operations vitally depend on a racialized and feminized laboring substrate.

While *Tropic* comments on the reverberations of globalization writ large, it primarily focuses on NAFTA as shorthand for global capitalism's characteristic features: the deregulation of trade, the outsourcing of labor, the exploitation of the floating wage scale, and the decimation of local businesses. It registers the impact of NAFTA on both sides of the border, from the "international breast milk" shipped northward to LAX (Los Angeles International Airport), emblematic of the increasing feminization of the immigrant labor force, to the American beers, sodas, hamburgers, and ketchup flooding the menu at the "Cantina de Miseria y Hambre."[80] *Tropic* also captures the migratory flows of displaced populations moving northward in search of work who then become the living infrastructure for the machinations of global capitalism.

The image of the freeway as a "great root system" signals the novel's interest in the evolving and coerced routes of people, products, and labor precipitated by the demands of global consumerism, and the ways in which these circuits interact with histories of immigration, colonization, so-called urban renewal, and displacement in the global city of Los Angeles.[81] *Tropic* depicts a Los Angeles transformed by free trade and the reconfiguration of global and metropolitan infrastructural networks, which accelerate an influx of products, people, labor, and capital. In part of what Grace Chang terms a "calculated pull" by the United States and other Global North nations, job-seeking migrants land in well-resourced cities such as LA.[82] Here, they become part of a service sector industry that supports the city's larger operations. Encompassing occupations like domestic, garment, food preparation, janitorial, and childcare work, these low-wage service jobs are overwhelmingly occupied by racialized immigrant women, both in the United States and abroad.[83] In *Tropic*, such work is performed by *"all the people who do the work of machines: / human washing machines, / human vacuums, / human garbage disposals."*[84] Given that this work supports the imperatives of global capital while remaining unseen and unvalued, it resonates with the function of infrastructure as a network of invisible reinforcement that supports a larger totality.

In Yamashita's novel, this unseen network of maintenance labor ("Washing dishes. Chopping vegetables. Cleaning floors. . . . Cleaning up. Keeping up") is embodied most fully by the undocumented migrants Bobby Ngu and Rafaela Cortes.[85] Partners in a janitorial business prior to their split, Bobby and Rafaela perform the material, embodied work required by an ostensibly dematerialized world of wireless communication and transaction. They "wipe up the conference tables. Dust everything. Wipe down the computer monitors. Vacuum staples and hole punches and donuts out of carpets."[86] Rafaela further provides the much-needed labor for Gabriel Balboa's vacation home, "sweeping both dead and living things from over and under beds."[87] This scene of industrious cleaning not only opens the novel, thereby setting the stage for a narrative indebted to maintenance labor, but also showcases Gabriel's incompetence and dependency: "Even though he tried, he was not a hands-on sort of person. . . . After all, he was a journalist; he just wanted a quiet place to write. Maintenance was the problem."[88]

Yet, despite the necessary labor she performs for Gabriel and others, Rafaela feels the weight of anti-immigrant dependency discourse: "But she [Rafaela] kept talking, saying we're not wanted here [in Los Angeles]. Nobody respects our work. Say we cost money. Live on welfare. It's a lie."[89] As *Tropic of Orange* demonstrates, workers such as Bobby and Rafaela are not external to the system or parasitic on it. Rather, they provide the manual labor that enables it to run. Further, they are part of a long-standing history of racialized infrastructural labor central to LA's growth. During one of his final segments, Manzanar pays homage to the early systems of support that sustained the city—"the railroads and the harbors and the aqueduct"—and more specifically, the "migrant and immigrant that created the initial grid on which everything else began to fill in."[90] The construction of early transit networks, a precursor to our contemporary age of free trade, was contingent on exploited migrant labor. And so, as the novel foregrounds the global economy's maintenance labor substrate, we view capitalism's privileged citizens—ostensibly autonomous individuals—as enmeshed in a network of support, rather than the reverse.

In amplifying the low-wage, racialized work that supports cosmopolitan wealth, *Tropic* re-embodies the invisible living infrastructure—what Abdou-Maliq Simone terms "people *as* infrastructure"—underpinning globalization.[91]

In so doing, it recuperates the category of dependency frequently used to devalue migrant laborers, reversing a dominant narrative of globalization that works to obscure them. This narrative emphasizes the hypermobility of capital and a new international class, as well as the phenomena of time-space compression ensuing from advanced telecommunications and modes of transit.[92] For proponents of this narrative, globalization inserts us into an efficient cyborgian realm in which technological prostheses free us from the inconveniences of the material world, rendering us hyper-able. Yet, as Saskia Sassen argues, the global economy cannot be disconnected from the local sites and laboring bodies that set it into motion.[93] As such, *Tropic* traces the material flows that circulate within this cross-border region—both "waves of floating paper money: pesos and dollars and reals, all floating across effortlessly" and "oranges, bananas, corn, lettuce, guarachis, . . . electrodomestics, live-in domestics, living domestics, gardeners, dishwashers, . . . undocumenteds, illegals, aliens."[94]

The novel's centering of low-wage labor thereby fleshes out globalization's dominant narrative, which omits the work of racialized immigrant women as well as the work of laborers overseas. Sassen identifies the dominant construct of global economy as selectively pieced together through an overvaluation of corporate culture and a disavowal of nonexpert jobs that, for many, do not register as part of the same system. The externalization of low-wage labor hinges on the racialization of this labor force—that is, the framing of immigration and ethnicity as *other*. "Although these types of workers and jobs are never represented as part of the global economy," Sassen writes, "they are in fact *part of the infrastructure* of jobs involved in running and implementing the global economic system."[95] And so, through the eyes of the character Arcangel we see—in poetic detail—the Black and brown laboring bodies that comprise the global economy's unseen layers:

> Haitian farmers burning and slashing cane,
>
> workers stirring molasses into white gold.
>
> Guatemalans loading trucks with
>
> crates of bananas and corn.
>
> Indians, who mined tin in the Cerro Rico
>
> and saltpeter from the Atacama desert,

chewing coca and drinking aguardiente to

dull the pain of their labor.

. . .

He saw

the mother in Idaho peeling a banana for her child.[96]

Arcangel's poetry and performance art stems from his critiques of the US-Mexico border, which he summons in his poetic condemnation of the villain SUPERNAFTA. A spokesperson for the Global South's laboring poor, he speaks of the expansive grid of manual labor—what he terms "noble work"—that sources raw materials for consumption in the United States.[97] This exchange is noticeably uneven; Arcangel juxtaposes the notoriously brutal work of sugarcane cutting and tin mining with the effortless act of "peeling a banana." That workers need to "dull the pain of their labor" further emphasizes the disabling function of free trade imperatives, with the workers' pain offering a somatic archive of resource extraction. In return for sinking the entirety of labor power into "*draining their / homeland of its natural wealth*," the workers receive "*progress, / technology, / loans.*"[98] They exchange material goods for the dematerialized rhetoric of development.

With the inclusion of "hidden and cheap" racialized laboring bodies onto the stage of the global economy, we can view the system of multinational capitalism as a parasitic ecology of disablement, wherein the devalued labor of allegedly dependent subjects in fact enables the global economy's beneficiaries.[99] *Tropic* thus reverses the thought system that imagines the low-wage migrant laborer as a disabling public burden and the global citizen as a self-governing ideal, positioning the two as mutually imbricated. Through its emphasis on infrastructure, *Tropic* outlines the "great root system[s]" that prop up a multiethnic, economically unequal Los Angeles.[100]

Both Butler's *Sower* and Yamashita's *Tropic* employ transit infrastructure to dispel the dependency rhetoric that divides ethnic subjects into "deserving" and "undeserving" categories and obscures the violent economic conditions driving migration en masse to the United States. While *Sower* foregrounds the manufactured dependency that forces California migrants to take to the freeways, *Tropic* depicts migrant labor as a systemic prosthesis, a living infrastructure that sustains the fantasies of hyper-ability entertained by proponents of globalization. Finally, both novels underscore the disabling function of global economic systems, in which labor extraction and coerced migration operate in tandem to wear out the bodies of migrant workers. In the following pages, I consider how both novels render freeway infrastructure as a conduit for the generative and world-making properties of interdependency. They do so by fostering radical forms of disability consciousness and politics, accessed through the eccentric freeway conductor Manzanar Murakami and the hyperempath Lauren Olamina.

Toward the Crip Sacred and Infrastructural Sublime

Looking to Lauren and Manzanar, I tap into the crip visioning potential of both novels, in which the freeway becomes a portal for imagining interdependent ways of living and being-in-relation. Both characters demonstrate modes of perception that diverge significantly from the cognitive norms established in their respective fictional universes, and in this way, they are aligned with the categories of neurodiversity and neurodivergence. Grounded in disability political activism, the term *neurodiversity* insists on the recognition and respect of cognitive, mental, and neurological variation. As Ralph James Savarese and Emily Thornton Savarese have written, the "concept of neurodiversity can help us to remain attentive to a different sensibility—indeed a different way of being in, and perceiving the world—while at the same time reminding us of the need to construct the category of the human in the most capacious manner possible."[101] Signaling resistance to dominant psychiatric discourse, it honors the many ways that the world can be sensed, felt, and known.

Through their neurodivergence, Manzanar and Lauren attune us to alternate planes of infrastructural consciousness. In the passage cited earlier in this chapter, Manzanar zeroes in on the aesthetic properties and political potential of the otherwise mundane Harbor Freeway, conducting Los Angeles traffic like an orchestra: "Each of the maps was a layer of music, a clef, an instrument . . . a change of measure, a coda."[102] Lauren, too, experiences an amplified version of the world, attributable to her condition of *hyperempathy*. In the *Parables* universe, this term describes a congenital disability that causes those affected to intensely experience—sometimes to the point of paralysis—the physical sensations of others within their visual range. Due to this heightened vulnerability, Lauren develops a hyperaware sense of local geography and resource availability during her freeway exodus. She is closely tuned into any small detail that could harm or help her crew. In this way, she demonstrates how disability might in fact engender key survival skills in the midst of climate and resource apocalypse.

Both characters, then, employ neurodivergent practices of hyperattention, which underscore the webs of support undergirding both the world as it is lived and the world as it could be. In this way, they model politicized forms of infrastructural consciousness that train focus on the resources, practices, skills, and systems that enable life (and vulnerable life in particular) to flourish. And though the *Parable* series has received far more attention from disability critics than *Tropic*, I contend that Yamashita's portrayal of Manzanar also invites disability analysis, as multiple characters in *Tropic* interpret his freeway orchestration as potential evidence of madness (though the novel ultimately discredits these interpretations). For instance, during an interview, Buzzworm candidly asks Manzanar, "You're an educated man; you don't consider that you might be crazy?"[103]

The novel's description of Manzanar as a "sooty homeless man," one with deeply eccentric habits, further evokes what Craig Willse identifies as the "dominant discourse on homelessness in the United States," which has "its roots in medicine in general and psychiatry in particular."[104] Popular depictions of unhoused people as mentally unstable, excessive, and subhuman have "[sanctioned] social abandonment" of economically precarious populations, who face the continued withdrawal of housing resources in favor of increased policing and criminalization.[105] The deinstitutionalization movement, which emerged in the 1960s as an alliance between antipsychiatry groups and reformers of so-called big government, further fueled the connection between psychiatric disability and unhoused status.[106] Yamashita's *Tropic* invokes this history when describing the takeover of the Harbor Freeway by LA's unhoused population following an explosive, multilane accident: "As the homeless flocked onto the freeway, there were also the usual questions of shelter and jobs, drug rehabilitation, and the closing of mental health facilities."[107] The character of Manzanar, then, throws into relief the connections between disability, state management of vulnerable populations, and the retraction of social services and welfare.

It remains important, however, to resist a formal diagnosis of these characters, given that such a reading would center the narratives of medical authority rather than the interpretive frameworks of disability scholarship and activism. Instead, this section highlights the particular worldviews and thought systems brought into being by *crip wisdom*, a term coined by the disability justice collective Sins Invalid.[108] Through their depictions of these neurodivergent characters, both novels grant their readers access to what M. Jacqui Alexander has termed the "metaphysics of interdependence": a spiritual imperative to transcend the artificial and violent divisions enforced by global capitalism, (neo) colonization, and chattel slavery and, in doing so, to imagine modes of coexistence "premised in relationality and solidarity."[109]

For Manzanar, the Harbor Freeway most fully activates his alignment with the infrastructural web that props up Los Angeles and connects it to the world. From his vantage point on a freeway overpass, he notes the "Southern California pipelines of natural gas; the unnatural waterways of the Los Angeles Department of Water and Power, and the great dank tunnels of sewage . . . electric currents racing voltage into the open watts of millions of hungry energy-efficient appliances."[110] And while "the complexity of layers should drown an ordinary person," Manzanar's expansive consciousness allows him to hold all these layers in tandem, translating them into musical composition.[111]

With his sonic rewriting of the Harbor Freeway, Manzanar reimagines existing infrastructures as a means of writing the city anew and envisioning it beyond the mandates of global capitalism. This re-envisioning might be understood in Lefebvrian terms as the production of *differential space*, or the seizing of abstract space (the bureaucratic, gridlike space of capitalism) to serve potentially revolutionary ends.[112] In so doing, Manzanar practices a form of avowal I term the *infrastructural sublime*: an overpowering awareness of our enmeshment, via infrastructure, in a webbed systemic infinity, which ranges from the molecular vibrations of concrete and steel to the panoramic vistas of the global economy. This awareness highlights a shared dependency on the social, historic, and civic support systems that constitute much of human ecology, and it most explicitly delivers us to a disability politic of interdependency.

From an aggregate of individual, interacting movements arises the emergent phenomenon of traffic symphony, a gestalt formation not reducible to the sum of its parts, but rather a "great writhing concrete dinosaur" that supervenes on localized flows of traffic.[113] As single cells, the agents in this organism—the drivers who trundle en masse—cannot predict traffic patterns. They "[take] advantage unknowingly" of a momentary lag on the congested freeway, an occurrence that appears random to an agent embedded in the formation it comprises.[114] Traffic assumes the form of a Deleuzoguattarian assemblage, a confederation of diverse bodies with no central point of governance. As a systemic totality, the assemblage's massed energies produce a unique effect "distinct from the sum of the vital force of each materiality considered alone."[115] Though made up of individual drivers acting of their own accord, the overall traffic in turn affects the commutes of each constituent: "People in this traffic could count themselves lucky. They might reach their destinations ten to fifteen minutes early."[116]

Using music as an interface, Manzanar renders freeway traffic as palpable form, outlining the "contours of the swarm" from a jumble of parts.[117] In "[making] infrastructure sing," he demonstrates how the song itself—and his role as musical conduit—hinges on numerous systems of support: the interplay of cars, the vibratory properties of concrete and steel structures, the "man-made grid of civil utilities."[118] Although *Tropic* foregrounds the singularity of Manzanar's vision, referring to him as a "conductor" seems misleading, given that he does not exert his will over the freeway. On the contrary, the freeway sings itself through Manzanar. When he assumes his concrete podium, the collective pulse of traffic possesses him, inducing a succession of measured gestures punctuated by tears. The "vibration rumbling through the cement and steel" flows through his being; his body becomes a node of amplification for "the great heartbeat of a great city."[119] This vision requires a mesh of supporting actors whose travels provide for him the foundation of a musical ecology. Rather than being subjects distinct from and deliberately acting on their surroundings, Manzanar and the drivers are embedded in and continuous with their environs; they are obstructed by the whole while constituting its parts. His traffic symphony thus relays a multisited or distributive account of agency, wherein our capacity to act hinges on a multiplicity of entities both external to and conjoined with us.[120] Manzanar's perception of the "complexity of layers" comprising the city thus elicits awareness of our shared contingency on infrastructural support systems and presents the individual, city, and novel as multiply determined.[121]

This powerful sense of entanglement in LA's supporting operations, a feeling captured and conveyed through Manzanar's musical overtures, effectively delivers infrastructure from the realm of the functional mundane—its "inherent boringness"—to the realm of the aesthetic.[122] By mapping the city's grids through his symphonic opus, Manzanar approaches and exceeds the Kantian mathematical sublime, in which "the mind, overwhelmed by number, uses evidence of its own unifying perception to amalgamate the overwhelming many into the heroic one."[123] And while Kant speaks to the difficulty of apprehending infinity, stating, "the mere ability even to think [the infinite] as a *whole* indicates a faculty of mind transcending every standard of the senses," Manzanar's transcendent mind carries the capacity to grasp LA's countless layers, and does so through musical composition: "*There are maps and there are maps and there are maps.* The uncanny thing was that he could see all of them at once, filter some, pick them out like transparent windows and place them even delicately and consecutively in a complex grid of pattern, spatial discernment, body politic.... Each of the maps was a layer of music, a clef, an instrument, a musical instruction, a change of measure, a coda."[124] His apprehension of these musical layers brings us to a vision of the infrastructural sublime, a sense of deep embeddedness within the networks of support that make up a shared human ecology.

In its overwhelming magnitude, the sublime seemingly defies any sense of (infra-)structure, as it necessarily goes beyond that which has limits. The term *infrastructural sublime* thus holds an inherent tension, oscillating between the bounded and the infinite, between the exalted and the mundane. Yet, rather than negating the term, this tension points to the potential of the sublime to transform infrastructure, to expand it beyond its intended purpose of reproducing Los Angeles as it is—with all of its economic, racial, and disabling violence—and toward producing what the city could be. For instance, the maps of the city engendered by the infrastructural sublime, which chart the many dependencies that comprise Los Angeles, defy the ideology of self-ownership that too often justifies racial and economic disparities. This vision diverges, too, from the popular narrative of the freeway as imparting a sense of unfettered independence. Manzanar's is not a vision of self-ownership or of autopian freedom; rather, it is a vision of the self's dispersal across and contingency on human and material worlds.

The infrastructural sublime thus posits a model of subjectivity in which every body, human and nonhuman, is always influenced, permeated, or supported by a configuration of other networked bodies. As such, it prompts us to chart the interdependent relations linking subjects, environments, communities, and cities. As much of the scholarship on *Tropic* observes, Yamashita's depiction of borders and boundaries conveys the violence enacted by artificial divisions, as both imaginary constructs that cannot contain or describe the world as it is lived, as well as militarized entities with devastating effects.[125] The line "in the dust" separating Mexico from the United States is both a "slender endless serpent" and "as wide as an entire culture and as deep as the social and economic construct that nobody knew how to change."[126] The freeway, too, functions as a metropolitan border supporting socioeconomic striation, as the "new flat walls . . . [preventing] access to certain areas" represent, in many ways, the vertical walls that once encircled cities.[127]

In all of its magnitude and limitlessness, the infrastructural sublime rewrites the freeway's function as city border. The "thousand natural and man-made divisions" separating Los Angelenos from one another collapse into the unity of traffic symphony, transforming into a "mass of people flowing to work and play."[128] The separations between the self and its systems of support dissipate, creating a borderless subject contingent on the "Southern California pipelines of natural gas" and the "unnatural waterways of the Los Angeles Department of Water and Power."[129] In so doing, this sublime works to unbind city inhabitants from the divisions separating the homeless from the affluent, citizens from undocumented populations, and the seemingly discrete self from the "great flow" of metropolitan and global life.[130] Yet, open borders, borderless subjects, and interdependent networks still do not guarantee a seamlessly integrated Los Angeles / Tijuana / Mazatlán, even as the infrastructural sublime gestures toward a fantasy of unity. As El Gran Mojado points out, "We are not the world."[131] On the contrary, we see how cross-border and inner-city infrastructural networks also reproduce social inequity, and the ways in which borders, while porous, are unevenly so.

While gesturing toward a horizon of collective support, *Tropic of Orange* reminds us that the racialized processes and narratives that obscure particular infrastructural networks—the low-wage laboring substrate, the freeway as a mechanism of racial inequality—also reproduce the uneven topographies that characterize city and globe. That is, the sense of interdependency imparted by the infrastructural sublime does not necessarily imply reciprocity or apolitical global harmony. After all, as Rubenstein, Robbins, and Beal note, infrastructures "both produce and reveal a two-tiered version of citizenship in which much of the world's population has little or no access to goods and services in common."[132] *Tropic* therefore compels us to acknowledge the asymmetrical power relations between supported and unsupported subjects, which are too often disappeared by mythologies of dependency. This, indeed, is another political function of the infrastructural sublime: to give form and urgency to the abstracted, uneven support relations propping up city and globe—the dis-/enabling ecologies of power and provision that, again, "ordinary persons never bother to notice."[133]

For the road traveler and disabled religious visionary Lauren Oya Olamina, California's freeway networks similarly offer deliverance from everyday arrangements that promise only death and indebtedness. Just as the Harbor Freeway connects Manzanar to "the great heartbeat of a great city," so *Sower's* Highway 101 connects Lauren to the heartbeat of Earthseed; it is a "river of the poor" that she "[fishes]" for those "who would join us and be welcome."[134] While *Sower's* freeway frequently signals violence, resource polarization, and infrastructural collapse, it doubly functions as a site of sacred encounter, where those most disabled by current infrastructural arrangements might find each other and insist on another way: "Earthseed is being born right here on Highway 101."[135] In this way, the freeway "evokes/invokes the crossroads" embedded in M. Jacqui Alexander's theorization of the Crossing, which references both the Middle Passage as well as "the space of convergence and endless possibility" from which we "dream the craft of a new compass."[136] Against the meager social paradigms offered up by corporations and the state, Lauren's freeway navigation moves toward the sacred possibility of life and regeneration, yielding a multiracial, multi-abled "harvest of survivors" who "might be able to do it—grow our own food, grow ourselves and our neighbors into something brand new. Into Earthseed."[137]

Shaped by disability knowledge, this pathway toward survival plots a metaphysics of interdependence and mutual support that I term the *crip sacred*—sacred because Earthseed names a spiritual community and thought system, and sacred because its practice is fundamentally oriented toward life, and is thereby connected to the "pulse and energy of creation."[138] Following Alexander, who identified the "central understanding within an epistemology of the Sacred" as a "core/Spirit that is immortal," the concept of the sacred I mobilize here centralizes the "living matter that links us to each other, making that which is individual simultaneously collective."[139] The *crip* modifier, further, serves multiple purposes: it describes the influence of disabled experience on Earthseed philosophy and practices, the resonance of Earthseed tenets with disability justice movement principles, the crafting of alternate solidarities along the axes of vulnerability and dispossession, and the centering of disabled, vulnerable, and racialized life in the movement's present and future. The crip sacred, then, names a spiritual practice and life-giving horizon in which disability is legible as not only a viable way of living but also a divine engine of creation.

As feminist disability scholars have observed, Lauren's experience of hyperempathy plays a fundamental (though not singular) role in the creation and growth of Earthseed.[140] The movement's tenets of adaptation, change, and interconnection reflect her lived experiences as a Black disabled woman navigating an uninhabitable and unpredictable world, with the genre of the parable—the

movement's main method of delivery—signaling her middle-class, highly educated, and religious upbringing. According to Sami Schalk, adaptation and
change speak in particular to the survival strategies employed by hyperempaths
(or "sharers"), as they are "forced to adapt to the unruly sensations of their
bodyminds" and "change their relationship to the world in order to protect
themselves from harm."[141] Relatedly, hyperempathy heightens Lauren's sense of
interconnection with the broader world, placing her in direct communion with
its many pleasures and pains. From Lauren's perspective, however, hyperempathy yields more pain than pleasure—as she remarks, "There isn't much pleasure
around these days."[142] By involuntarily sharing the sensations of any living being
within sight, Lauren "[gets] a lot of grief that doesn't belong to [her]," rendering her particularly vulnerable to outside threats.[143] Yet, rather than denying her
status as "the most vulnerable person [she knows]," she adapts to this vulnerability by developing keen practices of hyperattention, taking notice of anything
that can inflict harm—or, conversely, enable survival.[144]

Hyperempathy, for instance, assists Lauren's navigation of the perilous California freeways, in which even a brief lapse of attention can result in robbery,
rape, or death. Zahra Moss conveys this danger during the group's first foray
onto the 118, when she alerts Lauren to the high stakes of inattention: "Keep
your eyes open. You get too wrapped up in your thinking, and you'll miss
things. People get killed on freeways all the time."[145] Lauren's vigilance serves
the group well, as they benefit from and at times adopt the tactics she employs
to maximize safety, which include scanning the landscape for strategic camp-
sites, learning best practices for combat to avoid unnecessary pain, and keeping
a strict night watch schedule. Lauren's thick descriptions of her environment,
which register minute details that would likely escape ordinary notice, suggest
that she is already well adapted to the particular demands of this journey. Anna
Hinton states it simply: "Living with a disability provides Lauren with the skills
that she needs to survive."[146]

Lauren's heightened experience of attention further enables her to recognize the unexpected skills offered by her freeway companions, lifting up survival strategies that might be illegible under normative rubrics of worth. She
places great value on informal skill sharing, emphasizing the importance of
this practice as a survival tactic for the underresourced and exploited. This
value is expressed early in the novel's freeway exodus, when Lauren and fel-

low Robledo survivors Zahra Moss and Harry Baiter discuss their travels northward. On hearing that Lauren and Harry do not plan to "dump [her]" on departure, Zahra cries with relief.[147] She sees herself as a potential liability on the upcoming journey, particularly given that she has "[no] money. Not a dollar."[148] Lauren, however, identifies a "useful skill" of Zahra's that may not typically register as valuable: her talent at stealing food and, relatedly, stealing "information about living out here"—that is, outside the once-protective walls of Robledo.[149]

As this exchange demonstrates, one of the most relevant skills in Lauren's hyperempathic arsenal is crip resourcefulness—the insistence that all people are inherently valuable and have something to offer, even and especially if their value does not register under dominant metrics. Racialized, working poor, and disabled members not only are accepted in Earthseed but are central to the movement's inception and growth; in the final chapters of *Sower*, additional Black and brown hyperempaths join Earthseed's ranks and assist in the establishment of Acorn, the collective's first settlement. Throughout the novel, Lauren's freeway cohort swells with disempowered subjects, including children, mixed-race couples (who, as Zahra Moss notes, "catch hell out here"), the formerly enslaved, and sharers.[150] When Lauren first encounters Travis, Natividad, and their six-month-old baby Dominic, she convinces them to join their group by, first, protecting their camp from dogs, and later by identifying a line of potential affinity: "You are our natural allies. . . . The baby won't weaken us much, I hope, and he'll have a better chance of surviving with five adults around him."[151] Similarly, when the mixed-race, formerly enslaved sharer Emery Tanaka Solis and her daughter Tori infiltrate the group's camp, Lauren decides to accept them as freeway companions simply because she "[thinks] they might be worth something."[152] While these travelers, marked as they are by race, class, and ability, are understood as disposable under capitalist ideologies, Earthseed forges an alternate set of values that frames their vulnerability as an asset. Both in word and practice, then, Earthseed presages the disability justice principle of collective liberation—the idea that "no body/mind is left behind" in the work of revolution.[153]

By honoring a broad variety of skill sets, identities, and embodiments within the Earthseed project, Lauren encourages the practice of shared support among a diverse group of disempowered people, framing interdependence as key to collective survival. And survival, as *Sower* makes clear, is one of Lauren's guiding goals, but it is survival not in the sense of mere existence, or as a battle won only by the most deserving, but as a collective promise forged in the context of struggle—survival, in the words of Alexis Pauline Gumbs, as "life after disaster, life in honor of our ancestors, despite the genocidal forces worked against them specifically so that we would not exist."[154] Survival, for Lauren, necessarily means the survival of the racialized, poor, and disabled collective. It also means the collective working in tandem to ensure the life force of other vulnerable subjects. The qualities she values in her freeway companions operate in service of this goal; she pays close attention to those who can do the work of mutual support. For instance, Lauren appreciates Travis and Natividad not only for mirroring her own mixed-race family, thereby furthering the possibility of Black and brown futures, but also for providing "two more pairs of eyes, two more pairs of hands" for keeping watch and giving care.[155]

Among the Earthseed converts, the work of care is interdependence in practice, and the basis of a communal infrastructure that can propagate and support all forms of life. In particular, Lauren and her freeway companions prioritize care for the most vulnerable, a value that shows up in multiple ways: protection of the collective's children and primary caregivers, deep consideration for injured companions, and attentiveness to the varying access needs of individual members. When the group sets up camp near the San Luis Reservoir, they recognize that both Natividad and Allie, as primary parent figures for Dominic and Justin, have "more reason to be tired and to need sleep than the rest of [the group]," so they do not include them in "[drawing] lots for a watch schedule."[156] Lauren also expresses admiration for the care ethic practiced in Hollister even in the midst of ecological disaster: "The earthquake had done a lot of damage . . . but the people hadn't gone animal. They seemed to be helping one another with repairs and looking after their own destitute. Imagine that."[157]

Alongside the novel's critiques of resource deprivation, Earthseed's emphasis on care is also connected, at least in part, to Lauren's neurodivergence. After witnessing the mutilated body of her brother Keith, she observes, "I would never wish anyone dead in that horrible way. . . . If hyperempathy syndrome were a more common complaint, people couldn't do such things."[158] She expresses a wish to "find other people who have it, and live among them," prefiguring her experience of building community with Grayson and Emery, the novel's other sharers.[159] In addition to enabling survival skills, then, Lauren's experience of hyperempathy also helps forge an ethic of collective care, foregrounding a disability consciousness grounded in mutual regard for the other.

The value of interdependence—expressed through the Earthseed collective's care work and philosophy—is thus vital to seeding the possibility of Black, brown, and disabled futures that can "take root among the stars."[160] Interdependence, after all, is the ongoing act of "[meeting] each other's needs as we build toward liberation," and of seeing the labor of "meeting needs," particularly for those whose needs go structurally unmet, as vital to large-scale revolution.[161] The final Earthseed verse in *Sower* in particular imparts this vision of interdependence, imagining it as akin to God:

> God is Change—
>
> Seed to tree,
>
> tree to forest;
>
> Rain to river,
>
> river to sea;
>
> Grubs to bees,
>
> bees to swarm.
>
> From one, many;
>
> From many, one. . . .
>
> The universe
>
> is God's self-portrait.[162]

In *Sower*, then, interdependence names not only a state of intersubjectivity and mutual support but also a spiritual practice that grants access to the crip sacred—a reverence for racialized, disabled, and vulnerable life that necessitates cosmological transformation.

Across both *Sower* and *Tropic*, California's freeways signal both the promises and perils of interdependency in the era of so-called free trade. As a multivalent figure of im/mobility, migration, and infrastructural inequity, they offer a means of mapping both the dominant dependency narratives propping up trade deregulation—the myths of state parasitism foisted onto undocumented migrants, the false independence of capitalism's global elites, and the coercive dependencies manufactured by transnational corporations—as well as the life-giving interdependencies accessed through Manzanar's freeway symphony and Earthseed's inception.

As the crossroads for a "heterogeneous mass" of migrants, Butler and Yamashita's freeways offer dynamic zones of convergence that "make different conversations and solidarities possible," such as the potential affinities between transnational feminist critiques of globalization and disability justice politics.[163] The disability justice principles of interdependence, access, and collective liberation issue powerful correctives to the ideologies of free trade and resource parasitism. Rather than adhering to global capital's ideology of individualism, both Lauren and Manzanar demonstrate a hyperawareness of the networked resources, skills, and support systems that enable survival and collective life for vulnerable populations—a heightened form of attention linked to their neurodivergent sensibilities. Their hypersensitivities make it possible for them to perceive and know the world beyond the ordering systems of Enlightenment rationality, and beyond the artificially constructed borders and divisions that enable resource deprivation on global and domestic scales. Through their freeway fictions, *Tropic* and *Sower* lift up the racialized and feminized infrastructures of care, domestic, and maintenance labor undergirding transnational capitalism and reroute them to serve Black, brown, and disabled lifeworlds.

However, this is not to position disability politics and neurodivergence as a silver bullet for global power imbalances, or to suggest that disabled people can (and should) be the world's saviors. As Butler's *Parable of the Talents* illustrates, even the paradigm shift modeled by Earthseed generates its own set of violent contradictions. The reflections of Lauren's daughter, Larkin, on Earthseed's legacy reveal the movement's eventual subjugation to the interests of capital and celebrity.[164] Following my analyses of Sapphire's *Push* and Delany's *Through the Valley of the Nest of Spiders*, the work of infrastructural freedom dreaming is never clean-cut or straightforward—it always yields its own set of contradictions.

Rather than offering a program for world revolution, then, the crip sensibilities modeled by Lauren and Manzanar outline a worldview in which liberation—or something like it—can be approached only once we honor the web of dependent relations binding us together. In Yamashita's *Tropic*, the seeding of this worldview emerges near the end of Manzanar's narrative, during which other freeway conductors adopt his musical practice:

> Little by little, Manzanar began to sense a new kind of grid, this one defined not by inanimate structures or other living things but by himself and others like him. He found himself at the heart of an expanding symphony of which he was not the only conductor. On a distant overpass, he could make out the odd mirror of his figure, waving a baton. And beyond that, another homeless person had also taken up the baton. And across the city, on overpasses and street corners, from balconies and park benches, people held branches and pencils, toothbrushes and carrot sticks, and conducted. . . . Manzanar nodded to himself. Not bad.[165]

At the center of yet another connective web, Manzanar witnesses the dissemination of his once-unique practice across the spectrum of LA's unhoused. Presumably, they too can see traffic as symphony, and below that, the infrastructural grids that support metropolitan life. Considering the characters' enmeshment in systems beyond their control, *Tropic of Orange* seemingly occludes many viable paths to political action. And yet, with the proliferation of the "heroic one" into the "overwhelming many," a move that makes a thousand new mapmakers, the novel suggests the political and aesthetic import of this interdependent worldview.

By foregrounding the social, economic, and prosthetic systems propping up *all* subjects, Manzanar challenges the pernicious myth of self-governance attributed to global capitalism's elites. Liberation, here, is contingent not on the achievement of self-ownership but on the recognition of and reverence for the many infrastructural support networks that coordinate contemporary life. Satisfied with his legacy, Manzanar "[lets] his arms drop. There was no need to conduct the music any longer. The entire city had sprouted grassroots conductors of every sort."[166] Together, they use music to map the interdependencies of worlds.

For both Lauren Oya Olamina and Manzanar Murakami, the freeway functions as a sacred portal toward an infrastructural consciousness in which dependency is not only depathologized but exalted. In the next and final chapter, I further elaborate on the divine, life-giving potential of crip wisdom via the infrastructural freedom dreams of the disability justice activist-writers Aurora

Levins Morales and Leah Lakshmi Piepzna-Samarasinha. Looking to their autobiographical meditations on healthcare infrastructure, which run the gamut from speculative fiction to realist life-narrative, I explore their crip-of-color responses to one of this book's central questions: What does care look like in the context of state abandonment, apocalypse, and isolation? I demonstrate how Levins Morales and Piepzna-Samarasinha, like Lauren Olamina, dream and call forth a "blaze of light," one that seeds other horizons of infrastructural support.[167]

"I am a Medicaid welfare queen." This staunch declaration opens Alice Wong's 2017 *New York Times* op-ed "My Medicaid, My Life," in which the seasoned disability activist and writer confronts continuing onslaughts against Medicaid and any state-funded program that grants disabled and low-income people access to life-giving support.[1] Boldly invoking and inhabiting the memory of Linda Taylor, Reagan's mythical welfare recipient, Wong's commentary is an experiment in time travel: it instantly traverses forty years of state divestment from social safety nets, linking Reagan's 1976 campaign strategy to Trump-era assaults on the Affordable Care Act (ACA). Present, too, are echoes of Johnnie Tillmon's 1972 *Ms.* magazine essay "Welfare Is a Woman's Issue," which begins with a similar set of statements: "I'm a woman. I'm a Black woman. I'm a poor woman. I'm a fat woman. I'm a middle-aged woman. And I'm on welfare."[2] Both Wong's and Tillmon's essays declare in no uncertain terms that freedom—for low-income, disabled, racialized, and disempowered populations—comes from, not despite, the social safety net, and that for many, freedom might look like an unashamed embrace of dependency rather than the achievement of un-fettered individualism. "When Republicans talk about freedom and choice," Wong writes, "they don't realize that Medicaid gives those very things to people with disabilities."

In affixing *Medicaid* to the reclaimed epithet *welfare queen*, Wong's essay invokes the method and spirit of crip-of-color critique in that it forges alliances between Black feminist / feminist-of-color struggles against antiwelfare policy and struggles for disability liberation, to which access to public health/care remains central.[3] This chapter turns to disability justice life-writing and poetry that navigates the health/care infrastructural landscape of the 2010s, from the debates preceding the passage of the 2010 ACA to the Trump administration's many chaotic attempts to further curtail state-supported health/care— attempts that continued even during the COVID-19 pandemic. In so doing, it bridges major welfare reform with the adjacent arena of health/care reform and, in particular, the state benefit programs of Medicaid, Medicare, Supplemental Security Income (SSI), and Social Security Disability Insurance (SSDI).

Looking to recent works by Leah Lakshmi Piepzna-Samarasinha and Aurora Levins Morales, both queer poets, performers, and activists in the disability justice movement, I examine how radical crip-of-color writers negotiate the ableist bureaucracies and diagnostic gatekeeping of the medical-industrial complex while simultaneously dreaming of other possible configurations of care.[4] Levins Morales's *Kindling: Writings on the Body* (2013) and Piepzna-Samarasinha's *Tonguebreaker* (2019) draw on poetry, life-writing, performance, and prayer to lift up the work of disabled survival within and despite paltry health/care options; in this way, these multigenre texts join a long tradition of disability writing and scholarship that has taken medicine to task. Yet, while medical authority has been a frequent object of disability critique, much first-wave disability scholarship emerged from a place of presumed access to health/care, with little attention paid to racial and class disparities in treatment and access, or to the impacts on disability status of environmental racism, infrastructural neglect, intergenerational trauma, coerced migration, and sexual/gendered violence. Not only do *Kindling* and *Tonguebreaker* foreground the systemic production of disability and illness within vulnerable populations, situating "our bodies . . . in the mix of everything we call political," but they also offer potent re-theorizations of *health* and *care* that center the pleasure and wisdom of disabled queers of color.[5]

I use *health/care infrastructure* to describe the confluence of insurance networks, safety net programs, care providers, medical facilities, and pharmaceutical companies that make up the current matrix of health support in the United States, with a particular focus on the parts of that system directly pertaining to the disability bureaucratic sector.[6] I begin by mapping out how such infrastructure emerges and makes itself present in these works, shaping the form of what I call *disability justice life-writing*. Taken together, *Kindling* and *Tonguebreaker* chart the complexity of disabled relationships to state-funded health/care in that they reject the state as a primary instrument of disabled protection yet they also understand that in our current world, disabled survival often relies on state support. Then, I turn to what Piepzna-Samarasinha calls "wild disability justice dreams" and focus on how *Kindling* and *Tonguebreaker* dream of alternate care infrastructures in both the present and the future.[7]

In a time of pandemic and manufactured neglect, more and more people are coalescing around shared infrastructural dreams for more and better support, and the insights of disability justice feel more urgent than ever. The ongoing destruction inflicted by COVID-19 has demonstrated the bitter consequences of a hollowed-out social safety net; the horrific state response in particular has exacerbated existing food, labor, and housing crises while highlighting the deadly repercussions of a profiteering health/care system that lacks decent and affordable options. What, then, does care look like in the context of abandonment, apocalypse, and social isolation, when the state wants people to subsist on less and less? How do we reclaim, define, and practice care outside existing models offered by the state and the medical-industrial complex, in which care all too often exists on a continuum with control and abuse? I argue that *Kindling* and *Tonguebreaker* offer wild disability justice blueprints for health and care in an era of deprivation, in which care suggests not restoration and movement back toward the status quo—the reacquisition of a fabled norm—but instead the serious and sustained tending of a lifeworld that centers the complexity of disabled queers of color, makes room for sickness and grief, and generates real moments of joy. "This book is a magic spell," writes Piepzna-Samarasinha about *Tonguebreaker*, "about what it means to be surrounded by death and live on."[8]

Let the spell begin.

Disability Justice Life-Writing

The preface for *Tonguebreaker* goes on to describe the sources for Piepzna-Samarasinha's poetic and performance magic: "Being surrounded by death and persisting is a disabled knowledge. It is a femme knowledge. It is a knowledge held in Black, brown, and Indigenous bodies."[9] The magic, in this case, is survival for those who "were never meant to survive," and the spell is the labor of staying alive and documenting the evidence of that work.[10] *Tonguebreaker* ends with a poem titled "Litany," a response to Audre Lorde's "A Litany for Survival," where Piepzna-Samarasinha states their intent to document: "I say I treasure, witness, and remember you, and the way / we survived who were never meant to survive."[11] Taken together, these beginning and ending lines convey the essence of what I am calling *disability justice life-writing*: a loving, politicized act of narration committed to telling the lives (and capturing the aliveness) of the multiply marginalized disabled people who live closest to death.

Before I go further, I want to revisit the framework of disability justice, which I reference in the book's introduction and throughout its chapters. This term names a framework of liberation that focuses on the most vulnerable within disability communities: the queer, trans, gender nonconforming/noncompliant, undocumented, incarcerated, Black, brown, Indigenous, low-income, and working poor members for whom legal rights are inaccessible. Cultivated by the Bay Area performance group Sins Invalid, disability justice emerges from what Patricia Berne calls the "cliffhangers" of the disability rights movement—that is, the many crip struggles left unaddressed by the passage of the 1990 Americans with Disabilities Act (ADA). While Berne honors the modes of access that the ADA made possible, she also calls for a different kind of disability movement. Disability rights activists, Berne argues, furthered a single-issue platform that prioritized legal reform, "litigation," and "the establishment of a disability bureaucratic sector at the expense of developing a broad-based popular movement."[12] In contrast, disability justice favors coalitional struggle, demanding an intersectional approach that recognizes ableism's coarticulation with "white supremacy, heteropatriarchy, colonialism, and capitalism."[13] Disability justice life-writing, then, describes the telling of a life (or lives) resonant with disability justice movement principles, as summarized in both Sins Invalid's "10 Principles of Disability Justice" and Berne's 2015 blog post "Disability Justice—a Working Draft."[14]

Both Piepzna-Samarasinha and Levins Morales have helped determine these principles, which include interdependence, collective access, and collective liberation. Once members of Sins Invalid, they have a shared history of performing, collaborating, and dreaming together in service of crip-of-color freedom. This collaborative spirit undergirds *Kindling*, *Tonguebreaker*, and "Disability Justice—a Working Draft," in which Berne uses an excerpt from Levins Morales's *Kindling* to launch her explanation of the movement. Further, Piepzna-Samarasinha makes multiple references in *Tonguebreaker* to Levins Morales's presence and friendship during their time in Oakland. For instance, in "Riches: Oakland 2010–2013," they describe a group ride in a sodden "leather ragtop" following a Sins Invalid performance, during which "Aurora has to hang her head out the window the whole way because the mold is so intense."[15] They cite this experience as evidence of their good fortune: "Four queer of color krip artists doing a show about sex and disability, getting paid, driving home late together? Riches. Lucky."[16]

In addition to their performance work in Sins, Piepzna-Samarasinha and Levins Morales have worked together in the adjacent movement of healing justice, a shared effort captured in the 2013 essay "A Babe-ilicious Healing Justice Statement" by the BadAss Visionary Healers, with Piepzna-Samarasinha as a listed coauthor. The statement begins by explaining the collective's genesis at the hands of Levins Morales, who wanted to create a "community wellness center and urban farm" that challenged dominant models of health and medicine.[17] For both writer-activists, life-writing offers an important platform from which to issue this challenge.[18] Across this rich body of collaboration, both Levins Morales and Piepzna-Samarasinha express a clear commitment to life-writing and narrative as itself a form of disabled survival work and a means of supporting other queer-of-color disabled lives in the struggle, as well as their own. "The thing about the stories you tell to save your life," writes Piepzna-Samarasinha, "is that you'll believe them."[19]

Their stories do not exist in isolation. Over the past several decades, life-writing has emerged as a vital outlet for writers to craft stories about disability on their own terms.[20] Works such as Nancy Mairs's *Waist-High in the World* (1997), Audre Lorde's *The Cancer Journals* (1980), and Harriet McBryde Johnson's *Too Late to Die Young* (2005) demonstrate how life-writing and auto/biography offer powerful alternatives to mainstream narratives of disability and illness, which largely traffic in the registers of pity, tragedy, or heroic overcoming. Rather than touting medical intervention or cure as the only acceptable response, disability auto/biography can describe the writer coming into a politicized disability identity, or critiquing structural racism and sexism in the medical-industrial complex (Lorde), or demonstrating how one can find community, pleasure, and joy while (and because of) living in a disabled body (Johnson, Mairs). Disability life-writing also has played a crucial role in the disability rights movement, as evidenced by Judith Heumann's *Being Heumann: An Unrepentant Memoir of a Disability Rights Activist* (2020) and the edited collection *Voices from the Edge:*

Narratives about the Americans with Disabilities Act (2004). How, then, does disability life-writing—a well-established genre of disability literature—shift form and narrative strategy when disability justice anchors the storytelling?

In accordance with the disability justice principles of intersectionality and cross-movement organizing, *Kindling* and *Tonguebreaker* connect their personal narratives about disability to broader struggles against health/care inequities and state-sanctioned racialized violence, linking disability politics to the ongoing safety net erosion that disproportionately harms racialized, low-income, and feminized populations. In particular, Levins Morales's *Kindling* turns to a particular segment of health/care infrastructure—state-funded support for people with disabilities—as a means of articulating a commitment to and theory of radical crip coalitional politics. Both *Kindling* and *Tonguebreaker*, I argue, resonate with a crip-of-color framework for a number of reasons: (1) they highlight the broader systems of infrastructural support that delimit or enable disabled, low-income, and/or racialized survival, (2) they leverage life-writing to issue key interventions into governing narratives around what disabled people deserve, and (3) they reconceptualize health not as a property of the individual body but as an iceberg-tip symptom of the unequal distribution of structural violence—evidence of what minoritized bodies have been made to bear across generations. Further, in their assessment of extant care infrastructures and dreams of radical interdependency, both *Kindling* and *Tonguebreaker* diverge from the emphasis on independence that disability scholars David Mitchell and Rachel Adams identify as a key feature of disability rights auto/biographies. In so doing, they create new paths for disability life-writing as a genre.[21]

These next pages will examine how health/care reform and infrastructure shape Piepzna-Samarasinha and Levins Morales's respective life narratives, with an extended focus on Levins Morales's experiences with Medicare, disability benefits, and the US medical-industrial complex. Indeed, *Kindling: Writings on the Body* is a book "born of desperation," written and compiled to "raise some money" for Levins Morales's mounting medical bills following an unexpected pain emergency in September 2012.[22] Instead of expressing shame for needing financial assistance, Levins Morales adopts a stance resonant with Alice Wong's "My Medicaid, My Life" in that she openly claims her chronic pain and requests for support. What's more, she refuses to see her financial needs as evidence of personal failure, as antiwelfare logics would suggest, but as an inevitable symptom of living in a nation without adequate health/care infrastructure.

The source of Levins Morales's desperation is clear: "Because I live in a rich country whose health care system is controlled by corporations, for profit, not public health, and whose policy makers, at the service of private wealth, not collective wellness, have been systematically slashing budgets and closing doors, *there is no social safety cushion for me*."[23] Absent a functional health/care safety net, *Kindling* operates as itself a form of self-made infrastructure in that all "proceeds from the sale of this book" go to "medical and attendant care."[24] Beyond the function of "[taking] a life . . . as its subject," for Levins Morales, life-writing also serves the purpose of saving a life—that is, of making a disabled life possible to live at all.[25] This is, however, not a celebration of the power of life narrative to fund personal medical expenses—a kind of crip Horatio Alger. Rather, she highlights the absurd cruelty of a system that forces people to earn, dollar by dollar, their access to health/care support.

The book's critiques of our "cruel and corrupt profit-driven medical system" were incubated in the shadow of the 2010 ACA, which Levins Morales directly addresses in a chapter titled "Will the Real Socialist Medicine Please Stand Up?"[26] "Socialist medicine" names but one of many accusations that Republicans lobbed against the ACA, a major piece of legislation that represents the most transformative health/care reform since the institution of Medicaid and Medicare in 1965. Steeped in controversy well before and after its passage, the ACA aimed to extend health/care coverage to tens of millions of previously uninsured individuals, as well as improve the US health/care delivery system overall. However, health policy scholars note that the law also created "new forms of exclusion," particularly following the 2012 *National Federation of Independent Business v. Sebelius* Supreme Court decision, which rendered Medicaid expansion—a key provision of the ACA—optional.[27] As Alice Wong notes in "My Medicaid, My Life," such limitations placed on Medicaid could determine life or death for disabled people, many of whom rely on Medicaid-funded personal care services and other forms of state support. The tragedy, in this case, is not disability, but the lack of infrastructure available for disabled survival: "The fragility and weakness of my body, I can handle. The fragility of the safety net is something I fear and worry about constantly."[28]

The accusations of "socialist medicine" further reflect the extension of antiwelfare rhetoric to the arena of state-funded health/care, in which public access to medical benefits and life-saving services is rigorously gatekept. As Jamila Michener observes, "Historically, the politics of health care in the United States parallels the politics of antipoverty policy in many ways."[29] Indeed, Medicaid, SSI, and SSDI have been subject to austerity rhetoric similar to that attached to welfare programs. Publications such as the *Washington Post* and the *Atlantic* have framed disability benefits as yet another source of government waste and fraud, with the latter running a 2013 article titled "Disability Insurance: America's $124 Billion Secret Welfare Program."[30] Relatedly, the successful passage of the 1990 ADA, as Lezlie Frye and Samuel Bagenstos have argued, was predicated at least in part on positioning the legislation in direct opposition to welfare and its stigma of dependency.[31] Further, the heated discourse around the ACA reflects a now decades-long history of fearmongering around the social safety net and the possibility of government intervention. "During the ACA debates," writes Allison K. Hoffman, "the mere mention of a public insurance plan option, which someone could choose instead of private insurance, provoked horror stories of socialized healthcare."[32]

In response, *Kindling* highlights the absurdity of referring to any potential version of the ACA as socialist: "When I hear the watered down, pathetic proposals for health care reform being tossed around by our politicians referred to in horrified tones as socialism, as if that's the terrible abyss we must avoid at all cost, I'm clear about whose abyss it is and whose cost."[33] Levins Morales has, in fact, descended into the "abyss"—she writes her critiques of US health/care reform from the vantage point of the Cuban health/care system, which, in the summer of 2009, offered her several months of free medical treatment. In the United States, she observes, "the word 'socialist' is used to scare people. In Cuba it heals."[34]

As Levins Morales explains in the book's introduction, the pain emergency that necessitated *Kindling*'s publication represents but one of her many experiences with chronic illness and medical debt. Self-identified as Puerto Rican and Jewish, Levins Morales describes her heavy exposure to pesticides during her early childhood in 1950s Puerto Rico, as well as her genetic inheritance of malfunctioning liver enzymes, both of which greatly compromise her body's capacity to process toxins. Across *Kindling*'s mixed-genre compilation of personal essays, poems, and performance texts, Levins Morales chronicles a litany of conditions that regularly devastate her body: tonic-clonic seizures, stroke, chronic fatigue, migraines, and multiple chemical sensitivity. And while *Kindling* at times describes the author's intimate personal details of sickness—the time her "mouth was flooded with a taste like sucking on key chains," for instance, or the long night of "excruciating pain in [her] right sacro-ileac joint"—it also dilates the scope of disability life-writing outward, situating Levins Morales's personal narrative within larger geopolitical matrices of power and domination.[35]

Throughout the book, she frames her experiences with chronic and environmental illness as coterminous with US empire, Western militarism, intergenerational trauma, and gendered-sexual violence. In the chapter "Some Thoughts on Environmental Illness," Levins Morales notes that US companies sold the pesticides saturating her childhood farm in Puerto Rico, and that many of these chemicals began as "nerve gases used in war."[36] Her environmental illness and subsequent medical debt, then, offers somatic testimony to the US colonial domination of Puerto Rico in that her body bears the poisonous legacies of US pesticide production while also paying the financial costs of colonial violence. US health/care infrastructure thus cannot mitigate or heal the harms of US colonial interference and is in fact yet another extractive system structured to deny colonized subjects access to care (even as US empire created the need for care in the first place). Additionally, Levins Morales connects her persistent sicknesses to the extreme sexual abuse imposed on her by a "group of men connected to [her elementary] school," as well as the red-baiting of her radical parents.[37]

Childhood sexual abuse, environmental toxins, and intergenerational trauma similarly figure into *Tonguebreaker*'s understanding of health and disability. The poem "Bad Road," for instance, locates the "pain tides" of chronic illness in the trauma of migration, incest, and a brutally inaccessible world, all of which shaped Piepzna-Samarasinha's body into "forty miles of perfect bad road."[38] She writes,

> I could tell you my mama
>
> molested me, I could tell you hers did too,
>
> I could tell you we had to walk a long long way and get on a boat . . .
>
> I could read you the particulate matter of the air, that they're
>
> spraying for
>
> pesticides today . . .
>
> —but does anyone want to hear all that?[39]

The persistent refrain of "I could tell you" marks the disability stories that no one "[wants] to hear," the stories in which disability provides not an opportunity for inspiration or individual cure but embodied evidence of a world structured by sexual, economic, and environmental violence. Piepzna-Samarasinha's infrastructural metaphor of "perfect bad road" speaks to the historic and economic production of disability in "a violent context of social and economic exploitation," as Nirmala Erevelles has so eloquently put it, with every "[bump] and [pothole]" leaving evidence of that production.[40] In this way, both *Kindling* and *Tonguebreaker* further an understanding of disabled experience that resonates with what the medical historian Alondra Nelson terms "social health," a politicized model of embodiment derived from the Black Panthers' health activism that links "the individual, corporeal body to the body politic."[41] Through somatic testimony and life narrative, Levins Morales and Piepzna-Samarasinha map the many threads connecting their personal experiences to the disabling systems of US empire, heteropatriarchy, colonization, and environmental devastation.

Their works further attest to the aspects of health/care infrastructure that low-income and/or disabled people must navigate regularly, systems such as paid attendant care, Medicaid/Medicare, and ssi/ssdi, with which the able-bodied largely remain unfamiliar. *Kindling*, for instance, is bookended by mentions of Levins Morales's care needs; the book's dedication begins with appreciation for "the multitudes who donated money to pay for my attendant care" and "the attendants who provide that care every day."[42] Following *Kindling*'s conclusion, the author biography restates the book's purpose of raising funds for medical costs, with the aforementioned statement that "proceeds from the sale of this book will pay for medical and attendant care" typeset in bold.[43] The biography page also provides a link to Levins Morales's personal website, where readers can get "updates on [her] condition" and/or "donate to her health care fund."[44] The book's introduction states plainly the out-of-pocket costs for the "round the clock attendants" hired during the early months of Levins Morales's pain emergency: "The cost of hiring them ourselves comes to $11,000 a month. We used up all my savings in the first month."[45] By highlighting the astronomical costs of attendant support, care that many disabled people require in order to survive, Levins Morales offers a reversal of the discourse that posits disabled people as drains on the public, instead framing the costs of US health/care infrastructure as drains on disabled people.

As this assessment of paid attendant care suggests, Levins Morales maps out a complicated set of relationships to US health/care infrastructures and state-funded support, in which she describes the simultaneous necessity and unviability of these systems for low-income and/or disabled people of color. She further explains this stance in a letter to Gloria Anzaldúa, who both Levins Morales and Piepzna-Samarasinha reclaim as a queer crip ancestor. Here, she expresses understanding about why the lesbian Chicana writer refused to identify as disabled and speculates on what Anzaldúa might have needed in order to do so: "You would have needed people . . . who would have understood to the core your reasons for brewing all those herbal teas, knowing it's dangerous to enter the doors of the medical-industrial complex, and that there are things we need in there."[46] A place of peril and a place of survival: Levins Morales thus describes the primary paradox of health/care from the stance of disability justice, in which state care exists on a continuum with racialized state violence (and they are often one and the same). *Kindling* describes the various indignities of navigating state health/care bureaucracy to get the "things we need," explicitly naming the "fourteen insulting pieces of mail from Social Security" that place "as many obstacles as possible in the way of my access to Medicare."[47] Through the descriptive strategy of enumeration and the modifier of "insulting," Levins Morales emphasizes how insurance gatekeeping—in addition to the exorbitant costs of attendant care—functions as yet another expression of state-sanctioned violence, highlighting how such expressions are coarticulated with ableism.

In prioritizing the lives of nonwealthy disabled people of color, disability justice life-writing reflects in no uncertain terms the reality of negotiating the health/care infrastructures that make disabled survival possible—that is, the complicated stance of living within extant networks of infrastructure while dreaming of more and better. Piepzna-Samarasinha, too, highlights the limits of state and legal support, which, as *Tonguebreaker* describes, must always be supplemented with other forms of self- and community care. In "Riches: Oakland 2010–2013," they depict their crip comrades as those with "three hustles, waiting on food stamps, crazy and not eligible for state disability, or making state disability stretch."[48] Piepzna-Samarasinha's brief gloss of their comrades simultaneously underscores the inadequacies of the state disability system: the strict diagnostic qualifications for resources, the stinginess of the resources themselves, and the economic necessity of pairing state disability with other forms of public assistance. State systems, by themselves, are not enough; Piepzna-Samarasinha and their companions "find [themselves]" at the "dollar section" of "that big Target on the Shellmound in West O," which they reclaim as a disability "community center."[49] They draw on shared, accumulated knowledge about Oakland in order to create beauty in lives otherwise circumscribed by manufactured scarcity. "No matter how fucked up your car is," Piepzna-Samarasinha writes, "how the registration's overdue from last year and you've got six unpaid parking tickets you can't pay so they're gonna triple, that view of Mt. Tam and the big real ocean makes you rich. Seeing other brown disabled poor people around you makes you rich."[50]

At the same time, Piepzna-Samarasinha articulates the limits of community care and of DIY health/care infrastructure constituted by and for disabled people. In the 2018 essay collection *Care Work: Dreaming Disability Justice*, they express the urgency of creating "emergent, resilient care webs" because "state systems are failing," and yet, "'community' is not a magic unicorn, a one-stop shop that always helps us do the laundry and be held in need."[51] As the COVID-19 pandemic made clear, community care—which many refer to as *mutual aid*—is vital for collective survival in a time of decimated infrastructure, and yet, it is often still not enough. In their end-of-year Twitter post, which Piepzna-Samarasinha cites in their book *The Future Is Disabled*, the mutual aid organization Mask Oakland speaks to this dilemma: "Every inspiring Mutual Aid project we know of is pretty burned out right now. . . . Public Health is like Water and Sewage Infrastructure: should not be left to unpaid Mutual Aid."[52] The group's usage of infrastructure as metaphor highlights the need for broad-based systemic change *in addition to* the activist teams, organizations, and pods providing care within a mutual aid context.[53] For Piepzna-Samarasinha, the answer is not to prioritize one particular system of care over another but to make all care networks and practices more possible, robust, and accessible: "I just want to echo my friend Dori: more care, more of the time."[54]

The *Kindling* chapter "A Day in the Life" grants us additional insight into how health/care infrastructure can shape the form of disability justice life-writing. The framing essay for Levins Morales's blog post series on Cuba, "A Day in the Life" catalogs her experiences over the course of one day with US state bureaucracy, a system that disabled people without wealth must regularly navigate. Levins Morales, as she explains in the book's introduction, "was raised middle class"; her father was the renowned Harvard University professor Richard Levins and her mother was the Puerto Rican writer-activist Rosario Morales, an original contributor to *This Bridge Called My Back*.[55] Despite her background, Levins Morales is still "unable to afford adequate medical care," which costs her in both money and time.[56] In this way, "A Day in the Life" articulates yet another example of what disability scholars have termed *crip time*.[57] This term describes the myriad ways that disability affects the experience of temporality, whether in terms of the perceived failure to conform to normative developmental timelines, or the hours, months, and years stolen by inefficient state bureaucracies.

The chapter begins by situating the reader in time and space, with the coordinates of place and date signaling the genre of journal writing: "Monday, May 4 2009 10:45 am. / Social Security Office, Berkeley, CA."[58] We know now where we are: in California, a place with comparatively robust Medicaid services and, accordingly, a high population of disabled people. We are in Berkeley, a progressive town with a storied history of disability activism, and we are in 2009, a few months into the newly minted Obama administration, with its agenda of health/care reform. Finally, we are in the Social Security office, a brick-and-mortar site of public service that for many nondisabled and nonelderly people exists only as a faceless (and placeless) government agency. The journal format further calls to mind Audre Lorde's auto/biographical writings on illness: *The Cancer Journals* (1980), which documented Lorde's experiences with breast cancer, and "A Burst of Light" (1988), a long-form essay written following the metastasis of her breast cancer to her liver. Lorde's cancer writings constitute, in the words of Rudolph P. Byrd, "the first public reflections by an African American woman, and specifically a black lesbian feminist, on the nature of health, disease, mortality, and social struggle."[59] They are therefore indispensable precursors to contemporary disability justice life-writing, which carries forward the light of Lorde's legacy.

Kindling mirrors Lorde's cancer trilogy in a number of ways. Both writers, for instance, reflect at length on the racial determinants and political economy of health in the United States. Levins Morales's observations on the "real costs . . . of being a patient in this particularly ferocious manifestation of late stage capitalism" echo, both in content and tone, Lorde's commentary on the "economics of disease in america," in which "the first consideration concerning cancer is not what does this mean in my living, but how much is this going to cost?"[60] Both writers, too, model medical self-advocacy for queer women of color and ultimately seek treatment outside of the US health/care system, with Levins Morales turning to Cuba's CIREN (the International Center for Neurological Restoration) and Lorde turning to the Lukas Klinik in Switzerland. Lastly, Lorde and Levins Morales both offer lengthy meditations on the altered temporalities generated by disability and illness. For instance, Lorde takes the shortened time frame of a terminal diagnosis as impetus to "live the rest of my

life, however long or short, with as much sweetness as I can decently man-
age. . . . I'm going to write fire until it comes out my ears, my eyes, my nose-
holes. . . . I'm going to go out like a fucking meteor!"[61] For Lorde, disability
and illness speed up time, distilling for her the essence of her life's work.

In contrast, "A Day in the Life" highlights the painful lengthening of time
imposed on many nonwealthy disabled people by state health/care systems.
The chapter begins like this: "It takes an hour and a half, even with the help of
a very friendly social worker, to fill out all the paperwork on my application for
disability benefits and Medicare. I turned fifty-five in February and the premi-
ums on my already costly insurance shot up to $1200 a month. Even with all my
papers in order, and clear evidence that I have not been able to work for three
years, it will take another year before the government starts paying for a portion
of my medical expenses, which overshadow every other item in my budget."[62]
As this opening paragraph makes clear, one manifestation of state-sanctioned
ableism is the systematic theft of time from disabled people: an hour and a half;
a year. Leveraging the narrative strategy of time logs and enumeration, the passage conveys the numbing temporal abuse inflicted by inefficient state bureaucracies, allowing us to see this abuse as a form of infrastructural violence. Not
only does applying to SSI/SSDI, Medicare, and Medicaid gobble up precious
hours for disabled people subject to the state, it also elongates their experience
of time into a seemingly never-ending horizon of waiting rooms, glitching web-
sites, and government forms. The infrastructure of disability assumes human,
material, and temporal form in this passage; Levins Morales mentions the "very
friendly social worker" who assists her with her paperwork, but no measure
of individual competence can alleviate the structural slowness of state disability systems. In this way, "A Day in the Life" lends concrete detail to the often-
disregarded state institutions that constitute daily reality for most disabled
people and regularly steal their time.

The remainder of this chapter's three sections drive home the frustration
encapsulated by the stated "hour and a half" of application time.[63] While "A
Day in the Life" measures out, block by block, a nine-to-five schedule, the time-
consuming nature of state bureaucracy and disability services means that Levins
Morales can address a total of only three tasks within this period. After the Social Security office, she stops by The Luggage Center in Berkeley for "duffle bags
and suitcases" to carry a "load of medical supplies."[64] An hour and a half later,
at 2 p.m., she arrives at her final destination, the now-shuttered Wheelchairs of

Berkeley, where again, she must wait for hours to have her wheelchair serviced. These last two stops are made in preparation for Levins Morales's forthcoming travels to Cuba, where she is scheduled to receive a comprehensive course of free medical treatment. The many hours she logs in order to receive paltry state support, in addition to the exorbitant costs of US health/care, provide evidence for why Levins Morales is seeking care elsewhere—in the aforementioned "abyss" of socialized medicine.[65]

While Cuba may seem like a health/care abyss to anti-ACA policy pundits, Levins Morales's experience at the Wheelchairs of Berkeley frames US disability support as an abyss of time. Alongside two other clients, a Black man and a white man similarly seeking repairs, she "[sits], steeping in . . . frustration and boredom in the front of the store," all of them together "like patients in a hospital emergency room," until she is called into the "repair alcove" an "hour after [her] appointment time."[66] While Levins Morales waits, she observes that the Black man in the wheelchair, whose "manual chair is literally held together with red plastic tape," has to restart his authorization process all over again because "he asked for a new chair instead of a replacement chair."[67] Indeed, navigating the paperwork for state support is a labyrinthine process with no margin for error. As the anthropologist Javier Auyero has argued, these acts of waiting for state services are not incidental or politically neutral; rather, they are "*temporal processes in and through which political subordination is reproduced.*"[68] In his analysis of the grueling wait times at Argentinian welfare offices, Auyero theorizes waiting as a key mode through which states exercise their power over vulnerable segments of the population and, in so doing, make racialized, disabled, and low-income people into compliant, worn-down subjects.

Levins Morales mirrors Auyero's analysis in "Patients," a poem in the "Stricken" section of *Kindling*, which begins,

> Why do they call us "the patient"
>
> We are not patient. We endure.
>
> The anxious tedium of public hospital
>
> waiting rooms, because waiting
>
> is the punishment of the poor;
>
> interminable buses to inconvenient places[69]

Taken together, Levins Morales and Auyero render evident the relationship between medical subordination—the clinical category of *patient*—and the subordination produced by state bureaucracies, thus revealing another potential node of affinity between disability politics and feminist/queer-of-color critique. In addition to what Auyero terms the "visible fists" of the state—that is, "police forces and armies"—state discipline also takes hold in these acts of waiting, in which the time of disempowered subjects is rendered both disposable and an endlessly extractable resource, one that enables the continued underresourcing of public assistance.[70]

Through its meticulous logging of dates and time stamps, as well as its detailed narration of time's passage, "A Day in the Life" marshals the temporal documentation characteristic of journal writing to underscore the flagrant time wasting inflicted by state entities onto disabled and low-income people, framing this wasted time as yet another mode of ableist state control. It thus demonstrates how disability justice life-writing can testify to the often-invisible workings of state health/care infrastructure. And so, while Levins Morales's "A Day in the Life" allows me to examine extant forms of infrastructure, or what currently exists, the following pages examine how *Kindling* and *Tonguebreaker* contend with what *could be*—the kinds of health/care and community infrastructures necessary for the flourishing of disabled, racialized, queer, and working-class life.

Creating Infrastructures of Abundance

In the face of manufactured scarcity, Piepzna-Samarasinha and Levins Morales express their queer and crip longing for *more*—more resources, more support, "more care, more of the time."[71] For instance, Piepzna-Samarasinha's *Tonguebreaker* employs poetry and life narration to frame disability as a source of riches, asking, "Who would I be if I did not value the abundance of us?"[72] In a different register, Levins Morales testifies to the generosity of Cuban health/care, remarking, "Frugality is important in a poor and blockaded nation, but the administrators of clinics and hospitals, the developers of health care priorities, are directed by their society to provide as much as possible, not as little."[73] This engine of queer desire, of asking for more and believing we deserve it, creates the narrative momentum propelling forward their "wild disability justice dreams," in which both writers manifest infrastructures of abundant care capable of supporting disabled life and brilliance. For Piepzna-Samarasinha, this manifestation unfolds through the narrative modes of fantasy, magic, and speculation, which enable them to "time travel" and "see a future that is cripped the fuck out."[74] Key to this speculation is a staunch insistence on the sacredness of crip life, an ideological reframe of disability that necessitates both a total revisioning of care infrastructure and the definition of care itself. Toward this end, *Tonguebreaker* theorizes care (and its distribution) not from the standpoint of disability tragedy, pity, or hope for cure, which all too often informs current practices of health/care, but from the standpoint of disabled divinity—what chapter 3 of this book termed the *crip sacred*. Because even as their body is "40 miles of bad road," Piepzna-Samarasinha declares,

> my life is worth living anyway.
>
> I love every jounce on this bad, bad
>
> underfunded budget cut frost heave road . . . this body
>
> is reason enough
>
> for being.[75]

In *Tonguebreaker*, disability operates as lifeforce, source of creation, method of survival, and wellspring of brilliance, and it should be cherished as such.

Piepzna-Samarasinha's *Tonguebreaker* thus functions as an invocation toward a world of plenty for their fellow "crip femme brown survivors."[76] A frequently future-oriented collection of poetry and performance texts, it engages in forms of radical dreaming that the Chinese American activist icon Grace Lee Boggs once termed *visionary organizing*, and that others have termed *prefigurative politics*: the practice of calling radical futures into being by living them in the present.[77] As Piepzna-Samarasinha once said to the broadcast journalist Laura Flanders, "I think the imagination is one place that we are powerful. I think that we don't have the state, we don't have the prisons, we don't have the cops . . . thank God. What we do have is the wild, queer, feminist-of-color, decolonial imagination."[78]

The preface to *Tonguebreaker*, subtitled "the epistemology of breaking / how you make a book," describes the brutal conditions under which Piepzna-Samarasinha had to call on the "wild, queer, feminist-of-color, decolonial imagination" to support themself and others. Much of the book was conceived and written from 2014 to 2018, encompassing what Piepzna-Samarasinha calls "the femme suicide years," a span of time during which the community lost a multitude of "beloved femme writers living at the intersections of multiple margins": "Taueret Davis ... Bryn Kelly, Amanda Arkansassy Harris, Basil Arbogast, and Jerika Bolen."[79] Also present in this sensorium of death were the many horrific murders of "Black people, trans women of color, Indigenous folks and brown folks," as well as the rise of the Trump administration in 2016.[80]

With the election of Trump, Piepzna-Samarasinha writes, "things became even more apocalyptic. . . . Things felt too much to bear, and then there was more to bear, and more."[81] Among the administration's many targets was the ACA—a clear attack on sick and disabled people. On the day Trump was sworn into office, he issued Executive Order 13765, which clearly stated the administration's intent to repeal the ACA. Two months later, Republicans in the House of Representatives introduced the American Health Care Act, also known as "Trumpcare," a bill that, at its core, proposed deep cuts to Medicaid. In response, the disability rights organization Americans Disabled for Attendant Programs Today (ADAPT) orchestrated a "die-in" outside Senate Majority Leader Mitch McConnell's office, a major protest that garnered a wealth of media attention. Like Wong's op-ed, the ADAPT protestors drew key connections between public access to health/care support and disability freedom, posing the two as inextricable. Their spokesperson, Marilee Adamski-Smith, put it succinctly: "AHCA will take away our freedom to live in our own homes."[82] Highlighting the greatly reduced access to medical, home, and community care effected by these proposed cuts, disability protestors made clear the stakes of these assaults on health/care support systems: the intensification of death and suffering for disabled people nationwide.

In the midst of so much infrastructural violence, *Tonguebreaker* propels us toward a future in which infrastructures and worlds are remade in the image of queer brown femme disabled life—a multiply marginalized positionality that Piepzna-Samarasinha themself occupies as a self-identified "queer disabled femme writer ... of Burgher/Tamil Sri Lankan and Irish/Roma ascent."[83] In this way, it functions as what Sidonie Smith calls an "autobiographical manifesto," a politicized form of life narrative that "attempts to actively position the subject in a potentially liberated future distanced from . . . constraining and oppressive identifications," and in so doing, it departs from autobiography's often retrospective function.[84] Toward this end, the first section of the book is titled "femme futures," with the first line of the first poem asking its readers, "Where does the future live in your body? / Touch it."[85] The future Piepzna-Samarasinha invokes is not a dematerialized lifeworld in which physical bodies and lived experiences no longer matter, and in which disability no longer exists—an ableist fantasy often prophesied in the world of science fiction. Rather, they extrapolate their imagined futures from the immanence of "femme of color disabled [bodies]," which constitute the fleshy coordinates for *Tonguebreaker*'s world-building practice.[86]

Following this, the poem ends with a refrain of *When*:

> When I hear my femme/myself say, *When I get dementia and I am held*
>
> *with respect when I am between all worlds.* . . .
>
> When I hear us plan the wheelchair accessible femme of color trailer
>
> park. . . .
>
> When I hear us dream our futures,
>
> believe we will make it to one,
>
> We will make one.
>
> The future lives in our bodies
>
> Touch it.[87]

The persistent repetition of *When* acts as itself a magic spell, an invocation toward a future with accessible housing and health/care for elderly femmes of color, in which care infrastructures offer disabled femmes respectful support rather than just the bare minimum. Not just *if* we will get respect, not just *if* we will have accessible housing, but *when*. Through its future-oriented divinations, *Tonguebreaker* thus enacts another element of disability justice life-writing in that it narrates not only the crip femme-of-color lives that are, but the lives that could and will be.

For Piepzna-Samarasinha, disabled femme-of-color lives *are* possible in the future because our knowledge, skills, and expertise are magic. Because, as *Tonguebreaker* insists again and again, disability is magic, and disability is divine. Yet, as the feminist disability scholar Alison Kafer has argued, imagining disability as part of the future remains a radical queer feminist act, because all too often, "disability is seen as the sign of no future, or at least of no good future."[88] Rather than taking this narrative as a given, however, Kafer explains that a "disability-free future" is, most of all, a failure of imagination: "If disability is conceptualized as a terrible unending tragedy, then any future that includes disability can only be a future to avoid."[89] No one is telling us, Piepzna-Samarasinha writes in "Crip

Magic Spells," that "disability is magic, / that crips are magicians. . . . We flourish the swords and wands of this artful way to live."[90] Evoking the Black disabled poet Lynn Manning and his classic poem "The Magic Wand," poems such as "Crip Magic Spells," "Sri Lankan Disabled Futures 2017," and "Crip Fairy Godmother" describe for us exactly what crip magic entails:[91]

> You will gain skill in learning to not predict the future
>
> You will learn every magic trick
>
> to shape-shift pain
>
> You become an alchemist
>
> and you are better than
>
> any of the most boring neurotypicals in the world.[92]

Speaking to a "baby crip" new to the art of disabled living, Piepzna-Samarasinha offers a poetic intervention in the form of a folktale: they are this new crip's "fairy godmother," and they are ready to transform, with the flick of a wand, dominant stories about disability. Rather than referencing the loss of skill and productivity, Piepzna-Samarasinha narrates disability as yielding an artful set of skills, or as the disabled poet Neil Marcus once put it, as offering an "ingenious way to live."[93] In "Crip Fairy Godmother," pain management becomes a form of alchemy, one of the many ways to "[survive] a million things they said would kill us."[94] Disability, rather than being seen as a form of living death, is re-visioned as a source that gives life; it is a portal to a set of robust resources, a "secret guild of other sickos," and freedom to "move as slow and weird as you want."[95]

What infrastructures of care, then, does Piepzna-Samarasinha envision as necessary for supporting crip-of-color lives in both the present and the future? As the 2018 essay collection *Care Work: Dreaming Disability Justice* attests, they are a writer-activist dedicated to rethinking care—its theory, praxis, and structural distribution. Toward this end, *Care Work* forwards the infrastructural concept of the "care web" in order to describe the informal support networks that sick and disabled communities of color create for each other, as well as "the contradictions and the cracks" inherent to community care in an age of infrastructural divestment.[96] Key to envisioning and enacting these radical crip support systems, the book argues, is a complete re-theorization of care itself—the wresting of the term from the medical-industrial complex, in which *care* all too often becomes synonymous with *cure*, or the restoration of a defective body to a fabled norm.

In their theorization of the care web, Piepzna-Samarasinha recontextualizes the term within long-standing labor histories in which care work was extracted from "Black, Indigenous, and brown femme people," who nonetheless "[kept] our communities alive after being both abandoned and policed by the state, and in the face of medical experimentation and denial of health insurance."[97] They protest mainstream definitions of care that propose a unidirectional, top-down, and paternalistic model in which medical authority determines the best course of action for sick and disabled people. This often involves eradicating or at least lessening the experience of disability, and it rarely takes disabled perspectives into account. Finally, they propose care as a collective rather than individual responsibility and as a justly distributed set of practices that replenish, rather than diminish, disabled femmes of color. They see it as a potential source of reciprocity, community building, and joy, rather than an "isolated, begrudgingly done task."[98] Above all, care means honoring the vulnerabilities and needs emergent from crip-of-color experiences, and seeing vulnerability "not as a crime" but as the basis of building worlds in which everyone gets enough.[99]

In *Tonguebreaker*, the work of crip-of-color infrastructural support must first begin with an ideological shift. Following this, works such as "Crip Fairy Godmother," "The Amethyst Room," and "Litany" leverage the genres of ritual and prayer to present disability as worthy of not only care, but reverence. "Crip Fairy Godmother" in particular references the Earthseed religion detailed in Octavia Butler's *Parable of the Sower* and discussed in chapter 3 of this book. It calls in the disabled brilliance of Butler's protagonist Lauren Olamina, who Piepzna-Samarasinha candidly refers to as "that crip."[100] Through Earthseed's spiritual mythos, "Crip Fairy Godmother" makes the argument for disabled divinity:

Shape god

You, you are god

Disability is adaptive, interconnected, tenacious, voracious, slutty,

silent,

raging,

life giving[101]

Echoed here, too, is Ntozake Shange's 1975 choreopoem *For Colored Girls Who Have Considered Suicide / When the Rainbow Is Enuf*, and the famous lines uttered by the lady in red:

> i found god in myself
>
> & i loved her / i loved her fiercely.[102]

Tonguebreaker thus enables a return to the idea of the *crip sacred* explored in this book's chapter 3. In "Crip Fairy Godmother," the "baby crip" addressed in the poem becomes god through their rebirth into disabled embodiment. This act of resurrection frames disability as a portal connected to "the pulse and energy of creation," which M. Jacqui Alexander identifies as the "central understanding within an epistemology of the Sacred."[103] In becoming sick, one becomes re-created in the divine image of disability.

Themes of divine rebirth similarly emerge in the script for "The Amethyst Room," a ritual prayer Piepzna-Samarasinha performed in 2012 with the queer and trans people of color (QTPOC) collective Mangos with Chili, and which they reprinted in *Tonguebreaker*. "If chronic illness and disability have ritual," the script begins,

> this bed is my altar
>
> the place I circle and return to
>
> the place I rest
>
> the place I am dismembered
>
> and am reborn
>
> over and over again.[104]

Part of the Mangos with Chili's Reclaiming the Rites series, "The Amethyst Room" proposes chronic illness as a QTPOC rite of passage, one specific to queer-of-color experience because it records the "trauma and life" accrued by the "ancestors who survived so much."[105] Chronic illness is, then, one primary mode through which QTPOC histories—so often subject to erasure—endure across generations. And chronic illness is sacred because it constitutes a web of cosmic ancestral connection—the "living matter," as Alexander has written, that "links us to each other, making that which is individual simultaneously collective."[106]

"Let me know," Piepzna-Samarasinha asks their ancestors, "that my pain is you reaching for me."[107]

Through the genre of ritual prayer, *Tonguebreaker* gives structure, form, and ceremony to the process of racialized disablement, honoring it as a somatic crucible of QTPOC legacies, and one that should be recognized as such. In so doing, it highlights another informal care infrastructure operating in service of crip-of-color survival: the wisdom, knowledge, and support of other disabled queers of color who came before us, whose "sick bodies have smarts that nondisabled bodies don't have."[108] In other words, if disability is sacred, then we revere it by recognizing crip-of-color ancestry as itself a support structure, one that allows disabled queers of color to live as they are and not as they should be.

Evidence of this infrastructural support system is woven throughout *Tonguebreaker*, which testifies to all the ways that disabled queers of color have held each other across and beyond the earthly plane. For instance, in addition to claiming themself as a knowledgeable crip elder in "Crip Fairy Godmother," Piepzna-Samarasinha underscores the radical disability lineage encapsulated in movement texts such as *This Bridge Called My Back*, claiming queer luminaries such as Audre Lorde, June Jordan, and Gloria Anzaldúa as part of their disability justice inheritance. Their epistolary essay "A Requiem for Gloria," which reads as a response to Anzaldúa's missive "Speaking in Tongues: A Letter to Third World Women Writers," reimagines the Chicanx writer's legacy as a support structure for Piepzna-Samarasinha's own queer brown femme existence. "Dear gloria," they write, "I listen for your echo. my life like so many stands in the outline of yours."[109] Addressed to Anzaldúa's memory, the letter functions doubly as a prayer, declaring, "I want health care that is free for everyone. I want a world where no one will ever have to raise money on the internet for an ultrasound, IV antibiotics or a new wheelchair to replace the one stolen by another desperate crip."[110] With the repetitive chant of *I want*, Piepzna-Samarasinha's prayer channels their queer desire for more and better health/care infrastructures—and that desire is queer precisely because it interrupts present configurations of care to insist on other, more just arrangements.

By depicting disability as divine, and as having a sacred ancestral legacy, Piepzna-Samarasinha goes beyond the binary of deserving/undeserving that shapes the terms of state assistance programs, and beyond the tactics of inclusion and independence touted by disability rights activism. Both of these approaches, while not politically aligned, nonetheless situate disability within the terms of a world that already exists, a present world that is "impoverished and toxic" for disabled queers of color.[111] This is not the "cripped the fuck out" future that Piepzna-Samarasinha prophesies, where disabled femmes of color "[remake] the world" through "our recombinant bodies, our lurches, our Crazy brilliant ideas."[112] Rather, *Tonguebreaker* frames the disability justice principle of interdependency as a world-building ethos that might generate livable futures for her "cripbrownfemme" kin.[113] To recap, Sins Invalid's "Ten Principles of Disability Justice" defines interdependency as a practice of "[meeting] each other's needs as we build toward liberation, without always reaching for state solutions which can readily extend its control further over our lives."[114] This definition emphasizes the importance of shared support among disabled people as a prerequisite for freedom, arguing that crip liberation cannot come from the breadcrumbs given by the state.

Flouting the stigma of dependency undergirding Trumpcare's proposed Medicaid cuts, Piepzna-Samarasinha understands interdependency as not only an acceptable and inevitable way of arranging life, but a form of disability magic. In "Crip Magic Spells," they advise their "baby crip" addressee,

> Asking for help is the first and last spell you'll ever have to learn
>
> It's the one everything else rests on.
>
> It's the simplest, hardest thing.[115]

The crux of disability magic, as the poem makes clear, is the art and skill of dependency—of "asking for just what you need" and unlearning the shame associated with doing so.[116] As they tell the baby crip, "Know that everyone deserves to get exactly what we need / There is no such thing as not disabled enough."[117] Against the internalized austerity narratives that police disability— *"burden, whiner, don't ask them for too much"*—"Crip magic spells" recuperates and wields dependency as a form of "femme," "crip," and "submissive" protection against a world that wants to starve disabled people out of existence, and that weaponizes dependency in order to deny us the future.[118] "If we were really, *really* never meant to survive Audre," Piepzna-Samarasinha writes, "what does it mean to insist / that if we're going to live, it will be glorious. . . . That we will get to live to be old."[119] In its vision of an "orgasmic crone hood," a stage of life disabled femmes of color rarely get to experience, *Tonguebreaker* connects the achievement of liberatory crip futures to the unequivocal embrace of interdependency—thereby again highlighting the link between freedom and dependency that disability justice life-writing consistently underscores.[120]

Instead of denying the body's vulnerabilities, then, both Levins Morales and Piepzna-Samarasinha lean into them, with Levins Morales writing that "the only path out is deeper."[121] That is, deeper into everything "cripbrownfemme" existence teaches us about the intersections of structural ableism, turbocapitalism, and white supremacy, and deeper into the "political truths" held by disabled bodies.[122] And while Piepzna-Samarasinha calls on the future-oriented genre of speculation to envision radical antistate infrastructures of care, Levins Morales highlights the infrastructures extant in the world we currently inhabit, and more precisely, the "socialist medicine" that anti-ACA pundits wielded as an object of fear. Indeed, "A Day in the Life" functions as a prelude to her reprinted blog posts on Cuban health/care, which describe her two-month experience receiving medical treatment in Havana and compare socialist approaches to the profit-driven US system. "From the moment of my arrival [in Cuba]," Levins Morales reflects, "the difference between the two medical systems was profoundly evident."[123] Navigating a litany of ailments, including chronic fatigue immune dysfunction syndrome (CFIDS), epilepsy, and the aftermath of a stroke, Levins Morales sought out Cuban medicine once she had used up the "allotted number of once a week, forty-five-minute physical therapy sessions" afforded by her stingy US health plan.[124] She reflects, "I just woke up one day with a wish that had become a decision: I'm going to Cuba."[125]

The Cuban blog series thus functions as a kind of window into other infrastructural arrangements of care, all of which operate from a set of profoundly different ideologies on disability, well-being, and basic resource distribution. As Levins Morales observes, CIREN offers a holistic and integrative approach to health—in contrast to the "fragmented nature" of the US system—in which a "specialist" is assigned for "each separate molecule" of the body.[126] She marvels that her treatment plan includes "neurologists, neurosurgeons, physical therapists, traditional Chinese medicine practitioners, [and] homeopaths," as well as an acupuncturist, psychologist, and psychiatrist, all of whom work together to determine a comprehensive course of healing tailored to her needs.[127] Absent a profit motive and market competition, Cuban doctors and scientists do not need to "create patentable, profitable products" for pharmaceutical corporations, nor do they need to delegitimize so-called alternative medicines in order to fortify more mainstream methods.[128] And when Levins Morales does en-counter issues with the Cuban health/care system, she notes that many of these challenges can be linked to the ongoing US trade blockade, which greatly limits the basic supplies—food, fresh produce, soap, and toilet paper—to which Cu-bans have access.

Kindling further underscores where Cuban health/care infrastructure aligns with disability justice principles and imaginaries, envisioning a relationship with medical systems in which disability is not an object of hatred or extinction. So while Levins Morales highlights the healing possibilities afforded by the Cuban health/care model and approaches to well-being, this is not a wholesale acceptance of the narrative of cure, nor is it a stated hope to leave her disabled body behind. In *Kindling*, care and healing names a process in which sick and disabled people, particularly sick and disabled people of color, are given what they "require in order to thrive"—that is, "nourishment, equilibrium, water, connection, justice."[129] It does not entail "[fixing] [bodies] into a perfect able-bodied mold," as Piepzna-Samarasinha puts it; rather, healing centers disabled people within their own decision-making process, which at times might include medical intervention.[130] Toward this end, Levins Morales notes how in Cuba, "both [her] psychologist and [her] psychiatrist operated from a model of easy-going self-acceptance, rather than trying to 'fix' [her] toward an unreal model of perfect happiness."[131] She also praises the "amazing massages" administered by her physical therapist and the "electrical and magnetic treatments" that "dra-matically" drop her pain levels, exclaiming, "I am SO well cared for here!"[132]

In many ways, too, Levins Morales's experience in the Cuban medical sys-tem offers an answer to Piepzna-Samarasinha's prayer for free health/care and "guaranteed free personal care attendant service," as medical treatment there comes at no cost to Cuban citizens and is subsidized for many others.[133] *Kindling* and *Tonguebreaker*'s shared emphases on economically accessible health/care thus mark a departure from first-wave disability critiques of medical author-ity, which often presumed easy access to health/care and stressed the violence of ableism over medical racism and classism. Disability justice approaches to medical care, then, not only encompass a robust skepticism of medical knowl-edge but also insist on free, holistic health/care that centers the needs and de-sires of multiply marginalized disabled people. By testifying to a medical system that does not turn on profit, Levins Morales presents Cuban health/care as a more humane alternative to the US medical-industrial complex, stating boldly,

"So, no, the Obama administration is not proposing socialist medicine, but I am."[134] From her vantage point in Cuba, she tells her readers that other infrastructures are not only possible, they are already here.

Across earthly and cosmic planes, *Kindling* and *Tonguebreaker* put forth infrastructures of care that operate in alignment with the framework of disability justice, particularly the principles of interdependency, collective access, and collective liberation.[135] Throughout *Tonguebreaker*, Piepzna-Samarasinha employs the metaphysical genres of prayer and spellcasting to name, call forth, and honor the infrastructural care webs upholding disabled femme futures, worlds in which "stairs live in a museum," "perfume is an ancient hate crime," and "there are places to stim on every street corner in tiny libraries of joy."[136] In honoring these communal systems of support, they provide a crucial reframe of the dependency stigma so often weaponized against disabled people. Here, dependency is not only an assumed part of life, but crucial to the magic, art, and brilliance of disabled living. Levins Morales, too, defects from the violent sensorium of present-day US health/care to testify to other, more humane infrastructural arrangements, which she locates in the Cuban medical system. Resonant throughout both works is an insistence that care can look and operate otherwise, and that the structural transformation of care requires a conceptual overhaul—of what the term means, who is expected to practice it, and who deserves to receive it.

In the face of the breadcrumbs offered by US state institutions, *Kindling* and *Tonguebreaker* envision care infrastructures that could support disabled queers of color without seeking to fix us, and that could supplant austerity with generosity. For both writer-activists, this is the meaning of care: not the offering of meager resources toward the bare sustenance of life, but the seeding of conditions for a "glorious" present and future, one that underscores the richness of crip-of-color wisdom, comradery, and lifeforce.[137] It is an unshakable faith in the sacredness of disabled life, even when there is too much to bear and too much telling us otherwise. It is the wild, unexpected work of infrastructural freedom dreaming in a context that punishes us for wanting to live. In the book's epilogue, I speak to my own queer longings for more and better, in which my love for my best friend meant that I was dreaming, day and night, of infrastructure.

At the end, I return to the beginning. To the beginning of Leah Lakshmi Piepzna-Samarasinha's *Tonguebreaker* (2019), and to the source of my infra-structural dreams. To revisit, *Tonguebreaker* starts with this incantation: "This book is a magic spell about what it means to be surrounded by death and live on."[1] Now nearly three years after the death of my best friend, and over four years into the COVID-19 pandemic, I know, intimately, what this means.

Tonguebreaker took shape in an atmosphere of femme death, of queer, Black and brown, and disabled death. My book does, too. And while Piepzna-Samarasinha's book functions, in many ways, as memorial and eulogy for be-loved community members such as Bryn Kelly and Taueret Davis, the deaths did not stop there. In the first few months of the initial COVID-19 shutdowns in the United States, the passing of Lucia Leandro Gimeno and Stacey Park Milbern, both cherished organizers in queer-of-color and disability justice movements, sent tectonic waves of grief across radical queer and crip circles. I had never met either one in person, never knew either beyond a friend-of-a-friend connection, but in administering to the grief of their loved ones, in delivering meals and at-tending virtual memorials and reading (so many) tributes, I felt some intimacy with their web of memory, touching and tending to this vast garden of mourning as if it were my own. In a way, it was.

And it was, in part, because I know what it's like to learn that someone you love—someone who taught you how to navigate a hostile world and to live big in spite of it—will never get to be old. I know that Piepzna-Samarasinha's invocation of an "orgasmic cronehood" was in part a protection spell against the shortened lifespans inflicted on many sick and disabled femmes of color.[2] Because one of the biggest grieving points across queer-of-color, sick, disabled, working-class/low-income communities is that countless numbers of our beloveds are dead before they get to be old. A byproduct of chronic stress and systemic resource deprivation, this structural loss of wisdom is yet another way crip and queer time gets stolen, another way our time is reformatted as an endlessly extractable resource for hypercapitalist consumption. Another way the precious resource of elder knowledge and experience—their blueprints for survival—gets taken from us. Because even while disability justice life-writing can reflect joy and pleasure and generosity, the telling of a disabled life is so often about one's proximity to death.

My best friend was thirty-four. She was born a year before me, in 1985, but now, at thirty-eight, I am older than she will ever get to be. She entered the world of disability and illness suddenly, with marked changes in her vision and balance, then received a diagnosis of glioblastoma multiforme, a deadly form of brain cancer with an average survival time of twelve to eighteen months. She made it to ten.

I moved down to Atlanta the May prior to her passing in August 2019, intent on spending the summer as part of her cancer care team. No stranger to illness, I had lost many people in my life to cancer—my grandmother, my aunt, my uncle, my dissertation adviser—but no one who had witnessed me wobble my way through a painful adolescence and who shared the brutal, searing experience of growing up as a nonwhite outsider in Atlanta's conservative suburbs. No one who had introduced me to Cheryl Dunye and Michelle Tea and Laurie Anderson and Kara Walker and the Butchies, and no one with whom I had spent hours, shaking with laughter, over the dated drawings and language in the 1977 manual *The Joy of Lesbian Sex*. No one who—by dint of her shamelessness, gayness, and sheer force of spirit—had nurtured me into my freedom. Together, we had "set about creating"—in the words of the inimitable Toni Morrison—"something else to be."[3]

For all these reasons, and more besides, I knew I had to walk alongside her as she approached the shadow of death. Yet—even as I had seen the work that cancer does on the body, even as I had shared in mourning with others, I felt utterly unprepared for the particular crisis of care that emerged shortly after my arrival. I have described the contours of this crisis elsewhere, so let me summarize it briefly: after I made my summer move, it gradually became apparent that my best friend was mired—psychologically, emotionally, and materially—in a dynamic of what I viewed as care abuse perpetuated by her romantic partner and primary caregiver, another queer person of color.[4]

While I will not recount the details at length, I will say this much: his actions primarily took the form of social isolation and interpersonal control. Because he was granted her medical power of attorney, and because he presented himself as her sole chance for survival, his power over her future ran unchecked. Under a set of authoritarian demands, her friends and family were not allowed to acknowledge the fact that she was dying, for fear of risking excision from her social world. What's more, we were only able to care for her to the very limited degree allowed by her partner, who withheld information about her care protocol. The summer, then, became a season of appeasement, focused not on her but on her partner—we navigated his turbulent moods, complied with the demand for denial, so that we could accompany her through the process of death.

As in Piepzna-Samarasinha's letter to Anzaldúa, my grief turned me into a muscle of infrastructural desire, into an endless refrain of "I want." I wanted so much more and better. I wanted a hospital system that could understand the weight of platonic love. I wanted a social worker who did not default to my friend's romantic partner as the sole carrier of medical information. I wanted to bypass Kaiser Permanente's insurance song and dance and the bureaucratic labyrinth preceding every crumb of care. I wanted healthcare infrastructure that wouldn't underscore this nation's hatred of poor people, of racialized people, of sick and disabled and queer people. I wanted infrastructure that could support a collective, diffuse, and horizontal model of caregiving rather than a private, individualized, and top-down model. I wanted to destroy governing understandings of care as a family matter, a sparse resource resentfully given, and a luxury service. I wanted an arrangement of care that would allow me to access the wellspring of soul connection between me and my friend, which I could now touch only in the most superficial of ways.

From the sterile chamber of her hospital room, I remember feeling so much queer desire: for a healthcare system that could recognize friendship as life connection, for ways to tell my friend she wasn't a burden, for other and more expansive structures of care to hold her in her final days. And yet, even under that regime of restriction and denial, there were still moments of loving attachment. Sometimes, there was even joy. Because, to borrow the words of M. Jacqui Alexander, we could not "afford to cease yearning for each others' [*sic*] company," even as so many forces conspired to make it otherwise.[5]

Our most profound moment of connection took place at Piedmont Atlanta Hospital, in a drab in-patient room outfitted with beige plastic panels. By the door, an informational whiteboard listed an ever-rotating roster of nurses and a daily care schedule. Outside of my friend's care regimen, much of our time in that room was spent cutting through the tedium of hospital life. We streamed *Queer Eye* on a laptop, and as the Fab Five West Elm–ified yet another straight person's house, my friend would cry about whether or not she would get to see Kansas City again, where most of her extended family lived and where the *Queer Eye* makeovers were taking place. "Yes," we reassured her, "you'll get to see Kansas City again. Of course, you'll see it again."

It was at Piedmont where I read her the essay "After Peter," part of Alexander Chee's stunning 2018 essay collection *How to Write an Autobiographical Novel*. Chee's essay was one of a number of texts I shared with her that summer, along with June Jordan's 1977 essay "The Creative Spirit: Children's Literature," recently reprinted in the 2016 anthology *Revolutionary Mothering: Love on the Front Lines*, and parts of Ocean Vuong's 2019 novel *On Earth We're Briefly Gorgeous*. When we were alone in her hospital room, I often felt compelled to read to her, even though this wasn't something we had ever done before. I'm not sure why I started doing this. In hindsight, I think I wanted to find some way to tell her how our love made it possible for me to live, that even in death she would be the home I would return to always. That my life, as Piepzna-Samarasinha wrote in their letter to Anzaldúa, "[stood] in the outline of [hers]," and that I would always be "[listening] for [her] echo."[6] I needed, however, to say these things without breaking the vow of silence I had made implicitly to her and her partner, in which I could not acknowledge the possibility of her dying, even as she was doing so right before me.

So, I borrowed from the long-standing queer tradition of speaking in code. This time, the code was Chee's essay. "After Peter" is a requiem for his former lover, friend, and comrade Peter D. Kelloran, who fought alongside Chee in the 1990s San Francisco gay activist scene, where they participated in ACT UP/SF and Queer Nation. Like many other gay men of his generation, Peter died of HIV/AIDS, passing in May 1994 after years of protesting government inaction against the epidemic. I first came across this essay at a 2018 reading in Amherst Books, where I listened to Chee read it aloud, his eyes beaded with tears. Moved by this open display of grief, I bought his book. I did not know that four months later, the essay would speak to me in a different way.

In many ways, "After Peter" was not a perfect analogue for my particular experience of loss. Chee begins the essay with an admission—that he was "a minor character in Peter's story" and was not among the first group of people notified of his passing.[7] The two were also, for a brief span of time, romantically involved. It's true, too, that Peter's death from HIV/AIDS slots into queer history in a way that my friend's sudden diagnosis of brain cancer does not. And while "After Peter" reads in many ways like a portrait and loving homage to a single person, the character of Peter also functions as a portal to a particular time in Chee's life, when he was twenty-two, a new arrival to San Francisco, and throwing himself into the heady world of direct-action AIDS activism. "At this time in San Francisco," he writes, "it seemed that the world might either go up in flames or be restored in a healing past imagining. . . . I think now, twenty years later, this feeling might always be true."[8]

Still, there were places in the essay with which I felt parallel. Like Peter, my friend was "a kind of art prodigy, good at ceramics, drawing, design."[9] We had met initially as art majors at Georgia's Governor's Honors Program, a state-funded summer camp for high-achieving high school juniors and seniors. At the time of her diagnosis, she was designing textiles for major retailers, and one of her rugs had been recently included in a *Vogue* photo spread. I had long given up on the idea of making a living from art, and I admired her fearless insistence on doing so. I admired many things about her, including but not limited to her fearlessness and utter self-possession, which remained as constant at the age of thirty-four as it did at seventeen. As a mixed-race Chicana teenager, she founded a chapter of the Gay-Straight Alliance (GSA) at her majority-white, conservative high school, serving as the chapter's president. I was also a teenage member of the GSA, but as an "ally." It would take me many years to publicly claim my sexuality. Like Peter, who was listed among Chee's "personal pantheon of heroes from that time," my friend "inspired me to be an artist, to protest, to live as queerly, as confidently, and as openly as I wanted."[10]

By reading "After Peter" aloud, I was able to say this to her, and many other things without risking entry into the territory of mourning. When I wanted to say *I'll miss you*, I read, "I can't help but long for Peter still, the sight of him . . . a star in my eye."[11] When I wanted to say *thank you*, I read, "In the end I wonder if it is a mistake to think about what was lost. If it isn't better to think about what [Peter] gave me."[12] When I wanted to tell her how she helped me find a way to exist freely, how her friendship blunted the sharp corners of my once-unlivable world, I read to her Chee's paean to the gay men who should have been his elders: "The men I wanted to follow into the future are dead. Finding them had made me want to live, and I did. I do. I feel I owe them my survival."[13] As we sat in the afterglow of the essay, tearful and stunned, I could feel the curtain between us momentarily part.

She made me want to live. I owe her my survival. Queer-of-color and disability justice life-writing helped me tell her this. Chee's essay thus offered a safety net in a healthcare infrastructural landscape that would not let us love each other in the way we always had. And while platonic love does not often register within hospitals and waiting rooms, "After Peter" provided a holding container and mirror for our friendship, as it spelled out some of the ways that queer people have acted as infrastructure for one another through sickness and death, when nothing else in the world would hold us. To borrow a metaphor from Piepzna-Samarasinha's *Tonguebreaker*, the essay acted as an "adaptive device," a "piece of beautiful supportive tech / that [put] in work to keep [us] alive."[14] And alive not just in the sense of having a sentient body, but in the sense of feeling the place where one connects to the "pulse and energy of creation."[15] Alive like touching the bridge that forever connects my world to hers.

At the end of her life, I was dreaming of infrastructure. And now, in the middle of the COVID-19 pandemic, I am still dreaming. But as the feminist, queer, and crip-of-color literary pantheon has taught me, I am not alone; there is in fact a storied tradition of infrastructural freedom dreaming—of reimagining what is and reaching toward what could be. I have mapped some of these dreams across the imagined classrooms of Sapphire's *Push*, the flooded landscapes of Jesmyn Ward's *Salvage the Bones*, the erotic sanitation fantasies of Samuel Delany's *Through the Valley of the Nest of Spiders*, the apocalyptic freeways of Karen Tei Yamashita's *Tropic of Orange* and Octavia Butler's *Parable of the Sower*, and finally, the hospitals, waiting rooms, and care webs documented by the writer-activists Leah Lakshmi Piepzna-Samarasinha and Aurora Levins

Morales. While navigating the US landscape of infrastructural violence, I have also been held by feminist, queer, and/or crip-of-color friends, colleagues, and comrades, who helped me find a way to survive in academia and in life. Because of them, I know that feminist, queer, and crip friendship makes me rich. I know that "we are dangerous when we find each other. at the bottom of the stairs. in the crip seats. in the waiting room at kaiser or acupuncture. on tumblr. we are dangerous."[16] I know we are most dangerous when we dream.

Notes

Acknowledgments

1   Smith, *Homie: Poems*, 81.

Introduction

1   Piepzna-Samarasinha, *Care Work*, 122.
2   Kafai, *Crip Kinship*.
3   Kelley, *Freedom Dreams*, x.
4   For more on the implicit centering of able-bodiedness in antiracist political movements, see Harriet Tubman Collective, "Disability Solidarity"; Minich, *Accessible Citizenships*; and Lee, *Pedagogies of Woundedness*.
5   Jackson, "Working Publics," 11.
6   Frye, "Birthing Disability," 100.
7   Ferguson, *Aberrations in Black*, 26.
8   Lowe, *Immigrant Acts*, 29.
9   See Bagenstos, "Americans with Disabilities Act"; and Frye, "Cripping the 'Crack Baby' Epidemic."
10 Frye, "Cripping the 'Crack Baby' Epidemic," 86.
11 For more on disability and austerity policies, see McRuer, *Crip Times*.
12 See Erevelles, *Disability and Difference*; Puar, *Right to Maim*; Frye, "Cripping the 'Crack Baby' Epidemic"; Nishida, *Just Care*; and Ben-Moshe, *Decarcerating Disability*.
13 Simone, "People as Infrastructure," 407 (emphasis in original).
14 Nishida, *Just Care*, 9.
15 Ben-Moshe, *Decarcerating Disability*, 15–17.
16 Bhattacharya, "Mapping Social Reproduction Theory," 2.
17 See, for instance, Piepzna-Samarasinha, *Care Work*; Nishida, *Just Care*; Hobart and Kneese, "Radical Care"; and Glenn, *Forced to Care*.
18 Donegan, "How Domestic Labor Became Infrastructure."
19 See Mink, *Welfare's End*; Abramovitz, *Regulating the Lives of Women*; Gordon, *Pitied but Not Entitled*; and Poole, *Segregated Origins of Social Security*. Recently,

Priya Kandaswamy has argued convincingly for the Freedmen's Bureau as an underexplored site of analysis for US welfare history; see *Domestic Contradictions*.

20 See Mink, *Welfare's End*; and Roberts, "Welfare's Ban."

21 Influential texts like Charles Murray's *Losing Ground: American Social Policy, 1950–1980* and Lawrence Mead's *Beyond Entitlement: The Social Obligations of Citizenship* advocated for major overhauls of the existing welfare system, which ranged from its complete abolishment (Murray) to establishing work as a prerequisite for aid (Mead). Their books claimed that welfare dependency would discourage welfare's recipients from wage-earning work, trapping them in a cycle of poverty and enabling them to continue self-indulgent lifestyles.

22 See Fraser and Gordon, "Genealogy of Dependency." "Whereas industrial usage had cast some forms of dependency as natural and proper," write Fraser and Gordon, "postindustrial usage figures all forms as avoidable and blameworthy" (323).

23 For more on the eventual association of ssi with the more stigmatized elements of welfare, see Berkowitz and DeWitt, *Other Welfare*.

24 Personal Responsibility and Work Opportunity Reconciliation Act of 1996, Pub. L. No. 104–193 (1996), 2110, 2112. Hereafter cited as PRWORA.

25 Kornbluh and Mink, *Ensuring Poverty*, ix.

26 Cohen and Jackson, "Ask a Feminist," 776.

27 Salamanca, "Unplug and Play," 34.

28 Ruth Wilson Gilmore uses the term *organized abandonment* to describe the purposeful starvation of the welfare/social functions of the state, creating gaps that are then filled in by prisons and policing. See Gilmore and Gilmore, "Beyond Bratton." Dean Spade's concept of administrative violence, described in *Normal Life: Administrative Violence, Critical Trans Politics, and the Limits of Law*, describes how state agencies such as the Department of Child Welfare, US Immigration and Customs Enforcement, and the Environmental Protection Agency actively manufacture and distribute life chances at the population level. Finally, Puar's concept of debility is mobilized as part of a conceptual triad (capacity, debility, disability) to intervene into the disabled/nondisabled binary. Derived from the context of settler colonialism, debility further describes processes of bodily incapacitation that unfold without access to legal recourse, accommodations, or the rights associated with the liberal category of disability in settler states. See Puar, *Right to Maim*.

29 Rubenstein, Robbins, and Beal, "Infrastructuralism," 576.

30 Fraser, "Contradictions of Capital and Care," 112.

31 See Glenn, *Forced to Care*; and Mohanty, *Feminism without Borders*.

32 See Gilmore, *Golden Gulag*.

33 See Ferguson, *Aberrations in Black*; Hong, *Ruptures of American Capital*; and Chambers-Letson, *After the Party*.

34 Ferguson, *Aberrations*, 10.

35 Ferguson, *Aberrations*, 10, 4.

36 See Minich, *Accessible Citizenships*; Lee, *Pedagogies of Woundedness*; and Harriet Tubman Collective, "Disability Solidarity."

37 Lorde, "Burst of Light," 130.

38 Lorde, "Burst of Light," 44.

39 Lorde, "Burst of Light," 41–42.

40 Moraga, "La Jornada," xxxvii.

41 Sins Invalid, "10 Principles of Disability Justice."

42 Moraga and Anzaldúa, *This Bridge*, 196.

43 Moraga and Anzaldúa, *This Bridge*, 195.

44 Moraga and Anzaldúa, *This Bridge*, 196.

45 Rushin, "Bridge Poem," xxxiii.

46 Lorde, "Master's Tools," 96.

47 Moraga, "La Jornada," xl.

48 Moraga, "La Jornada," xli.

49 Moraga, "La Jornada," xxxix.

50 Moraga, "La Jornada," xxxix.

51 Moraga, "La Jornada," xli.

52 Mingus, "Interdependence."

53 See Garland-Thomson, "Integrating Disability"; and Kittay, *Love's Labor*.

54 Garland-Thomson, "Integrating Disability," 21.

55 Cohen, "Punks, Bulldaggers, and Welfare Queens," 438.

56 Hong and Ferguson, *Strange Affinities*, 1–2.

57 Mohanty, *Feminism without Borders*, 25.

58 For feminist disability reclamations of Audre Lorde, see Bailey and Mobley, "Work in the Intersections"; Bolaki, "Challenging Invisibility"; and Kim and Schalk, "Radical Politics of Self-Care."

59 Lorde, "Master's Tools," 94.

60 Lorde, "Master's Tools," 95.

61 Lorde, "Master's Tools," 95.

62 Lorde, "Litany for Survival."

63 Lorde, "Master's Tools," 95.

64 Lorde, "Master's Tools," 95.

65 Lorde, "Master's Tools," 96.

66 Piepzna-Samarasinha, *Future Is Disabled*, 75.

67 See Piepzna-Samarasinha, *Care Work*; and Nishida, *Just Care*.

68 Erevelles, *Disability and Difference*, 17. In response to reclamatory accounts of disability, Erevelles provocatively asks, "How is disability celebrated if its very existence is inextricably linked to the violence of social/economic conditions of capitalism?" (17). I reference this quote here because I see it as one of the most important early interventions into white-centric, rights-based disability studies.

69 Sandahl, "Queering the Crip," 37.

70 For further explanations (and demonstrations) of disability as methodology, see Schalk, *Bodyminds Reimagined*; and Minich, "Enabling Whom?"

71 Minich, "Enabling Whom?"

72 Berne, "Disability Justice."

73 Kafai, *Crip Kinship*, 17.

74 Butler, *Parable*, 3.

75 Butler, *Parable*, 5.

76 Moraga, "La Jornada," xli.

77 Piepzna-Samarasinha, *Tonguebreaker*, 117.

78 Moraga and Anzaldúa, *This Bridge*, 196.

1. Cripping the Welfare Queen

1 Abdur-Rahman, *Against the Closet*, 136.

2 Ward, *Salvage the Bones*, 2.

3 Ward, *Salvage the Bones*, 2.

4 Lewis, *Abolish the Family*, 30. See also Weeks, "Abolition of the Family."

5 I return here to Audre Lorde's formulation. See Lorde, "Master's Tools," 95.

6 For more on the long-standing history of disgust for Black mothers, see Hancock, *Politics of Disgust*.

7 See Abramovitz, *Regulating the Lives of Women*.

8 *New York Times*, "'Welfare Queen' Becomes Issue," 51.

9 Moynihan, *Negro Family*.

10 *Culture of poverty* is a social theory concept that holds low-income communities responsible for their own poverty, particularly over generational cycles. See Lewis, "Culture of Poverty."

11 PRWORA, 2113 (emphasis mine).

12 See Mientka, "'Welfare-to-Work' Programs"; Muennig, Rosen, and Wilde, "Welfare Programs"; Wilde et al., "Impact of Welfare Reform"; and Muennig et al., "More Money, Fewer Lives."

13 Muennig et al., "More Money, Fewer Lives."

14 For more on the connection between dependency, Black motherhood, and welfare reform, see Roberts, *Killing the Black Body*; Cohen, "Punks, Bulldaggers, and Welfare Queens"; and Abdur-Rahman, *Against the Closet*.

15 Cohen, "Punks, Bulldaggers, and Welfare Queens," 438.

16 See Roberts, *Killing the Black Body*; Spillers, "Mama's Baby, Papa's Maybe"; Collins, *Black Feminist Thought*; Hancock, *Politics of Disgust*; Lubiano, "Black Ladies, Welfare Queens"; and Gumbs, "m/other ourselves."

17 See Gumbs, "m/other ourselves."

18 Frye, "Cripping the 'Crack Baby' Epidemic," 70.

19 Lubiano defines cover stories as narratives that "cover or mask what they make invisible with an alternative presence; a presence that redirects our attention, that covers or makes absent what has to remain unseen if the *seen* is to function as the *scene* for a different drama. One story provides a cover that allows another story (or stories) to slink out of sight" ("Black Ladies, Welfare Queens," 324).

20 Schram, *After Welfare*, 59.

21 Schram, *After Welfare*, 59.

22 Welfare Indicators Act of 1994, Pub. L. No. 103–432, 4462–4465 (1994).

23 Gumbs, "We Can Learn," 206.

24 Singer, *Erotic Welfare*.

25 Gumbs, "We Can Learn," 207.

26 PRWORA, 2111.

27 Cohen, "Punks, Bulldaggers, and Welfare Queens," 438.

28 Sapphire, *Push*, 34.

29 Michelle Jarman first noted the connection between Sapphire's *Push* and disability politics, in "Cultural Consumption."

30 See Jarman, "Cultural Consumption."

31 Jarman, "Cultural Consumption," 164.

32 Sapphire, *Push*, 132.

33 James and Wu, "Race, Ethnicity, Disability, and Literature," 4.

34 See Sanyika, "Katrina and Black New Orleans," 35.

35 Giroux, "Reading Hurricane Katrina," 174.

36 Ward, *Salvage the Bones*, 217 (emphasis in original).

37 Ward, *Salvage the Bones*, 189, 85.

38 Ward, *Salvage the Bones*, 102.

39 See Mississippi State Department of Health, "Personal Responsibility Education Program"; Bares, "Each Unbearable Day," 29.

40 Bares, "Each Unbearable Day," 29.

41 Ward, *Salvage the Bones*, 102.

42 Abdur-Rahman, *Against the Closet*, 134.

43 Sapphire, *Push*, 3.

44 Sapphire, *Push*, 8, 5.

45 Sapphire, *Push*, 15.

46 Eldred and Mortensen, "Reading Literacy Narratives," 512.

47 Henry Louis Gates, in his introduction to *"Race," Writing, and Difference*, recounts the story of Phillis Wheatley, whose display of reason through poetry composition earned her entry into the category of the human. As Gates notes, in the Enlightenment era, writing was seen as the "*visible* sign of reason" (emphasis in original), and within a Cartesian value system that privileged reason "over all

human characteristics," Black people were "'reasonable,' and hence 'men,' if—and only if—they demonstrated mastery of the 'arts and sciences'" (8). Presaging disability critiques of rationality as the baseline through which humanness is determined, Gates notes that "writing," in the system of Enlightenment-era values, "was not an activity of mind, rather, it was a commodity [slaves] were forced to trade for their humanity" (9). See Gates, "Introduction: Writing 'Race.'"

48   Ferguson, *Aberrations in Black*, 25.

49   See, for instance, Dubey, *Signs and Cities*; McNeil, "Un-'freak'ing Black Female Selfhood"; and Doane and Hodges, *Telling Incest*.

50   Erevelles, *Disability and Difference*, 26.

51   Jarman, "Cultural Consumption," 164.

52   Smith, *New Urban Frontier*, 7.

53   Sapphire, *Push*, 127.

54   Dubey, *Signs and Cities*, 59.

55   Sapphire, *Push*, 74.

56   Sapphire, *Push*, 77.

57   As Premilla Nadasen notes in *Welfare Warriors*, "Liberals, conservatives, and many radicals concurred that jobs programs would solve the problem of rising welfare rolls and the long-term problem of poverty" (136).

58   Nadasen, *Welfare Warriors*, xvi.

59   Nirmala Erevelles makes this argument in her reading of Hortense Spillers's "Mama's Baby, Papa's Maybe." Erevelles writes that while "the dominant paradigm has conceived of disabled bodies as having little economic value except in the very limited contexts where their extra-ordinariness was made hypervisible," it is in "becoming disabled that the Black body is at the height of its profitability" (*Disability and Difference*, 39). The "scene[s] of *actual* mutilation, dismemberment, and exile" enacted in the Middle Passage rendered, for Erevelles, the Black body a commodity *through* acts of purposeful disablement (Spillers, 67).

60   Sapphire, *Push*, 31.

61   Sapphire, *Push*, 119.

62   Sapphire, *Push*, 118.

63   Sapphire, *Push*, 118.

64   Sapphire, *Push*, 120.

65   Sapphire, *Push*, 121.

66   Kim, *Curative Violence*, 6.

67   Abdur-Rahman, *Against the Closet*, 142–43; Sapphire, Push, 30.

68   For more on this history, see Collins, "Shifting the Center"; and Glenn, "From Servitude to Service Work." For more transnational dimensions of racialized care extraction, see Parreñas, *Servants of Globalization*; and Choy, *Empire of Care*.

69   Ward, "Q & A," 265.

70   Spillers, "Mama's Baby, Papa's Maybe," 65.

71 Gumbs, "m/other ourselves," 23.

72 Gumbs, introduction to *Revolutionary Mothering*, 9.

73 Ward, *Salvage the Bones*, 213.

74 Edwards, "Sex after the Black Normal,"158.

75 Bares, "Each Unbearable Day," 32.

76 Berne, "Disability Justice"; Berne et al., "Ten Principles of Disability Justice," 228.

77 Edwards, "Sex after the Black Normal," 158.

78 Ward, *Salvage the Bones*, 38.

79 Yaeger, "*Beasts.*"

80 Yaeger, "*Beasts.*"

81 See Yaeger, "*Beasts.*"

82 Ward, *Salvage the Bones*, 2.

83 Ward, *Salvage the Bones*, 2.

84 Ellison, *Invisible Man*, 7.

85 For more on the trope of electricity in *Invisible Man*, see Ford, "Crossroads and Cross-Currents."

86 Ward, *Salvage the Bones*, 4.

87 Gurton-Wachter, "Stranger Guest."

88 Garland-Thomson, "Integrating Disability," 20, 28.

89 Jackson, *Becoming Human*, 166.

90 Ward, *Salvage the Bones*, 29.

91 Ward, *Salvage the Bones*, 3.

92 Ward, *Salvage the Bones*, 21.

93 Ward, *Salvage the Bones*, 106, 168.

94 Ward, *Salvage the Bones*, 96.

95 Ward, *Salvage the Bones*, 96.

96 Ward, *Salvage the Bones*, 129 (emphasis mine).

97 Ward, *Salvage the Bones*, 255.

98 Teish, *Jambalaya*, 120.

99 Ward, *Salvage the Bones*, 252–53.

100 Ward, *Salvage the Bones*, 255 (emphasis mine).

101 Fjord, "Disasters, Race, and Disability," 46.

102 See Ralli, "Who's a Looter?"; and Treaster and Kleinfield, "New Orleans Is Inundated."

103 See ABC News, "Troops Told 'Shoot to Kill.'"

104 Ward, *Salvage the Bones*, 14.

105 Ward, *Salvage the Bones*, 226–27.

106 For more on the nonprofit industrial complex, see INCITE!, *Revolution Will Not Be Funded*.

107 Sapphire, *Push*, 54.

108 Sapphire, *Push*, 54–55.

109 Piepzna-Samarasinha, *Care Work*, 35.

110 Sapphire, *Push*, 95.

111 Moraga, "La Jornada," xxxvii.

112 Sapphire, *Push*, 96.

113 Piepzna-Samarasinha, *Care Work*, 33.

114 Lorde, "Uses of the Erotic," 56.

115 Musser, "Re-membering Audre," 348.

116 Sapphire, *Push*, 96.

117 Chinn, "Feeling Her Way," 188.

118 Musser, "Re-membering Audre," 357.

119 Sapphire, *Push*, 95–96.

120 Abdur-Rahman, *Against the Closet*, 141. Also see Morris, *Close Kin*; and Dubey, *Signs and Cities*.

121 Sandoval, *Methodology of the Oppressed*, 63, 62.

122 Moraga and Anzaldúa, *This Bridge*; Smith, *Home Girls*; and Anzaldúa, *Making Face*.

123 Ward, *Salvage the Bones*, 254–55.

124 Ward, *Salvage the Bones*, 258.

125 Ward, *Salvage the Bones*, 205 (emphasis in original).

126 Nishida, *Just Care*, 130.

127 brown, *Pleasure Activism*, 3.

2. Refuse Work

1 Harrison, "Fraud and Waste," 148.

2 Harrison, "Fraud and Waste," 148.

3 Hawkins, *Ethics of Waste*, viii

4 Kapadia, *Insurgent Aesthetics*, 33; Roane, *Dark Agoras*, 4.

5 Clintonlibrary42, "Pres. Clinton Signing Welfare Reform."

6 Piepzna-Samarasinha, *Care Work*, 33.

7 Clift, "Reagan Condemns Welfare System."

8 Clift, "Reagan Condemns Welfare System."

9 Bucher and Dickel, "Affinity for the Lumpen," 289.

10 Delany, *Through the Valley*, 219. Also, I borrow the term *medical apartheid* from Washington, *Medical Apartheid*.

11 For more on assessing HIV/AIDS through a queer and disability studies lens, see McRuer, *Crip Theory*; and Bell, "I'm Not the Man."

12 Delany, *Through the Valley*, 98, 219. While the novel uses the term *public* to describe the services provided by the Kyle Foundation, the term typically refers to state-funded services and institutions rather than those bankrolled by philanthropic foundations.

13 Delany, *Through the Valley*, 114.

14 Delany, *Through the Valley*, 555.

15 See Ferguson, *Aberrations in Black*; Abdur-Rahman, *Against the Closet*; and Stallings, *Funk the Erotic*.

16 Morrison, *Bluest Eye*, 83; and Stallings, *Funk the Erotic*, 131.

17 Delany, *Through the Valley*, 219.

18 See Boris and Parreñas, introduction to *Intimate Labors*.

19 Delany, *Through the Valley*, 79.

20 Shaviro, "Mad Man."

21 Delany, *Shorter Views*, 133.

22 Delany, *Through the Valley*, 199.

23 Delany, *Through the Valley*, 39.

24 Delany, *Through the Valley*, 35.

25 Delany, *Times Square Red*, 111.

26 Mollow and McRuer, introduction to *Sex and Disability*, 1.

27 Rodríguez, "Queer Sociality," 336.

28 Delany, *Through the Valley*, 20.

29 Delany, *Through the Valley*, 219–20 (emphasis mine).

30 Delany, *Through the Valley*, 46.

31 The bathroom orgy's emphasis on interabled contact names but one place in *Through the Valley* where disability emerges as a method for reimagining sexual and social connection. Delany's reference to the disabled theater group Wry Crips, as well as his expressed appreciation to the late disability critic Josh Lukin (who he describes as an "astute reader of the first edition"), suggests a writer in conversation with disability theories and politics, particularly as they intersect with questions of race, class, and sexuality (Delany, *Through the Valley*, 763). For more on Delany's relationship to disability, see Bell, "I'm Not the Man"; and Shotwell, *Against Purity*, specifically the chapter "Worlds to Come: Imagining Speculative Disability Futures."

32 Kristeva, *Powers of Horror*, 2, 9. According to Kristeva, human wastes such as semen, urine, feces, and vomit incite disgust because they challenge the separation between self and other on which rational subjectivity depends, reminding us of the superficial and easily penetrable barriers that separate the body from the not-so-outside world. As such, the abject represents a threat that must be cordoned off in order to maintain a fiction of order and cohesion.

33 Kristeva, *Powers of Horror*, 4.

34 Dohmen, "Disability as Abject," 769.

35 Kristeva, *Powers of Horror*, 4.

36 Scott, *Extravagant Abjection*, 12, 4.

37 Delany, *Shorter Views*, 66. For more on Delany and abjection, see Wachter-Grene, "On the Unspeakable"; and Griffiths, "Queer.Black Politics."

38 Musser, *Sensual Excess*, 16.

39 Scott, *Extravagant Abjection*, 128.

40 Musser, *Sensual Excess*, 86.

41 Davis, "Nude Venuses," 55.

42 Wendell, *Rejected Body*, 61.

43 Kristeva, "Liberty, Equality, Fraternity, and . . . Vulnerability," 251 (emphasis in original).

44 Wade, "It Ain't Exactly Sexy," 88.

45 Wade, "It Ain't Exactly Sexy," 90.

46 Scott, *Extravagant Abjection*, 163.

47 Delany, *Through the Valley*, 48.

48 Delany, *Through the Valley*, 50.

49 Delany, *Through the Valley*, 50.

50 Delany, *Through the Valley*, 39.

51 Griffiths, "Queer.Black Politics," 308.

52 Musser, *Sensual Excess*, 5, 14.

53 Musser, *Sensual Excess*, 73; Bersani, "Is the Rectum a Grave?"

54 Musser, *Sensual Excess*, 5.

55 Musser, *Sensual Excess*, 88.

56 Musser, *Sensual Excess*, 5.

57 Delany, *Through the Valley*, 45.

58 Delany, *Through the Valley*, 192.

59 Boris and Parreñas, introduction to *Intimate Labors*, 2.

60 For more on feminist disability theories of care, see Nishida, *Just Care*; Kelly, *Disability Politics and Care*; and Piepzna-Samarasinha, *Care Work*.

61 Boris and Parreñas, introduction to *Intimate Labors*, 2.

62 Nagle, *Picking Up*, 24, 25.

63 Delany, *Through the Valley*, 126.

64 Delany, *Through the Valley*, 126.

65 Delany, *Through the Valley*, 97.

66 During the strike, 1,300 Black employees from the Memphis Department of Public Works protested the horrific laboring conditions foisted on them by an increasingly austere city government. Though part of the waged labor system, 40 percent of Memphis sanitation workers qualified for welfare as a supplement to their paltry wages, while the city refused to update dangerous and outmoded garbage equipment. The tragic and unnecessary deaths of Echol Cole and Robert Walker, two sanitation workers crushed in a malfunctioning trash compacter, ultimately set the strike into motion. See Honey, "Martin Luther King, Jr."

67 Benelli, "Sweeping the Streets," 455; City of New York Department of Sanitation, *Doing More with Less*.

68 Benelli, "Sweeping the Streets," 454.

69 Benelli, "Sweeping the Streets," 456; see also Goldberg, "Welfare Recipients or Workers?"

70 For a longer history of the relationship between welfare and work, see Piven and Cloward, *Regulating the Poor*.

71 See Schram, *After Welfare*.

72 Weeks, *Problem with Work*, 7.

73 Weeks, *Problem with Work*, 12.

74 Delany, *Through the Valley*, 59.

75 Delany, *Through the Valley*, 79.

76 Weeks, *Problem with Work*, 8 (emphasis mine).

77 Delany, *Through the Valley*, 225.

78 Delany, *Through the Valley*, 271.

79 Delany, *Through the Valley*, 271.

80 Delany, *Through the Valley*, 271.

81 For more on Delany and his depictions of enslavement within interracial BDSM scenarios, see Scott, *Extravagant Abjection*.

82 As Sunaura Taylor observes, the politico-economic shift to industrialism and the sale of labor-power "lessened the ability of impaired people to make meaningful contributions to their households," as they could not produce at the rates determined by capitalist production ("Right Not to Work"). See also Gleeson, *Geographies of Disability*.

83 Social Security Administration, "Understanding SSI Eligibility Requirements."

84 Frye, "Cripping the 'Crack Baby' Epidemic," 85.

85 For instance, in their "Ten Principles of Disability Justice," Sins Invalid states that they "value our people as they are, for who they are, and understand that people have inherent worth outside of capitalist notions of productivity" (Berne et al., 228).

86 Taylor, "Right Not to Work."

87 Delany, *Through the Valley*, 74.

88 Delany, *Through the Valley*, 240.

89 Delany, *Through the Valley*, 388, 389, 391.

90 Delany, *Through the Valley*, 740, 741.

91 Delany, *Through the Valley*, 741.

92 Weeks, *Problem with Work*, 29.

93 Delany, *Through the Valley*, 387.

94 Delany, *Through the Valley*, 387.

95 Delany, *Through the Valley*, 387–88.

96 Delany, *Through the Valley*, 389.

97 Delany, *Through the Valley*, 271.

98 Delany, *Through the Valley*, 271.

99 Delany, *Through the Valley*, 387.

100 Delany, *Through the Valley*, 400.

101 Delany, *Through the Valley*, 517.

102 Delany, *Through the Valley*, 518.

103 Delany, *Through the Valley*, 519.

104 Delany, *Through the Valley*, 219.

105 Delany, *Through the Valley*, 503.

106 Delany, *Through the Valley*, 97 (emphasis in original).

107 Weeks, *Problem with Work*, 64. See also Mink, *Welfare's End*; and Collins, "Afro-American Work/Family Nexus."

108 Lévi-Strauss, *Elementary Structures of Kinship*, 32.

109 Rubin writes, "The Oedipal crisis is precipitated by certain items of information. The children discover the differences between the sexes, and that each child must become one or the other gender. They also discover the incest taboo, and that some sexuality is prohibited—in this case, the mother is unavailable to either child because she 'belongs' to the father" ("Traffic in Women," 193).

110 See Freud, *Three Essays*.

111 Delany, *Through the Valley*, 293.

112 Delany, *Through the Valley*, 293.

113 Piaget, *Language and Thought*.

114 Eng, *Feeling of Kinship*, 16.

115 For more on crip temporalities and crip time, see Kafer, *Feminist, Queer, Crip*; and Samuels, "Six Ways."

116 Delany, *Through the Valley*, 82.

117 Delany, *Through the Valley*, 465.

118 Delany, *Through the Valley*, 466.

119 See Abdur-Rahman, *Against the Closet*.

120 Abdur-Rahman, *Against the Closet*, 116, 117.

121 To note, this attachment is expressed in a number of ways throughout the novel, not the least of which is Eric's sexual delight in being called a n—.

122 Delany, *Through the Valley*, 419.

123 Delany, *Through the Valley*, 419.

124 Freeman, "Queer Belongings," 299.

125 Abdur-Rahman, *Against the Closet*, 127.

126 Delany, *Through the Valley*, 28.

127 Delany, *Through the Valley*, 731.

128 Delany, *Through the Valley*, 560, 562.

129 Delany, *Through the Valley*, 561.

130 Delany, *Through the Valley*, 761.

131 Shaviro, "Through the Valley"; Delany, *Through the Valley*, 440.

132 Delany, *Through the Valley*, 371.

133 *Ethics* theorizes a monistic metaphysics that understands God as a singular substance, in which every living entity is either God or a mode of God, with modes

defined as "things that . . . are dependent on other things" (Hampe, Renz, and Schnepf, introduction to *Spinoza's "Ethics,"* 6).

134 Delany, *Through the Valley,* 542.

3. Lines of Transit, Migration, Mobility

1 Butler, *Sower,* 210.
2 For more on Lauren Olamina as a disabled character, see Schalk, *Bodyminds Reimagined*; Pickens, "Aesthetics of the Novel"; Bailey and Jamieson, "Palimpsests"; Hinton, "Making Do"; Whatcott, "Crip Collectivity"; and Piepzna-Samarasinha, *Care Work.*
3 Butler, *Sower,* 210.
4 Butler, *Sower,* 80.
5 Yamashita, *Tropic,* 35.
6 Yamashita, *Tropic,* 57.
7 Yamashita, *Tropic,* 57.
8 Yamashita, *Tropic,* 57.
9 Yamashita, *Tropic,* 57.
10 In *Bodyminds Reimagined,* Sami Schalk uses the term *(dis)ability* to highlight ability and disability as a mutually constitutive system of meaning, arguing that the term "highlights the mutual dependency of disability and ability to define each other" (6). Building on Schalk, I use the term *dis-/enabling* to capture the relationship of ability to disability within processes of infrastructural violence, in which the hyper-ability of elite classes produces debilitation for vulnerable classes. See Schalk, *Bodyminds Reimagined.*
11 See Chang, *Disposable Domestics*; and Marchevsky and Theoharis, *Not Working.*
12 Marchevsky and Theoharis, *Not Working,* 35.
13 Banham, *Los Angeles,* 5.
14 Villa, *Barrio-Logos.*
15 Villa, *Barrio-Logos,* 84.
16 Manzanas and Benito, *Cities, Borders, and Spaces,* 54.
17 Yamashita, *Tropic.*
18 Butler, *Sower,* 165.
19 Butler, *Sower,* 166.
20 Rowell, "Interview with Octavia E. Butler," 62.
21 Butler, *Sower,* 116.
22 Yamashita and Imafuku, "Latitude of the Fiction Writer."
23 Yamashita, *Tropic,* 55.
24 Lefebvre, *Production of Space,* 53.
25 Meyer, "Shaping of Purpose," 27.

26   See Kim, "Cripping East Los Angeles."

27   Goodman, *After the Planners*, 67; Villa, *Barrio-Logos*, 71.

28   For more on the social model, see Shakespeare, "Social Model of Disability"; and Oliver, "Thirty Years On."

29   See Erevelles, *Disability and Difference*.

30   Butler, *Sower*, 166.

31   Butler, *Sower*, 232.

32   Wendell, *Rejected Body*.

33   Wendell, *Rejected Body*, 37.

34   Butler, *Sower*, 12.

35   Butler, *Sower*, 169.

36   Yamashita, *Tropic*, 206.

37   Yamashita, *Tropic*, 207.

38   Yamashita, *Tropic*, 27.

39   Yamashita, *Tropic*, 189–90.

40   Displaying what the LA historian Scott Kurashige terms "the two-sided face of postwar development," the growth of the freeway system repatterned Los Angeles's lifestyles and landscapes, facilitating the exportation of wealth to the suburbs while splitting the social and economic fabric of the inner city (*Shifting Grounds of Race*, 240). As Kurashige and others have noted, the unfolding of the freeways devastated communities of color, many of whom viewed themselves as "the sacrificial lambs of freeway planners" (241).

41   Yamashita, *Tropic*, 82.

42   Yamashita, *Tropic*, 33.

43   I borrow this concept from Bill Brown's "Thing Theory," where he writes, "We begin to confront the thingness of objects when they stop working for us: when the drill breaks . . . when their flow within the circuits of production and distribution, consumption and exhibition, has been arrested, however momentarily" (4).

44   Yamashita, *Tropic*, 26.

45   Thoma, "Traveling the Distances," 7.

46   Hong, *Ruptures of American Capital*, 134–135. See also Chacón and Davis, *No One is Illegal*.

47   Minich, *Accessible Citizenships*, 2.

48   US Citizenship and Immigration Services, "Early American Immigration Policies."

49   Chang, *Disposable Domestics*, 2.

50   See Brown, *Black Utopias*; Rivera, "Future Histories and Cyborg Labor"; and Allen, "Octavia Butler's *Parable* Novels."

51   Butler, *Sower*, 78.

52   Butler, *Sower*, 307.

53   Butler, *Sower*, 307.

54   See Jackson and Butler, "Sci-Fi Tales"; and Cobb, "Interview with Octavia Butler."

55 Cobb, "Interview with Octavia Butler," 55.

56 Cobb, "Interview with Octavia Butler," 55.

57 Marchevsky and Theoharis, *Not Working*, 16.

58 Butler, *Sower*, 280.

59 Butler, *Sower*, 202.

60 Butler, *Sower*, 10, 109.

61 Butler, *Sower*, 116.

62 Butler, *Sower*, 116.

63 Butler, *Sower*, 273.

64 Butler, *Sower*, 273, 274.

65 Butler, *Sower*, 167, 191.

66 Schalk, *Bodyminds Reimagined*, 103. For more on the genre of critical dystopia, see Moylan, *Demand the Impossible*.

67 Chang, *Disposable Domestics*, 3.

68 Butler, *Sower*, 26.

69 Butler, *Sower*, 307.

70 Butler, *Sower*, 307.

71 Butler, *Sower*, 78.

72 Butler, *Sower*, 111.

73 Butler, *Sower*, 111.

74 Butler, *Sower*, 112.

75 Butler, *Sower*, 111–12.

76 Butler, *Sower*, 113.

77 Butler, *Sower*, 112.

78 Butler, *Sower*, 113.

79 Chang, *Disposable Domestics*, 124.

80 Yamashita, *Tropic*, 91, 130.

81 Yamashita, *Tropic*, 37. I borrow the term *global city* from Saskia Sassen, who uses it to describe cities whose economic significance and activity are extranational. See Sassen, *Global City*.

82 Chang, *Disposable Domestics*, 3.

83 For more on racialized immigrant women's labor, see Hong, *Ruptures of American Capital*.

84 Yamashita, *Tropic*, 200 (emphasis in original).

85 Yamashita, *Tropic*, 79.

86 Yamashita, *Tropic*, 16.

87 Yamashita, *Tropic*, 3.

88 Yamashita, *Tropic*, 5.

89 Yamashita, *Tropic*, 80.

90 Yamashita, *Tropic*, 237.

91 See Simone, "People as Infrastructure."

92 David Harvey coined the term *time-space compression* in *The Condition of Post-modernity* to refer to the condensation of space through advanced technologies of telecommunication and transit, a shift concomitant with the increasing rate of capital turnover.

93 See Sassen, "Global City."

94 Yamashita, *Tropic*, 200, 162.

95 Sassen, "Global City," 81 (emphasis mine).

96 Yamashita, *Tropic*, 145.

97 Yamashita, *Tropic*, 143.

98 Yamashita, *Tropic*, 146.

99 Yamashita, *Tropic*, 200.

100 Yamashita, *Tropic*, 37.

101 Savarese and Savarese, "Superior Half of Speaking."

102 Yamashita, *Tropic*, 57.

103 Yamashita, *Tropic*, 110.

104 Yamashita, *Tropic*, 35; Willse, *Value of Homelessness*, 94.

105 Willse, *Value of Homelessness*, 95.

106 For more on disability and deinstitutionalization, see Ben-Moshe, *Decarcerating Disability*.

107 Yamashita, *Tropic*, 122.

108 Sins Invalid, "This October."

109 Alexander, *Pedagogies of Crossing*, 6, 8.

110 Yamashita, *Tropic*, 57.

111 Yamashita, *Tropic*, 57.

112 In *The Production of Space*, Lefebvre states that abstract space "carries within it the seeds of a new kind of space . . . 'differential space'" (52). Such a space carries the potential for "the dissolution of old relations on the one hand and the generation of new relations on the other" (52).

113 Yamashita, *Tropic*, 37.

114 Yamashita, *Tropic*, 34.

115 Bennett, *Vibrant Matter*, 24.

116 Yamashita, *Tropic*, 34.

117 Bennett, *Vibrant Matter*, 32.

118 Yaeger, "Dreaming of Infrastructure," 17; Yamashita, *Tropic*, 57.

119 Yamashita, *Tropic*, 34, 35.

120 "Distributive agency," according to Jane Bennett, is an understanding of agency in which a "subject" is not "the root cause of an effect"; rather, "there are instead always a swarm of vitalities at play" (*Vibrant Matter*, 32).

121 Yamashita, *Tropic*, 57.

122 Rubenstein, Robbins, and Beal, "Infrastructuralism," 576. Rubenstein, Robbins, and Beal further note infrastructure's proximity to the sublime, writing, "Because of

[its] very vastness . . . infrastructure tends to have the same stupefying effect as the Kantian sublime" (576). To note, the mathematical sublime is not the only Kantian sublime—Kant also elaborates on the category of the dynamically sublime.

123 Yaeger, "Dreaming of Infrastructure," 15.

124 Kant, *Critique of Judgement*, 85; Yamashita, *Tropic*, 56–57. Emphasis in original.

125 For instance, on the relationship between Yamashita's use of magical realism and border politics, Anne Mai Yee Jansen asserts that *Tropic* "[uses] Los Angeles as a microcosm of border politics, depicting the city as the center of social change" ("(Dis)Integrating Borders," 106). On the border politics of *Tropic*, see also Ling, *Across Meridians*; Hsu, "*Tropic of Orange* and Chaos Theory"; Rody, *Interethnic Imagination*; Lee, "We Are Not the World"; and Mermann-Jozwiak, "Yamashita's Post-National Spaces."

126 Yamashita, *Tropic*, 253, 254.

127 Manzanas and Benito, *Cities, Borders, and Spaces*, 54.

128 Yamashita, *Tropic*, 57, 56.

129 Yamashita, *Tropic*, 57.

130 Yamashita, *Tropic*, 193. I borrow the language of "unboundedness" from Ana Mª Manzanas and Jesús Benito's discussion of *Tropic*, in which they conceptualize Yamashita's Los Angeles as an enactment of the urban geographer Edward Soja's concept of the *postmetropolis*, which examines the disaggregation of lines, borders, walls, and boundaries in contemporary cities. They write, "Within the two simultaneous processes of *unbounding* the city and *unbounding* the wall, [Yamashita] introduces a real crossing, a collision of races, classes, and realities on the freeway, the very premises of freedom" (*Cities, Borders, and Spaces*, 50). See Soja, *Postmodern Geographies*.

131 Yamashita, *Tropic*, 259.

132 Rubenstein, Robbins, and Beal, "Infrastructuralism," 577.

133 Yamashita, *Tropic*, 57.

134 Yamashita, *Tropic*, 35; Butler, *Sower*, 210.

135 Butler, *Sower*, 210.

136 Alexander, *Pedagogies of Crossing*, 8.

137 Butler, *Sower*, 280, 210.

138 Alexander, *Pedagogies of Crossing*, 326.

139 Alexander, *Pedagogies of Crossing*, 326.

140 For more on this analysis and conversation, see Schalk, *Bodyminds Reimagined*.

141 Schalk, *Bodyminds Reimagined*, 100.

142 Butler, *Sower*, 12.

143 Butler, *Sower*, 12.

144 Butler, *Sower*, 12.

145 Butler, *Sower*, 167.

146 Hinton, "Making Do," 173.

147 Butler, *Sower*, 162.

148 Butler, *Sower*, 162.

149 Butler, *Sower*, 162.

150 Butler, *Sower*, 191.

151 Butler, *Sower*, 200.

152 Butler, *Sower*, 271.

153 Berne et al., "Ten Principles of Disability Justice," 229.

154 Gumbs, "Shape of My Impact."

155 Butler, *Sower*, 200.

156 Butler, *Sower*, 245.

157 Butler, *Sower*, 242.

158 Butler, *Sower*, 108.

159 Butler, *Sower*, 108.

160 Butler, *Sower*, 73.

161 Berne et al., "Ten Principles of Disability Justice," 228.

162 Butler, *Sower*, 299.

163 Butler, *Sower*, 166; Alexander, *Pedagogies of Crossing*, 7.

164 See Nilges, "We Need the Stars."

165 Yamashita, *Tropic*, 238.

166 Yamashita, *Tropic*, 254.

167 Butler, *Sower*, 5.

4. Care at the End of the World

1 Wong, "My Medicaid."

2 Tillmon, "Welfare Is a Women's Issue."

3 I use the slash to separate *health* from *care* to trouble the relationship between these terms and their usage in the US medical-industrial complex and to call into question how mainstream medicine defines both *health* and *care*. Health/care, as it presently operates, does not always or perhaps even regularly offer affirming and sustaining care to patients, particularly those at the intersection of multiple oppressions.

4 Alondra Nelson, in *Body and Soul: The Black Panther Party and the Fight against Medical Discrimination*, offers a useful description of the medical-industrial complex, which she defines as "health radicals' term for the confluence of business interests, the medical profession, the insurance industry, and pharmaceutical companies that drove the commodification of healthcare" (12).

5 Levins Morales, *Kindling*, 10.

6 The disability scholar Akemi Nishida introduces the term *US public healthcare assemblage* to name one portion of this infrastructural network. This assemblage is made up of disabled people receiving paid attendant care, often through Medicaid or other forms of state support, and the racialized immigrant women of color

who serve as their (often poorly paid) home health aides. See Nishida, "Relating through Differences."

7   Piepzna-Samarasinha, *Care Work*, 122.
8   Piepzna-Samarasinha, *Tonguebreaker*, 13.
9   Piepzna-Samarasinha, *Tonguebreaker*, 13.
10 Lorde, "Litany for Survival."
11 Piepzna-Samarasinha, *Tonguebreaker*, 139.
12 Berne, "Disability Justice."
13 Berne, "Disability Justice."
14 Berne et al., "Ten Principles."
15 Piepzna-Samarasinha, *Tonguebreaker*, 29, 30.
16 Piepzna-Samarasinha, *Tonguebreaker*, 30.
17 Carter et al., "Babe-ilicious Healing Justice," 1.
18 I draw on Sidonie Smith and Julia Watson's definition of life-writing, which they describe as "writing that takes a life, one's own or another's, as its subject" (*Reading Autobiography*, 4).
19 Piepzna-Samarasinha, *Tonguebreaker*, 78.
20 For more on the disability/illness memoir boom, see Couser, *Recovering Bodies*.
21 See Adams, "Disability Life Writing"; and Mitchell, "Body Solitaire." Mitchell in particular argues that "even the most renowned disability autobiographers often fall prey to an ethos of rugged individualism that can reify the long-standing association of disability with social isolation" ("Body Solitaire," 312).
22 Levins Morales, *Kindling*, i, iv.
23 Levins Morales, *Kindling*, ii (emphasis mine).
24 Levins Morales, *Kindling*, author biography.
25 Smith and Watson, *Reading Autobiography*, 4.
26 Levins Morales, *Kindling*, dedication page.
27 Mulligan and Castañeda, introduction to *Unequal Coverage*, 3.
28 Wong, "My Medicaid."
29 Michener, *Fragmented Democracy*, 37.
30 Weissmann, "Disability Insurance"; McCoy, "Disabled, or Just Desperate?"
31 See Bagenstos, "Americans with Disabilities Act"; and Frye, "Cripping the 'Crack Baby' Epidemic."
32 Hoffman, "What Health Reform Reveals," 56.
33 Levins Morales, *Kindling*, 155.
34 Levins Morales, *Kindling*, 153.
35 Levins Morales, *Kindling*, 31, 49.
36 Levins Morales, *Kindling*, 66.
37 Levins Morales, *Kindling*, 66.
38 Piepzna-Samarasinha, *Tonguebreaker*, 39, 38.
39 Piepzna-Samarasinha, *Tonguebreaker*, 38–39.

40 Erevelles, *Disability and Difference*, 38; Piepzna-Samarasinha, *Tonguebreaker*, 38.

41 Nelson, *Body and Soul*, 11.

42 Levins Morales, *Kindling*, dedication page.

43 Levins Morales, *Kindling*, author biography.

44 Levins Morales, *Kindling*, author biography.

45 Levins Morales, *Kindling*, i.

46 Levins Morales, *Kindling*, 5.

47 Levins Morales, *Kindling*, 155.

48 Piepzna-Samarasinha, *Tonguebreaker*, 29.

49 Piepzna-Samarasinha, *Tonguebreaker*, 29.

50 Piepzna-Samarasinha, *Tonguebreaker*, 29.

51 Piepzna-Samarasinha, *Care Work*, 35.

52 Piepzna-Samarasinha, *The Future Is Disabled*, 329; Mask Oakland (@maskoakland), "Every inspiring Mutual Aid project we know of is pretty burned out right now . . ." Twitter, December 24, 2021, 12:20 a.m., https://twitter.com/maskoakland/status/1474248471385313282.

53 For more information on the term *pod*, see Mingus, "Pods and Pod Mapping."

54 Piepzna-Samarasinha, *Care Work*, 65.

55 Levins Morales, *Kindling*, iii.

56 Levins Morales, *Kindling*, iii.

57 For more on crip temporalities and crip time, see Kafer, *Feminist, Queer, Crip*; and Samuels, "Six Ways."

58 Levins Morales, *Kindling*, 95.

59 Byrd, "Create Your Own Fire," 19.

60 Levins Morales, *Kindling*, 96; Lorde, "Burst of Light," 122.

61 Lorde, "Burst of Light," 103.

62 Levins Morales, *Kindling*, 95.

63 Levins Morales, *Kindling*, 95.

64 Levins Morales, *Kindling*, 100.

65 Levins Morales, *Kindling*, 155.

66 Levins Morales, *Kindling*, 101.

67 Levins Morales, *Kindling*, 101.

68 Auyero, *Patients of the State*, 2. Emphasis is in the original.

69 Levins Morales, *Kindling*, 57.

70 Auyero, *Patients of the State*, 6.

71 Piepzna-Samarasinha, *Care Work*, 65.

72 Piepzna-Samarasinha, *Tonguebreaker*, 71.

73 Levins Morales, *Kindling*, 99.

74 Piepzna-Samarasinha, *Tonguebreaker*, 125.

75 Piepzna-Samarasinha, *Tonguebreaker*, 40.

76 Piepzna-Samarasinha, *Tonguebreaker*, 70.

77　See Chang, "Reimagining Revolution." For more on prefigurative politics, see Boggs, "Marxism, Prefigurative Communism."

78　Flanders and Friends, "Beyond Disability Rights," at 4:51.

79　Piepzna-Samarasinha, *Tonguebreaker*, 14.

80　Piepzna-Samarasinha, *Tonguebreaker*, 14.

81　Piepzna-Samarasinha, *Tonguebreaker*, 14.

82　Stein, "'No Cuts to Medicaid!'"

83　Piepzna-Samarasinha, *Tonguebreaker*, author biography.

84　Smith, "Autobiographical Manifesto," 194.

85　Piepzna-Samarasinha, *Tonguebreaker*, 19.

86　Piepzna-Samarasinha, *Tonguebreaker*, 21.

87　Piepzna-Samarasinha, *Tonguebreaker*, 21–22 (emphasis in original).

88　Kafer, *Feminist, Queer, Crip*, 3.

89　Kafer, *Feminist, Queer, Crip*, 2.

90　Piepzna-Samarasinha, *Tonguebreaker*, 42.

91　See Manning, "Magic Wand."

92　Piepzna-Samarasinha, *Tonguebreaker*, 26.

93　See Williams, "Neil Marcus Dies at 67."

94　Piepzna-Samarasinha, *Tonguebreaker*, 27.

95　Piepzna-Samarasinha, *Tonguebreaker*, 25, 26.

96　Piepzna-Samarasinha, *Care Work*, 35.

97　Piepzna-Samarasinha, *Care Work*, 37.

98　Piepzna-Samarasinha, *Care Work*, 46.

99　Piepzna-Samarasinha, *Tonguebreaker*, 28.

100　Piepzna-Samarasinha, *Tonguebreaker*, 26.

101　Piepzna-Samarasinha, *Tonguebreaker*, 27.

102　Shange, *For Colored Girls*, 63.

103　Alexander, *Pedagogies of Crossing*, 326.

104　Piepzna-Samarasinha, *Tonguebreaker*, 99.

105　Piepzna-Samarasinha, *Tonguebreaker*, 99.

106　Alexander, *Pedagogies of Crossing*, 326.

107　Piepzna-Samarasinha, *Tonguebreaker*, 100.

108　Piepzna-Samarasinha, *Tonguebreaker*, 101.

109　Piepzna-Samarasinha, *Tonguebreaker*, 109; Anzaldúa, "Speaking in Tongues."

110　Piepzna-Samarasinha, *Tonguebreaker*, 106.

111　Muñoz, *Cruising Utopia*, 27.

112　Piepzna-Samarasinha, *Tonguebreaker*, 125.

113　Piepzna-Samarasinha, *Tonguebreaker*, 110.

114　Berne et al., "Ten Principles."

115　Piepzna-Samarasinha, *Tonguebreaker*, 43.

116　Piepzna-Samarasinha, *Tonguebreaker*, 43.

117 Piepzna-Samarasinha, *Tonguebreaker*, 43.

118 Piepzna-Samarasinha, *Tonguebreaker*, 43.

119 Piepzna-Samarasinha, *Tonguebreaker*, 44.

120 Piepzna-Samarasinha, *Tonguebreaker*, 44.

121 Levins Morales, *Kindling*, 7.

122 Piepzna-Samarasinha, *Tonguebreaker*, 110; Levins Morales, *Kindling*, 7.

123 Levins Morales, *Kindling*, 148.

124 Levins Morales, *Kindling*, 96.

125 Levins Morales, *Kindling*, 97.

126 Levins Morales, *Kindling*, 96.

127 Levins Morales, *Kindling*, 97.

128 Levins Morales, *Kindling*, 154.

129 Levins Morales, *Kindling*, 10.

130 Piepzna-Samarasinha, *Tonguebreaker*, 103.

131 Levins Morales, *Kindling*, 150.

132 Levins Morales, *Kindling*, 122, 126, 122.

133 Piepzna-Samarasinha, *Tonguebreaker*, 106.

134 Levins Morales, *Kindling*, 156.

135 Berne et al., "Ten Principles," 228.

136 Piepzna-Samarasinha, *Tonguebreaker*, 125.

137 Piepzna-Samarasinha, *Tonguebreaker*, 44.

Epilogue

1 Piepzna-Samarasinha, *Tonguebreaker*, 13.

2 Piepzna-Samarasinha, *Tonguebreaker*, 44.

3 Morrison, *Sula*, 52.

4 Kim, "Love in the Time of Sickness."

5 Alexander, *Pedagogies of Crossing*, 269.

6 Piepzna-Samarasinha, *Tonguebreaker*, 109.

7 Chee, *How to Write*, 74.

8 Chee, *How to Write*, 79.

9 Chee, *How to Write*, 88.

10 Chee, *How to Write*, 90.

11 Chee, *How to Write*, 90.

12 Chee, *How to Write*, 91.

13 Chee, *How to Write*, 79.

14 Piepzna-Samarasinha, *Tonguebreaker*, 48.

15 Alexander, *Pedagogies of Crossing*, 326.

16 Piepzna-Samarasinha, *Tonguebreaker*, 123.

Bibliography

ABC News. "Troops Told 'Shoot to Kill' in New Orleans." September 2, 2005. https://www.abc.net.au/news/2005-09-02/troops-told-shoot-to-kill-in-new-orleans/2094678.

Abdur-Rahman, Aliyyah. *Against the Closet: Black Political Longing and the Erotics of Race*. Durham, NC: Duke University Press, 2012.

Abramovitz, Mimi. *Regulating the Lives of Women: Social Welfare Policy from Colonial Times to the Present*. Boston: South End Press, 1998.

Adams, Rachel. "Disability Life Writing and the Problem of Dependency in *The Autobiography of Gaby Brimmer*." *Journal of Medical Humanities* 38, no. 1 (2017): 39–50. https://doi.org/10.1007/s10912-016-9421-5.

Alexander, M. Jacqui. *Pedagogies of Crossing: Meditations on Feminism, Sexual Politics, Memory, and the Sacred*. Durham, NC: Duke University Press, 2006.

Allen, Marlene D. "Octavia Butler's *Parable* Novels and the 'Boomerang' of African American History." *Callaloo* 32, no. 4 (2009): 1353–65. https://doi.org/10.1353/cal.0.0541.

Anzaldúa, Gloria, ed. *Making Face, Making Soul / Haciendo Caras: Creative and Critical Perspectives by Feminists of Color*. San Francisco: Aunt Lute Books, 1990.

Anzaldúa, Gloria. "Speaking in Tongues: A Letter to Third World Women Writers." In *This Bridge Called My Back: Writings by Radical Women of Color*, 4th ed., edited by Cherríe Moraga and Gloria Anzaldúa, 163–72. Albany: SUNY Press, 2015.

Auyero, Javier. *Patients of the State: The Politics of Waiting in Argentina*. Durham, NC: Duke University Press, 2012.

Bagenstos, Samuel. "The Americans with Disabilities Act as Welfare Reform." *William and Mary Law Review* 44, no. 3 (2003): 921–1027.

Bailey, Moya, and Ayana A. H. Jamieson. "Guest Editors' Introduction: Palimpsests in the Life and Work of Octavia E. Butler." *Palimpsest* 6, no. 2 (2017): v–xiii.

Bailey, Moya, and Izetta Autumn Mobley. "Work in the Intersections: A Black Feminist Disability Framework." *Gender and Society* 33, no. 1 (2019): 19–40. https://doi.org/10.1177/0891243218801523.

Banham, Reyner. *Los Angeles: The Architecture of Four Ecologies*. New York: Penguin Books, 1971.

Bares, Annie. "'Each Unbearable Day': Narrative Ruthlessness and Environmental and Reproductive Injustice in Jesmyn Ward's *Salvage the Bones*." *MELUS: Multi-Ethnic*

Literature of the United States 44, no. 3 (2019): 21–40. https://doi.org/10.1093/melus/mlz022.

Bell, Chris. "I'm Not the Man I Used to Be." In *Sex and Disability*, edited by Robert McRuer and Anna Mollow, 208–28. Durham, NC: Duke University Press, 2012.

Benelli, Natalie. "Sweeping the Streets of the Neoliberal City: Racial and Class Divisions among New York City's Sanitation Workers." *Journal of Workplace Rights* 16, no. 3 (2011): 453–74. https://doi.org/10.2190/WR.16.3-4.l.

Ben-Moshe, Liat. *Decarcerating Disability: Deinstitutionalization and Prison Abolition.* Minneapolis: University of Minnesota Press, 2020.

Bennett, Jane. *Vibrant Matter: A Political Ecology of Things.* Durham, NC: Duke University Press, 2010.

Berkowitz, Edward D., and Larry DeWitt. *The Other Welfare: Supplemental Security Income and U.S. Social Policy.* Ithaca, NY: Cornell University Press, 2013.

Berne, Patricia. "Disability Justice—a Working Draft by Patty Berne." *Sins Invalid*, June 10, 2015. https://www.sinsinvalid.org/blog/disability-justice-a-working-draft-by-patty-berne.

Berne, Patricia, Aurora Levins Morales, David Langstaff, and Sins Invalid. "Ten Principles of Disability Justice." *WSQ: Women's Studies Quarterly* 46, no. 1 & 2 (2018): 227–30. https://doi.org/10.1353/wsq.2018.0003.

Bersani, Leo. "Is the Rectum a Grave?" *October* 43 (Winter 1987): 197–222.

Bhattacharya, Tithi. "Introduction: Mapping Social Reproduction Theory." In *Social Reproduction Theory: Remapping Class, Recentering Oppression*, edited by Tithi Bhattacharya, 1–20. London: Pluto Press, 2017.

Boggs, Carl. "Marxism, Prefigurative Communism, and the Problem of Workers' Control." *Radical America* 11, no. 6 (1977): 99–122.

Bolaki, Stella. "Challenging Invisibility, Making Connections: Illness, Survival, and Black Struggles in Audre Lorde's Work." In *Blackness and Disability: Critical Examinations and Cultural Interventions*, edited by Christopher M. Bell, 47–74. East Lansing: Michigan State University Press, 2011.

Boris, Eileen, and Rhacel Salazar Parreñas. *Intimate Labors: Cultures, Technologies, and the Politics of Care.* Redwood City, CA: Stanford University Press, 2010.

brown, adrienne maree. *Pleasure Activism: The Politics of Feeling Good.* Chico, CA: AK Press, 2019.

Brown, Bill. "Thing Theory." *Critical Inquiry* 28, no. 1 (2001): 1–22. https://doi.org/10.1086/449030.

Brown, Jayna. *Black Utopias: Speculative Life and the Music of Other Worlds.* Durham, NC: Duke University Press, 2021.

Bucher, Michael, and Simon Dickel. "An Affinity for the Lumpen: Depictions of Homelessness in Delany's *Bread and Wine* and *The Mad Man*." *African American Review* 48, no. 3 (2015): 289–304. https://doi.org/10.1353/afa.2015.0023.

Butler, Octavia E. *Parable of the Sower.* London: Headline, 2019.

Byrd, Rudolph P. "Introduction: Create Your Own Fire: Audre Lorde and the Tradition of Black Radical Thought." In *I Am Your Sister: Collected and Unpublished Writings of Audre Lorde*, edited by Rudolph P. Byrd, Johnnetta Betsch Cole, and Beverly Guy-Sheftall, 3–38. Oxford: Oxford University Press, 2009.

Carter, Tieraney, Rico Kleinstein Chenyek, M'kali-Hashiki, Marcelo Felipe Garzo Montalvo, Leah Lakshmi Piepzna-Samarasinha, and Jonah Aline Daniel. "A Babe-ilicious Healing Justice Statement from the BadAss Visionary Healers (BAVH)." *Nineteen Sixty-Nine: An Ethnic Studies Journal* 2, no. 1 (2013): 1–13.

Chacón, Justin Akers, and Mike Davis. *No One Is Illegal: Fighting Racism and State Violence on the U.S.-Mexico Border*. Chicago: Haymarket Books, 2006.

Chambers-Letson, Joshua. *After the Party: A Manifesto for Queer of Color Life*. New York: New York University Press, 2018.

Chang, Grace. *Disposable Domestics: Immigrant Women Workers in the Global Economy*. Cambridge, MA: South End Press, 2000.

Chang, Momo. "Reimagining Revolution: Q&A with Grace Lee Boggs." *Hyphen: Asian America Unabridged*, March 1, 2012. https://hyphenmagazine.com/blog/2012/03/reimagining-revolution-qa-grace-lee-boggs.

Chee, Alexander. *How to Write an Autobiographical Novel: Essays*. Boston: Mariner Books, 2018.

Chinn, Sarah E. "Feeling Her Way: Audre Lorde and the Power of Touch." *GLQ: A Journal of Lesbian and Gay Studies* 9, no. 1 (2003): 181–204.

Choy, Catherine Ceniza. *Empire of Care: Nursing and Migration in Filipino American History*. Durham, NC: Duke University Press, 2003.

City of New York Department of Sanitation. *2009 Annual Report: Doing More with Less*. New York: City of New York Department of Sanitation, 2009. https://dsny.cityofnewyork.us/wp-content/uploads/2017/12/about_2009_Annual_Report_0915.pdf.

Clift, Eleanor. "Reagan Condemns Welfare System, Says It's Made Poverty Worse instead of Better." *Los Angeles Times*, February 16, 1986. https://www.latimes.com/archives/la-xpm-1986-02-16-mn-8585-story.html.

Clintonlibrary42. "Pres. Clinton Signing Welfare Reform (1996)." YouTube, February 18, 2016, 28:36. https://www.youtube.com/watch?v=siuSgG_6xKc.

Cobb, Jelani. "Interview with Octavia Butler." In *Conversations with Octavia Butler*, edited by Conseula Francis, 49–64. Oxford: University Press of Mississippi, 2009.

Cohen, Cathy. "Punks, Bulldaggers, and Welfare Queens: The Radical Potential of Queer Politics?" *GLQ: A Journal of Lesbian and Gay Studies* 3, no. 4 (1997): 437–65.

Cohen, Cathy, and Sarah J. Jackson. "Ask a Feminist: A Conversation with Cathy J. Cohen on Black Lives Matter, Feminism, and Contemporary Activism." *Signs: Journal of Women in Culture and Society* 41, no. 4 (Summer 2016): 775–92.

Collins, Patricia Hill. "The Afro-American Work/Family Nexus: An Exploratory Analysis." *Western Journal of Black Studies* 10, no. 3 (1986): 148–55.

Collins, Patricia Hill. *Black Feminist Thought: Knowledge, Consciousness, and the Politics of Empowerment.* New York: Routledge, 2009.

Collins, Patricia Hill. "Shifting the Center: Race, Class, and Feminist Theorizing about Motherhood." In *Mothering: Ideology, Experience and Agency,* edited by Evelyn Nakano Glenn, Grace Chang, and Linda Rennie Forcey, 45–66. New York: Routledge, 1994.

Couser, G. Thomas. *Recovering Bodies: Illness, Disability, and Life Writing.* Madison: University of Wisconsin Press, 1997.

Davis, Lennard. "Nude Venuses, Medusa's Body, and Phantom Limbs: Disability and Visuality." In *The Body and Physical Difference: Discourses of Disability,* edited by Sharon L. Snyder and David T. Mitchell, 51–70. Ann Arbor: University of Michigan Press, 1997.

Delany, Samuel R. *Shorter Views: Queer Thoughts and The Politics of the Paraliterary.* Middletown, CT: Wesleyan University Press, 1999.

Delany, Samuel R. *Through the Valley of the Nest of Spiders.* Printed by the author, 2019.

Delany, Samuel R. *Times Square Red, Times Square Blue.* New York: New York University Press, 1999.

Doane, Janice, and Devon Hodges. *Telling Incest: Narratives of Dangerous Remembering from Stein to Sapphire.* Ann Arbor: University of Michigan Press, 2001.

Dohmen, Josh. "Disability as Abject: Kristeva, Disability, and Resistance." *Hypatia* 31 (2016): 762–78.

Donegan, Moira. "How Domestic Labor Became Infrastructure." *Atlantic,* April 14, 2021. https://www.theatlantic.com/ideas/archive/2021/04/why-care-work -infrastructure/618588/.

Dubey, Madhu. *Signs and Cities: Black Literary Postmodernism.* Chicago: University of Chicago Press, 2003.

Edwards, Erica R. "Sex after the Black Normal." *Differences* 26, no. 1 (2015): 141–67. https://doi.org/10.1215/10407391-2880636.

Eldred, Janet Carey, and Peter Mortensen. "Reading Literacy Narratives." *College English* 54, no. 5 (1992): 512–39. https://doi.org/10.2307/378153.

Ellison, Ralph. *Invisible Man.* New York: Vintage International, 1995.

Eng, David. *The Feeling of Kinship: Queer Liberalism and the Racialization of Intimacy.* Durham, NC: Duke University Press, 2010.

Erevelles, Nirmala. *Disability and Difference in Global Contexts: Enabling a Transformative Body Politic.* New York: Palgrave Macmillan, 2011.

Ferguson, Roderick A. *Aberrations in Black: Toward a Queer of Color Critique.* Minneapolis: University of Minnesota Press, 2003.

Fjord, Lakshmi. "Disasters, Race, and Disability: [Un]Seen through the Political Lens on Katrina." *Journal of Race and Policy* 3, no. 1 (2007): 46–66.

Flanders, Laura, and Friends. "Beyond Disability Rights; Disability Justice: Leah Lak-shmi Piepzna-Samarasinha." YouTube, June 30, 2015, 26:02. https://www.youtube.com/watch?v=n_sw6Hjtfg8.

Ford, Douglas. "Crossroads and Cross-Currents in *Invisible Man*." MFS *Modern Fiction Studies* 45, no. 4 (Winter 1999): 887–904.

Fraser, Nancy. "Contradictions of Capital and Care." *New Left Review*, no. 100 (August 2016): 99–117.

Fraser, Nancy, and Linda Gordon. "A Genealogy of Dependency: Tracing a Keyword of the U.S. Welfare State." *Signs* 19, no. 2 (1994): 209–336.

Freeman, Elizabeth. "Queer Belongings: Kinship Theory and Queer Theory." In *A Companion to Lesbian, Gay, Bisexual, Transgender, and Queer Studies*, edited by George E. Haggerty and Molly McGarry, 295–314. Hoboken, NJ: Wiley-Blackwell, 2007.

Freud, Sigmund. *Three Essays on the Theory of Sexuality: The 1905 Edition*. Translated by Ulrike Kistner. New York: Verso Books, 2017.

Frye, Lezlie. "Birthing Disability, Reproducing Race: Uneasy Intersections in Post–Civil Rights Politics of U.S. Citizenship." PhD diss., New York University, 2016.

Frye, Lezlie. "Cripping the 'Crack Baby' Epidemic: A Feminist Disability Genealogy of Welfare Reform." *Feminist Formations* 34, no. 2 (2022): 69–98. https://doi.org/10.1353/ff.2022.0023.

Garland-Thomson, Rosemarie. "Integrating Disability, Transforming Feminist Theory." NWSA *Journal* 14, no. 3 (2002): 1–32. https://doi.org/10.1353/nwsa.2003.0005.

Gates, Henry Louis. "Introduction: Writing 'Race' and the Difference It Makes." In *"Race," Writing, and Difference*, edited by Henry Louis Gates, 1–20. Chicago: University of Chicago Press, 1985.

Gilmore, Ruth Wilson. *Golden Gulag: Prisons, Surplus, Crisis, and Opposition in Globalizing California*. Berkeley: University of California Press, 2007.

Gilmore, Ruth Wilson, and Craig Gilmore. "Beyond Bratton." In *Policing the Planet: Why the Policing Crisis Led to Black Lives Matter*, edited by Jordan T. Camp and Christina Heatherton, 173–99. New York: Verso, 2016.

Giroux, Henry. "Reading Hurricane Katrina: Race, Class, and the Biopolitics of Disposability." *College Literature* 33, no. 3 (2006): 171–96. https://doi.org/10.1353/lit.2006.0037.

Gleeson, Brendan. *Geographies of Disability*. New York: Routledge, 1999.

Glenn, Evelyn Nakano. *Forced to Care: Coercion and Caregiving in America*. Cambridge, MA: Harvard University Press, 2012.

Glenn, Evelyn Nakano. "From Servitude to Service Work: Historical Continuities in the Racial Division of Paid Reproductive Labor." *Signs: Journal of Women in Culture and Society* 18, no. 1 (1992): 1–43. https://doi.org/10.1086/494777.

Goldberg, Chad Alan. "Welfare Recipients or Workers? Contesting the Workfare State in New York City." *Sociological Theory* 19, no. 2 (2001): 187–218. https://doi.org/10.1111/0735-2751.00136.

Goodman, Robert. *After the Planners*. New York: Touchstone, 1971.

Gordon, Linda. *Pitied but Not Entitled: Single Mothers and the History of Welfare*. Cambridge, MA: Harvard University Press, 1995.

Griffiths, Timothy M. "Queer.Black Politics, Queer.Black Communities: Touching the Utopian Frame in Delany's *Through the Valley of the Nest of Spiders*." *African American Review* 48, no. 3 (2015): 305–17.

Gumbs, Alexis Pauline. Introduction to *Revolutionary Mothering: Love on the Front Lines*, edited by Alexis Pauline Gumbs, China Martens, and Mai'a Williams, 9–10. Oakland, CA: PM Press, 2016.

Gumbs, Alexis Pauline. "m/other ourselves: a Black queer feminist genealogy for radical mothering." In *Revolutionary Mothering: Love on the Front Lines*, edited by Alexis Pauline Gumbs, China Martens, and Mai'a Williams, 19–31. Oakland, CA: PM Press, 2016.

Gumbs, Alexis Pauline. "The Shape of My Impact." *Feminist Wire*, October 29, 2012. https://thefeministwire.com/2012/10/the-shape-of-my-impact/.

Gumbs, Alexis Pauline. "'We Can Learn to Mother Ourselves': The Queer Survival of Black Feminism 1968–1996." PhD diss., Duke University, 2010. https://hdl.handle.net/10161/2398.

Gurton-Wachter, Lily. "The Stranger Guest: The Literature of Pregnancy and New Motherhood." *Los Angeles Review of Books*, July 29, 2016. https://lareviewofbooks.org/article/stranger-guest-literature-pregnancy-new-motherhood/.

Hampe, Michael, Ursula Renz, and Robert Schnepf. Introduction to *Spinoza's "Ethics": A Collective Commentary*, edited by Michael Hampe, Ursula Renz, and Michael Hampe, 1–16. Leiden: Brill Press, 2011.

Hancock, Ange-Marie. *The Politics of Disgust: The Public Identity of the Welfare Queen*. New York: New York University Press, 2004.

Harriet Tubman Collective. "Disability Solidarity: Completing the 'Vision for Black Lives.'" *Harvard Journal of African American Public Policy*, September 2017, 69–72.

Harrison, Burr. "Fraud and Waste in Public Welfare Programs: Debate in Congress (1951)." In *Welfare: A Documentary History of U.S. Policy and Politics*, edited by Gwendolyn Mink and Rickie Solinger, 148–54. New York: New York University Press, 2003.

Harvey, David. *The Condition of Postmodernity: An Enquiry into the Origins of Cultural Change*. Cambridge, MA: Blackwell, 1990.

Hawkins, Gay. *The Ethics of Waste: How We Relate to Rubbish*. Lanham, MD: Rowman and Littlefield, 2005.

Heumann, Judith, and Kristen Joiner. *Being Heumann: An Unrepentant Memoir of a Disability Rights Activist*. New York: Penguin Random House, 2020.

Hinton, Anna. "Making Do with What You Don't Have: Disabled Black Motherhood in Octavia E. Butler's *Parable of the Sower* and *Parable of the Talents*." *Journal of Literary and Cultural Disability Studies* 12, no. 4 (2018): 441–57.

Hobart, Hi'ilei Julia Kawehipuaakakahaopulani, and Tamara Kneese. "Radical Care: Survival Strategies for Uncertain Times." *Social Text* 38, no. 1 (March 1, 2020): 1–16. https://doi.org/10.1215/01642472-7971067.

Hoffman, Allison K. "What Health Reform Reveals about Health Law." In *The Oxford Handbook of U.S. Health Law,* edited by I. Glenn Cohen, Allison K. Hoffman, and William M. Sage, 49–69. Oxford: Oxford University Press, 2016. https://doi.org/10.1093/oxfordhb/9780199366521.013.3.

Honey, Michael K. "Martin Luther King, Jr., the Crisis of the Black Working Class, and the Memphis Sanitation Strike (1968)." In *American Labor Struggles and Law Histories,* 2nd ed., edited by Kenneth M. Casebeer, 423–48. Durham, NC: Carolina Academic Press, 2017.

Hong, Grace Kyungwon. *The Ruptures of American Capital: Women of Color Feminism and the Culture of Immigrant Labor.* Minneapolis: University of Minnesota Press, 2006.

Hong, Grace Kyungwon, and Roderick A. Ferguson, eds. *Strange Affinities: The Gender and Sexual Politics of Comparative Racialization.* Durham, NC: Duke University Press, 2011.

Hsu, Ruth. "Karen Tei Yamashita's *Tropic of Orange* and Chaos Theory: Angels and a Motley Crew." In *Karen Tei Yamashita: Fictions of Magic and Memory,* edited by A. Robert Lee, 105–22. Manoa: University of Hawai'i Press, 2018.

INCITE! Women of Color against Violence. *The Revolution Will Not Be Funded: Beyond the Non-profit Industrial Complex.* Durham, NC: Duke University Press, 2007.

Jackson, Jerome, and Octavia E. Butler. "Sci-Fi Tales from Octavia E. Butler." *Crisis* 101, no. 3 (1994): 4–7.

Jackson, Shannon. "Working Publics." *Performance Research* 16, no. 2 (2011): 8–13. https://doi.org/10.1080/13528165.2011.578722.

Jackson, Zakiyyah Iman. *Becoming Human: Matter and Meaning in an Antiblack World.* New York: New York University Press, 2020.

James, Jennifer C., and Cynthia Wu. "Editors' Introduction: Race, Ethnicity, Disability, and Literature: Intersections and Interventions." *MELUS: Multi-Ethnic Literature of the United States* 31, no. 3 (2006): 3–13.

Jansen, Anne Mai Yee. "(Dis)Integrating Borders: Crossing Literal/ Literary Boundaries in *Tropic of Orange* and *The People of Paper.*" *MELUS: Multi-Ethnic Literature of the United States* 42, no. 3 (2017): 102–28. https://doi.org/10.1093/melus/mlx047.

Jarman, Michelle. "Cultural Consumption and Rejection of Precious Jones: Pushing Disability into the Discussion of Sapphire's *Push* and Lee Daniels's *Precious.*" *Feminist Formations* 24, no. 2 (2012): 163–85.

Johnson, Harriet McBryde. *Too Late to Die Young: Nearly True Tales from a Life.* New York: Henry Holt and Co, 2005.

Kafai, Shayda. *Crip Kinship: The Disability Justice and Art Activism of Sins Invalid.* Vancouver: Arsenal Pulp Press, 2021.

Kafer, Alison. *Feminist, Queer, Crip.* Bloomington: Indiana University Press, 2013.

Kandaswamy, Priya. *Domestic Contradictions: Race and Gendered Citizenship from Reconstruction to Welfare Reform*. Durham, NC: Duke University Press, 2021.

Kant, Immanuel. *Critique of Judgement*. Translated by James Creed Meredith. Oxford: Oxford University Press, 2007.

Kapadia, Ronak. *Insurgent Aesthetics: Security and the Queer Life of the Forever War*. Durham, NC: Duke University Press, 2019.

Kelley, Robin D. G. *Freedom Dreams: The Black Radical Imagination*. Boston: Beacon Press, 2002.

Kelly, Christine. *Disability Politics and Care: The Challenge of Direct Funding*. Vancouver: University of British Columbia Press, 2016.

Kim, Eunjung. *Curative Violence: Rehabilitating Disability, Gender, and Sexuality in Modern Korea*. Durham, NC: Duke University Press, 2017.

Kim, Jina B. "Cripping East Los Angeles: Enabling Environmental Justice in Helena María Viramontes's *Their Dogs Came with Them*." In *Disability Studies and the Environmental Humanities: Toward an Eco-Crip Theory*, edited by Sarah Jaquette Ray and J. C. Sibara, 502–30. Lincoln: University of Nebraska Press, 2017.

Kim, Jina B. "Love in the Time of Sickness: On Disability, Race, and Intimate Partner Violence." *Asian American Literary Review* 10, no. 2 (2019): 191–202.

Kim, Jina B., and Sami Schalk. "Reclaiming the Radical Politics of Self-Care: A Crip-of-Color Critique." *South Atlantic Quarterly* 120, no. 2 (2021): 325–42. https://doi.org/10.1215/00382876-8916074.

Kittay, Eva Feder. *Love's Labor: Essays on Women, Equality, and Dependency*. New York: Routledge, 1999.

Kornbluh, Felicia, and Gwendolyn Mink. *Ensuring Poverty: Welfare Reform in Feminist Perspective*. Philadelphia: University of Pennsylvania Press, 2019.

Kristeva, Julia. "Liberty, Equality, Fraternity, and . . . Vulnerability." Translated by Jeanine Herman. *Women's Studies Quarterly* 38, no. 1/2 (Spring/Summer 2010): 251–68.

Kristeva, Julia. *Powers of Horror: An Essay on Abjection*. Translated by Leon S. Roudiez. New York: Columbia University Press, 1982.

Kurashige, Scott. *The Shifting Grounds of Race: Black and Japanese Americans in the Making of Multiethnic Los Angeles*. Princeton, NJ: Princeton University Press, 2008.

Lee, James Kyung-Jin. *Pedagogies of Woundedness: Illness, Memoir, and the Ends of the Model Minority*. Philadelphia: Temple University Press, 2021.

Lee, Sue-Im. "We Are Not the World: Global Village, Universalism, and Karen Tei Yamashita's *Tropic of Orange*." *MFS Modern Fiction Studies* 53, no. 3 (2007): 501–27. https://doi.org/10.1353/mfs.2007.0049.

Lefebvre, Henri. *The Production of Space*. Translated by Donald Nicholson-Smith. Malden, MA: Blackwell, 1991.

Levins Morales, Aurora. *Kindling: Writings on the Body*. Cambridge, MA: Palabrera Press, 2013.

Lévi-Strauss, Claude. *The Elementary Structures of Kinship*. Edited by Rodney Need-ham. Translated by James Harle Bell and John Richard von Sturmer. Boston: Beacon Press, 1969.

Lewis, Oscar. "The Culture of Poverty." *Scientific American* 215, no. 4 (1966): 19–25.

Lewis, Sophie. *Abolish the Family: A Manifesto for Care and Liberation*. New York: Verso Books, 2022.

Ling, Jinqi. *Across Meridians: History and Figuration in Karen Tei Yamashita's Transna-tional Novels*. Palo Alto, CA: Stanford University Press, 2012.

Lorde, Audre. "A Burst of Light." In *I Am Your Sister: Collected and Unpublished Writings of Audre Lorde*, edited by Rudolph P. Byrd, Johnnetta Betsch Cole, and Beverly Guy-Sheftall, 81–152. Oxford: Oxford University Press, 2009.

Lorde, Audre. *The Cancer Journals*. San Francisco, CA: Spinsters, Ink, 1980.

Lorde, Audre. "A Litany for Survival." In *The Collected Poems of Audre Lorde*, 255–56. New York: W. W. Norton, 1977.

Lorde, Audre. "The Master's Tools Will Never Dismantle the Master's House." In *This Bridge Called My Back*, 4th ed., edited by Cherríe Moraga and Gloria Anzaldúa, 94–97. Albany: SUNY Press, 2015.

Lorde, Audre. "Uses of the Erotic: The Erotic as Power." In *Sister Outsider: Essays and Speeches*, 53–59. Berkeley, CA: Crossing Press, 1984.

Lowe, Lisa. *Immigrant Acts: On Asian American Cultural Politics*. Durham, NC: Duke University Press, 1996.

Lubiano, Wahneema. "Black Ladies, Welfare Queens, and State Minstrels: Ideological Warfare by Narrative Means." In *Race-ing Justice, En-Gendering Power: Essays on Anita Hill, Clarence Thomas, and the Construction of Social Reality*, edited by Toni Morrison, 323–63. New York: Pantheon, 1992.

Manning, Lynn. "The Magic Wand." *International Journal of Inclusive Education* 13, no. 7 (2009): 785. https://doi.org/10.1080/13603110903046069.

Mairs, Nancy. *Waist-High in the World: A Life Among the Nondisabled*. Boston, MA: Beacon Press, 1997.

Manzanas, Ana Mª, and Jesús Benito. *Cities, Borders, and Spaces in Intercultural Ameri-can Literature and Film*. New York: Routledge, 2011.

Marchevsky, Alejandra, and Jeanne Theoharis. *Not Working: Latina Immigrants, Low-Wage Jobs, and the Failure of Welfare Reform*. New York: New York University Press, 2006.

McCoy, Terrence. "Disabled, or Just Desperate? Rural Americans Turn to Dis-ability as Jobs Dry Up." *Washington Post*, March 30, 2017. https://www.washingtonpost.com/sf/local/2017/03/30/disabled-or-just-desperate/?utm_term=.2aa70dc44392.

McNeil, Elizabeth. "Un-'freak'ing Black Female Selfhood: Grotesque-Erotic Agency and Ecofeminist Unity in Sapphire's *Push*." *MELUS: Multi-Ethnic Literatures of the United States* 37, no. 4 (2012): 11–27. https://doi.org/10.1353/mel.2012.0070.

McRuer, Robert. *Crip Theory: Cultural Signs of Queerness and Disability*. New York: New York University Press, 2006.

McRuer, Robert. *Crip Times: Disability, Globalization, and Resistance*. New York: New York University Press, 2018.

Mead, Lawrence. *Beyond Entitlement: The Social Obligations of Citizenship*. New York: Free Press, 1986.

Mermann-Jozwiak, Elizabeth. "Yamashita's Post-National Spaces: 'It All Comes Together in Los Angeles.'" *Canadian Review of American Studies* 41, no. 1 (2011): 1–24. https://doi.org/10.3138/cras.41.1.1.

Meyer, Larry L. "The Shaping of Purpose." *Westways* 57 (June 1965): 26–28.

Michener, Jamila. *Fragmented Democracy: Medicaid, Federalism, and Unequal Politics*. Cambridge: Cambridge University Press, 2018.

Mientka, Matthew. "'Welfare-to-Work' Program Linked to Higher Deaths." *Medical Daily*, June 15, 2013. https://www.medicaldaily.com/welfare-work-program-linked -higher-deaths-246835.

Mingus, Mia. "Interdependence (Excerpts from Several Talks)." *Leaving Evidence* (blog), January 22, 2010. https://leavingevidence.wordpress.com/2010/01/22 /interdependency-exerpts-from-several-talks/.

Mingus, Mia. "Pods and Pod Mapping Worksheet." *Bay Area Transformative Justice Collective* (blog), June 2016. https://batjc.wordpress.com/resources/pods-and-pod -mapping-worksheet/.

Minich, Julie Avril. *Accessible Citizenships: Disability, Nation, and the Cultural Politics of Greater Mexico*. Philadelphia: Temple University Press, 2013.

Minich, Julie Avril. "Enabling Whom? Critical Disability Studies Now." *Lateral: Journal of the Cultural Studies Association* 5, no. 1 (2016). https://doi.org/10.25158/L5.1.9.

Mink, Gwendolyn. *Welfare's End*. Ithaca, NY: Cornell University Press, 1998.

Mississippi State Department of Health. "Personal Responsibility Education Program (PREP)." *Mississippi State Department of Health* (website), last reviewed on March 27, 2024. https://msdh.ms.gov/msdhsite/index.cfm/44,11790,362.html.

Mitchell, David T. "Body Solitaire: The Singular Subject of Disability Autobiography." *American Quarterly* 52, no. 2 (June 2000): 311–15.

Mohanty, Chandra Talpade. *Feminism without Borders: Decolonizing Theory, Practicing Solidarity*. Durham, NC: Duke University Press, 2003.

Mollow, Anna, and Robert McRuer. Introduction to *Sex and Disability*, edited by Robert McRuer and Anna Mollow, 1–34. Durham, NC: Duke University Press, 2012.

Moraga, Cherríe. "La Jornada: Preface, 1981." In *This Bridge Called My Back: Writings by Radical Women of Color*, 4th ed., edited by Cherríe Moraga and Gloria Anzaldúa, xxxv–xli. Albany: SUNY Press, 2015.

Moraga, Cherríe, and Gloria Anzaldúa, eds. *This Bridge Called My Back: Writings by Radical Women of Color*. 4th ed. Albany: SUNY Press, 2015.

Morris, Susana M. *Close Kin and Distant Relatives: The Paradox of Respectability in Black Women's Literature.* Charlottesville: University of Virginia Press, 2014.

Morrison, Toni. *The Bluest Eye.* Vintage International Edition. New York: Penguin Random House, 1970.

Morrison, Toni. *Sula.* New York: Vintage, 2004.

Moylan, Tom. *Demand the Impossible: Science Fiction and the Utopian Imagination.* New York: Methuen, 1986.

Moynihan, Daniel Patrick. *The Negro Family: The Case for National Action.* Washington, DC: Office of Policy Planning and Research and United States Department of Labor, 1965.

Muennig, Peter, Rishi Caleyachetty, Zohn Rosen, and Andrew Korotzer. "More Money, Fewer Lives: The Cost Effectiveness of Welfare Reform in the United States." *American Journal of Public Health* 105, no. 2 (2015): 324–28. https://doi.org/10.2105/AJPH.2014.302235.

Muennig, Peter, Zohn Rosen, and Elizabeth T. Wilde. "Welfare Programs That Target Workforce Participation May Negatively Impact Mortality." *Health Affairs* 32, no. 6 (2013): 1072–77. https://doi.org/10.1377/hlthaff.2012.0971.

Mulligan, Jessica M., and Heide Castañeda. Introduction to *Unequal Coverage: The Experience of Health Care Reform in the United States,* edited by Jessica M. Mulligan and Heide Castañeda, 1–34. New York: New York University Press, 2018.

Muñoz, José Esteban. *Cruising Utopia: The Then and There of Queer Futurity.* New York: New York University Press, 2009.

Murray, Charles A. *Losing Ground: American Social Policy, 1950–1980.* New York: Basic Books, 1984.

Musser, Amber Jamilla. "Re-Membering Audre: Adding Lesbian Feminist Mother Poet to Black." In *No Tea, No Shade: New Writings in Black Queer Studies,* edited by E. Patrick Johnson, 346–61. Durham, NC: Duke University Press, 2016.

Musser, Amber Jamilla. *Sensual Excess: Queer Femininity and Brown Jouissance.* New York: New York University Press, 2018.

Nadasen, Premilla. *Welfare Warriors: The Welfare Rights Movement in the United States.* New York: Routledge, 2004.

Nagle, Robin. *Picking Up: On the Streets and behind the Trucks with the Sanitation Workers of New York City.* New York: Farrar, Straus and Giroux, 2014.

Nelson, Alondra. *Body and Soul: The Black Panther Party and the Fight against Medical Discrimination.* Minneapolis: University of Minnesota Press, 2011.

New York Times. "'Welfare Queen' Becomes Issue in Reagan Campaign." February 15, 1976. https://www.nytimes.com/1976/02/15/archives/welfare-queen-becomes-issue-in-reagan-campaign-hitting-a-nerve-now.html.

Nilges, Mathias. "'We Need the Stars': Change, Community, and the Absent Father in Octavia Butler's *Parable of the Sower* and *Parable of the Talents.*" *Callaloo* 32, no. 4 (2009): 1332–52.

Nishida, Akemi. *Just Care: Messy Entanglements of Disability, Dependency, and Desire.* Philadelphia: Temple University Press, 2022.

Nishida, Akemi. "Relating through Differences: Disability, Affective Relationality, and the U.S. Public Healthcare Assemblage." *Subjectivity* 10 (2017): 89–103. https://doi.org/10.1057/s41286-016-0018-2.

O'Brien, Ruth, ed. *Voices from the Edge: Narratives about the Americans with Disabilities Act.* Oxford: Oxford University Press, 2004.

Oliver, Mike. "The Social Model of Disability: Thirty Years On." *Disability and Society* 28, no. 7 (2013): 1024–26. https://doi.org/10.1080/09687599.2013.818773.

Parreñas, Rhacel. *Servants of Globalization: Migration and Domestic Work.* Redwood City, CA: Stanford University Press, 2001.

Piaget, Jean. *The Language and Thought of the Child.* Translated by Marjorie Gabain and Ruth Gabain. 3rd ed. New York: Routledge Classics, 2002.

Pickens, Therí. "Octavia Butler and the Aesthetics of the Novel." *Hypatia* 30, no. 1 (2015): 167–80. https://doi.org/10.1111/hypa.12129.

Piepzna-Samarasinha, Leah Lakshmi. *Care Work: Dreaming Disability Justice.* Vancouver: Arsenal Pulp Press, 2018.

Piepzna-Samarasinha, Leah Lakshmi. *The Future Is Disabled: Prophecies, Love Notes, and Mourning Songs.* Vancouver: Arsenal Pulp Press, 2022.

Piepzna-Samarasinha, Leah Lakshmi. *Tonguebreaker.* Vancouver: Arsenal Pulp Press, 2019.

Piven, Frances Fox, and Richard A. Cloward. *Regulating the Poor: The Functions of Public Welfare.* New York: Vintage, 1993.

Poole, Mary. *Segregated Origins of Social Security: African Americans and the Welfare State.* Chapel Hill: University of North Carolina Press, 2006.

Puar, Jasbir. *The Right to Maim: Debility, Capacity, Disability.* Durham, NC: Duke University Press, 2018.

Ralli, Tania. "Who's a Looter? In Storm's Aftermath, Pictures Kick Up a Different Kind of Tempest." *New York Times,* September 5, 2005, sec. C.

Rivera, Lysa. "Future Histories and Cyborg Labor: Reading Borderlands Science Fiction after NAFTA." *Science Fiction Studies* 39, no. 3 (2012): 415–36. https://doi.org/10.5621/sciefictstud.39.3.0415.

Roane, J. T. *Dark Agoras: Insurgent Black Social Life and the Politics of Place.* New York: New York University Press, 2023.

Roberts, Dorothy. *Killing the Black Body: Race, Reproduction, and the Meaning of Liberty.* New York: Vintage Books, 1998.

Roberts, Dorothy. "Welfare's Ban on Poor Motherhood." In *Whose Welfare?*, edited by Gwendolyn Mink, 152–68. Ithaca, NY: Cornell University Press, 1999. https://doi.org/10.7591/9781501728891-008.

Rodríguez, Juana María. "Queer Sociality and Other Sexual Fantasies." *GLQ: A Journal of Lesbian and Gay Studies* 17, no. 2–3 (2011): 331–48.

Rody, Caroline. *The Interethnic Imagination: Roots and Passages in Contemporary Asian American Fiction*. Oxford: Oxford University Press, 2009.

Rowell, Charles H. "An Interview with Octavia E. Butler." *Callaloo* 20, no. 1 (1997): 47–66.

Rubenstein, Michael, Bruce Robbins, and Sophia Beal. "Infrastructuralism: An Introduction." *MFS Modern Fiction Studies* 61, no. 4 (2015): 575–86. https://doi.org/10.1353/mfs.2015.0049.

Rubin, Gayle. "The Traffic in Women: Notes on the 'Political Economy' of Sex." In *Toward an Anthropology of Women*, edited by Rayna R. Reiter, 157–210. New York: Monthly Review Press, 1975.

Rushin, Kate. "The Bridge Poem." In *This Bridge Called My Back: Writings by Radical Women of Color*, 4th ed., edited by Cherríe Moraga and Gloria Anzaldúa, xxxiii–xxxiv. Albany: SUNY Press, 2015.

Salamanca, Omar Jabary. "Unplug and Play: Manufacturing Collapse in Gaza." *Human Geography* 4, no. 1 (2011): 22–37.

Samuels, Ellen. "Six Ways of Looking at Crip Time." *Disability Studies Quarterly* 37, no. 3 (2017). https://doi.org/10.18061/dsq.v37i3.5824.

Sandahl, Carrie. "Queering the Crip or Cripping the Queer? Intersections of Queer and Crip Identities in Solo Autobiographical Performance." *GLQ: A Journal of Lesbian and Gay Studies* 9, no. 1 (2003): 25–56. https://doi.org/10.1215/10642684-9-1-2-25.

Sandoval, Chela. *Methodology of the Oppressed*. Minneapolis: University of Minnesota Press, 2000.

Sanyika, Mtangulizi. "Katrina and the Condition of Black New Orleans: The Struggle for Justice, Equity, and Democracy." In *Race, Place, and Environmental Justice after Hurricane Katrina: Struggles to Reclaim, Rebuild, and Revitalize New Orleans and the Gulf Coast*, edited by Robert D. Bullard and Beverly Wright, 153–212. Boulder, CO: Westview Press, 2009.

Sapphire. *Push*. New York: Vintage Books, 2009.

Sassen, Saskia. *The Global City: New York, London, Tokyo*. Princeton, NJ: Princeton University Press, 2001.

Sassen, Saskia. "The Global City: Strategic Site/New Frontier." *American Studies* 41, no. 2/3 (2000): 79–95.

Savarese, Emily Thornton, and Ralph James Savarese. "'The Superior Half of Speaking': An Introduction." *Disability Studies Quarterly* 30, no. 1 (2010). https://dsq-sds.org/article/view/1062/1230.

Schalk, Sami. *Bodyminds Reimagined: (Dis)Ability, Race, and Gender in Black Women's Speculative Fiction*. Durham, NC: Duke University Press, 2018.

Schram, Sanford. *After Welfare: The Culture of Postindustrial Social Policy*. New York: New York University Press, 2000.

Scott, Darieck. *Extravagant Abjection: Blackness, Power, and Sexuality in the African American Literary Imagination*. New York: New York University Press, 2010.

Shakespeare, Tom. "The Social Model of Disability." In *The Disability Studies Reader*, 4th ed., edited by Lennard J. Davis, 214–22. New York: Routledge, 2013.

Shange, Ntozake. *For Colored Girls Who Have Considered Suicide / When the Rainbow Is Enuf*. New York: Collier Books, 1975.

Shaviro, Steven. "The Mad Man." *The Pinocchio Theory* (blog), November 30, 2006. http://www.shaviro.com/Blog/?p=528.

Shaviro, Steven. "Through the Valley of the Nest of Spiders." *The Pinocchio Theory* (blog), May 25, 2012. http://www.shaviro.com/Blog/?p=1050.

Shotwell, Alexis. *Against Purity: Living Ethically in Compromised Times*. Minneapolis: University of Minnesota Press, 2016.

Simone, AbdouMaliq. "People as Infrastructure: Intersecting Fragments in Johannesburg." *Public Culture* 16, no. 3 (2004): 407–29.

Singer, Linda. *Erotic Welfare: Sexual Theory and Politics in the Age of Epidemic*. New York: Routledge, 1992.

Sins Invalid. "10 Principles of Disability Justice." *Sins Invalid* (blog), September 17, 2015. https://www.sinsinvalid.org/blog/10-principles-of-disability-justice.

Sins Invalid. "This October: Birthing, Dying, Becoming Crip Wisdom." *Sins Invalid* (blog), August 3, 2016. https://www.sinsinvalid.org/blog/this-october-birthing -dying-becoming-crip-wisdom.

Smith, Barbara, ed. *Home Girls: A Black Feminist Anthology*. New Brunswick, NJ: Rutgers University Press, 2000.

Smith, Danez. *Homie: Poems*. Minneapolis, MN: Graywolf Press, 2020.

Smith, Neil. *The New Urban Frontier: Gentrification and the Revanchist City*. New York: Routledge, 1996.

Smith, Sidonie. "The Autobiographical Manifesto: Identities, Temporalities, Politics." *Prose Studies* 14, no. 2 (1991): 186–212. https://doi.org/10.1080 /01440359108586439.

Smith, Sidonie, and Julia Watson. *Reading Autobiography: A Guide for Interpreting Life Narratives*. 2nd ed. Minneapolis: University of Minnesota Press, 2010.

Social Security Administration. "Understanding Supplemental Security Income (SSI) Eligibility Requirements." 2024 edition. https://www.ssa.gov/ssi/text-eligibility -ussi.htm.

Soja, Edward. *Postmodern Geographies: The Reassertion of Space in Critical Social Theory*. New York: Verso Books, 1989.

Spade, Dean. *Normal Life: Administrative Violence, Critical Trans Politics, and the Limits of Law*. Durham, NC: Duke University Press, 2015.

Spillers, Hortense. "Mama's Baby, Papa's Maybe: An American Grammar Book." *Diacritics* 17, no. 2 (1987): 64–81. https://doi.org/10.2307/464747.

Stallings, L. H. *Funk the Erotic: Transaesthetics and Black Sexual Cultures*. Champaign: University of Illinois Press, 2015.

Stein, Jeff. "'No Cuts to Medicaid!': Protesters in Wheelchairs Arrested after Release of Health Care Bill." *Vox*, June 22, 2017. https://www.vox.com/policy-and-politics /2017/6/22/15855424/disability-protest-medicaid-mcconnell.

Taylor, Sunaura. "The Right Not to Work: Power and Disability." *Monthly Review: An Independent Socialist Magazine* 55, no. 10 (March 1, 2004): 20. https://doi.org/10 .14452/MR-055-10-2004-03_2.

Teish, Luisah. *Jambalaya: The Natural Woman's Book of Personal Charms and Practical Rituals*. New York: HarperCollins, 1988.

Thoma, Pamela. "Traveling the Distances of Karen Tei Yamashita's Fiction: A Review Essay on Yamashita Scholarship and Transnational Studies." *Asian American Literature: Discourses and Pedagogies* 1 (2010): 6–15.

Tillmon, Johnnie. "From the Vault: 'Welfare Is a Women's Issue' (Spring 1972)." *Ms. Magazine*, March 25, 2021. https://msmagazine.com/2021/03/25/welfare-is-a -womens-issue-ms-magazine-spring-1972/.

Treaster, Joseph B., and N. R. Kleinfield. "New Orleans Is Inundated as 2 Levees Fail." *New York Times*, August 31, 2005, sec. A.

US Citizenship and Immigration Services. "Early American Immigration Policies." July 30, 2020. https://www.uscis.gov/about-us/our-history/overview-of-ins -history/early-american-immigration-policies#:~:text=The%20general%20 Immigration%20Act%20of,for%20new%20federal%20enforcement%20authorities.

Villa, Raúl Homero. *Barrio-Logos: Space and Place in Urban Chicano Literature and Culture*. Austin: University of Texas Press, 2000.

Wachter-Grene, Kirin. "'On the Unspeakable': Delany, Desire, and the Tactic of Transgression." *African American Review* 48, no. 3 (2015): 333–43. https://doi.org/10 .1353/afa.2015.0032.

Wade, Cheryl Marie. "It Ain't Exactly Sexy." In *The Ragged Edge: The Disability Experience from the Pages of the First Fifteen Years of "The Disability Rag,"* edited by Barrett Shaw, 88–90. Louisville, KY: Advocado Press, 1994.

Ward, Jesmyn. "Q&A with Jesmyn Ward." In *Salvage the Bones*, 263–66. New York: Bloomsbury USA, 2011.

Ward, Jesmyn. *Salvage the Bones*. New York: Bloomsbury USA, 2011.

Washington, Harriet A. *Medical Apartheid: The Dark History of Medical Experimentation on Black Americans from Colonial Times to the Present*. New York: Anchor Books, 2008.

Weeks, Kathi. "Abolition of the Family: The Most Infamous Feminist Proposal." *Feminist Theory* 24, no. 3 (2023): 433–53.

Weeks, Kathi. *The Problem with Work: Feminism, Marxism, Antiwork Politics, and Postwork Imaginaries*. Durham, NC: Duke University Press, 2011.

Weissmann, Jordan. "Disability Insurance: America's $124 Billion Secret Welfare Program." *Atlantic*, March 25, 2013. https://www.theatlantic.com/business/archive

/2013/03/disability-insurance-americas-124-billion-secret-welfare-program
/274302/.

Wendell, Susan. *The Rejected Body: Feminist Philosophical Reflections on Disability.*
New York: Routledge, 1996.

Whatcott, Jess. "Crip Collectivity beyond Neoliberalism in Octavia Butler's *Parable of
the Sower.*" *Lateral* 10, no. 1 (2021). https://csalateral.org/section/cripistemologies
-of-crisis/crip-collectivity-beyond-neoliberalism-octavia-butler-parable-of-the
-sower-whatcott/.

Wilde, Elizabeth T., Zohn Rosen, Kenneth A. Couch, and Peter Muennig. "Impact
of Welfare Reform on Mortality: An Evaluation of the Connecticut Jobs First
Program, a Randomized Controlled Trial." *American Journal of Public Health* 104,
no. 3 (2014): 534–38. https://doi.org/10.2105/AJPH.2012.301072.

Williams, Annabelle. "Neil Marcus, Whose Art Illuminated Disability, Dies at 67."
New York Times, December 28, 2021. https://www.nytimes.com/2021/12/28/arts
/neil-marcus-dead.html.

Willse, Craig. *The Value of Homelessness: Managing Surplus Life in the United States.*
Minneapolis: University of Minnesota Press, 2015.

Wong, Alice. "My Medicaid, My Life." *New York Times*, May 3, 2017. https://www
.nytimes.com/2017/05/03/opinion/my-medicaid-my-life.html.

Yaeger, Patricia. "*Beasts of the Southern Wild* and Dirty Ecology." *Southern Spaces*,
February 13, 2013. https://doi.org/10.18737/M7K317.

Yaeger, Patricia. "Introduction: Dreaming of Infrastructure." PMLA: *Publications of the
Modern Language Association of America* 122, no. 1 (2007): 9–26.

Yamashita, Karen Tei. *Tropic of Orange.* Minneapolis, MN: Coffee House Press, 1997.

Yamashita, Karen Tei, and Ryuta Imafuku. "The Latitude of the Fiction Writer: A
Dialogue." Ryuta Imafuku's Café Creole. Accessed May 1, 2017. http://www
.cafecreole.net/archipelago/Karen_Dialogue.html.

Index

abandonment, 22–23, 24, 55; organized, 10, 11, 166n28; state and, 19–20, 131; of unhoused people, 116

Abdur-Rahman, Aliyyah, 28, 43, 63–64, 87–89

abjection, 61–62, 68–70; eroticism and, 65, 70–73, 76, 78–79, 88–90, 173n32

ableism: carceral, 6–7; dependency and, 12, 17–18; intersectionality of, 20, 132, 153; labor and, 41–42, 79; of medical-industrial complex, 130, 138–39, 142, 144, 154–55; mobility and, 94–95, 101; sanitation and, 73–74; of science fiction, 147; welfare reform and, 4–5, 29, 32–34, 41–42

abortion, 36

abstract space, 100–101, 117

abundance, 144–45, 151

abuse: care, 1–2, 82, 158–59; child, 37–38, 55, 137–38; family, 108; of medical-industrial complex, 131, 142; sexual, 137–38; sexuality and, 69; welfare reform and, 28, 37–38

ACA. *See* Affordable Care Act

academia, 15

access: collective, 92–93, 124, 125–26, 132–33, 155; to desire and, 67, 69–70, 80–81, 88–89, 90; to health/care, 36, 129–30, 135–44, 146–47, 154–55; as socially engineered, 93–94, 101–2; to transit, 94–95, 101–2; waged labor and, 60–61, 75, 79, 80; to welfare, 7–9, 41, 106

accountability, 27–28, 57, 89–90

Act to Regulate Immigration, 105–6

ACT UP/SF, 160–61

Adams, Rachel, 134

Adamski-Smith, Marilee, 146

adaptation, 107–8, 121–22, 149–50, 162

ADC. *See* Aid to Dependent Children

aesthetics: of abjection, 69–70; of disability, 2, 4, 19–20, 29, 33, 56–57; of freeways, 56–57, 115–16, 118–21; of infrastructure, 118–20, 126–27; of medicalized language, 29; of mobility, 102–4

AFDC. *See* Aid to Families with Dependent Children

affinity: crip, 4; eroticism and, 85–87; political, 16–17, 33–34, 54–55, 68, 123, 126, 143–44

Affordable Care Act (ACA), 129–30, 135, 146, 153

agency, distributed, 118, 180n120

AHCA. *See* American Health Care Act

Aid to Dependent Children (ADC), 7, 59

Aid to Families with Dependent Children (AFDC), 9, 41–42

Alexander, M. Jacqui, 116–17, 120–21, 149–51, 159–60

Alien Contract Labor Laws, 106

American Health Care Act (AHCA), 146, 152–53

Americans Disabled for Attendant Programs Today (ADAPT), 146

Americans with Disabilities Act (ADA), 5, 23–24, 79, 132, 135–36

ancestors, 16–17, 23–24, 123–24, 138–39, 150–52

Anderson, Laurie, 158

52–54, 124–25, 138–40; erotic, 53–54, 61, 64–65, 80–82, 90; family and, 30, 55–57, 84, 159; gendered, 17–18; infrastructures of, 6–8, 15–17, 23–25, 30, 35–36, 41, 45, 49, 55–56, 61, 81, 83, 126, 131, 144–45, 147–51, 153–55, 159–60; interdependency and, 17–18, 55–57, 124–25; labor and, 6–7, 11, 24–25, 43, 52–54, 56, 67–68, 72–74, 76–77, 80–83, 149; mothering and, 31–32, 35–36, 54; outsourcing, 11–12; privatization of, 11, 14, 28, 30, 52, 55, 89–90; queer, 53–54; as racialized, 12–14, 17–18; relations of, 55–57; state and, 6–14, 43, 52, 57, 60, 131; world-making and, 52–53, 55–56. *See also* health/care

care web, 148–49

Chacón, Justin Akers, 105

Chang, Grace, 94, 106, 108–12

change, 17, 49, 67–68, 92–93, 121–22, 125; social, 12, 46–47; systemic, 67–68, 140. *See also* adaptation

chattel slavery, 79, 116–17

Chee, Alexander, "After Peter," 160–62

childcare, 6–7, 11, 17–18, 111–12

child support, 31

Chinese Exclusion Act, 105–6

Chinn, Sarah, 54

chronic fatigue immune dysfunction syndrome (CFIDS), 153

citizenship, 76–77, 84, 105–6, 112, 120

civil rights movement, 16, 74–75, 79

class, 10, 41–42; abjection and, 70–71; Black mothering and, 31–32, 36–37; care and, 11; dependency and, 129; disability and, 11, 101–2, 173n31; grief and, 158; health/care access and, 130, 134, 138–39, 143–44, 154–55, 159; labor and, 41–42, 74–75, 81, 112–14; mobility and, 93–94, 100–101; resource distribution and, 8–9; sexuality and, 66–67; social reproduction and, 11; survival and, 134; value and, 123–24; waste and, 68

Clinton, Bill, 3, 30, 60–61, 63–64, 84

coalitions, 14–16, 33–34, 107, 132, 134

Cohen, Cathy, 10; "Punks, Bulldaggers, and Welfare Queens," 16, 19–20, 31–32

collaboration, 77–78, 132–33

collective: abjection and, 61; access and, 92–93, 132–33, 155; care and, 13–14, 30, 54–55, 120, 124–25, 149, 159; erotic, 69–70; liberation and, 123, 126–27, 132–33, 155; survival and, 45, 48–49, 55, 123–24, 126, 140

Collins, Patricia Hill, 31–32, 84

colonialism, 8–9, 111–12, 116–17, 137–38

community, 54–55, 133–34; building, 108, 121, 124–25; care and, 13–14, 139–40, 149, 155; labor and, 73, 76–77, 79–81; queer, 61–62, 63, 65, 67, 81, 88–89; state and, 36–37, 41, 57, 63

company towns, 106, 108–11

consciousness, infrastructural, 95, 103–4, 115–19, 126–28

contact, 66–68, 80, 88–89, 173n31

control: bodily, 70–72, 73–74; care and, 83, 131, 159; disability and, 70, 73–74; state, 6–8, 19–20, 144

COVID-19 pandemic, 23–24, 130–31, 140, 157, 162–63

creation, 45–46, 48–49, 51, 52–53, 92, 108, 121–22, 144–45, 149–50, 162. *See also* destruction

crip affinity, 4

crip-of-color critique, 162–63; Black feminism and, 29, 33–34; freedom and, 24–25; free trade and, 94; infrastructures of care in, 148–51; as insurgent, 60; interdependency and, 56–57, 77–78, 90, 95, 149; literary form and, 29, 44–45; method of, 4, 12–14, 19–20, 56–57, 67–68, 130, 132–34; nuclear family and, 84–85; refusal of work, 78, 83; support imaginaries of, 12–14, 24–25; waste management and, 60–61, 67–68, 77–78; welfare reform and, 29, 33–34, 60

cripping, 19–20

Middle Passage, 120–21
migrants, migration, 92–97, 100–101, 103–4, 137–38; coerced, 130; free trade and, 105–9, 111–15, 125–26. *See also* immigrants, immigration
Milbern, Stacey Park, 157
military, militarism, 10, 137
Mingus, Mia, 16
Minich, Julie Avril, 12, 20, 105–6
Mink, Gwendolyn, 7–10, 84
minority literatures, 4–5
misogyny, 32
Mitchell, David, 134
mobility, 94–95, 102–4, 125–26; forced, 96–97; uneven conditions of, 100–102
Mohanty, Chandra Talpade, 11, 16–17
Mollow, Anna, 67
Moraga, Cherríe, 14–16, 24–25
Morales, Rosario, 140–41
moralism, morality, 8, 59–60, 75, 87–88
Morrison, Toni, 158; *The Bluest Eye*, 63–64, 87–88
mothers, mothering, 44–47, 54–56; Black, 28–37, 41–45, 50–51, 54, 168n6; deviant, 48–51, 56–57; migrant, 15; poor, 36, 41–42; revolutionary, 49, 56; single, 7–9, 28, 32–33, 41–42, 62–63; teenage, 32–33
movement, 93–95, 100–101, 103–4; freedom of, 95–96. *See also* mobility
Moynihan, Daniel Patrick, 30–32, 36, 41
Mundo Zurdo, El, 14–15, 17
Musser, Amber Jamilla, 54, 69–70, 72
mutual aid, 140
mutualism, 3–4, 15–18, 24–25, 30, 45, 47–48, 52–53, 55–56, 89–90, 121, 123–25
myth, mythology, 24–25, 29, 44–51, 55–56

Nadasen, Premilla, 41–42
NAFTA. *See* North American Free Trade Agreement
Nagle, Robin, 74
National Federation of Independent Business v. Sebelius, 135

nativism, 8–9, 105
necropolitics, 6
neglect, 3–4, 10, 36, 56–57, 62–63, 130
Nelson, Alondra, 137–38, 182n4
neurodiversity, 115–17, 124–26
New York City Department of Sanitation (DSNY), 74–75
Nishida, Akemi, 6–7, 18, 57, 182n6
nonprofit industrial complex, 52
nonworker, 7, 62–63, 78–81; disabled, 3, 8–9, 12–13; low-income mother as, 41–42. *See also* labor
normativity, 12, 20, 69–70, 74, 140–41; nonnormative, 31–32, 62, 86, 93–95; refusal of, 75–76, 83, 84–85, 87–88
North American Free Trade Agreement (NAFTA), 93–95, 100, 105–7, 111, 113–14
nourishment, 1–2, 13–14, 154
nurturance, 16–17, 43, 44–45, 49, 158

Obama, Barack, 62–63, 141
Obamacare. *See* Affordable Care Act
Oedipus complex, 84–87, 89–90

pain, 102, 113–14, 121–22; chronic, 134, 136–38, 147–48, 154
parable, 121–22
parasitism, 3–4, 29, 114, 125–26
parents, parenting, 124; "responsible," 28; welfare reform and, 31, 36–37, 41–42. *See also* mothers, mothering
Park, Stacey Milbern, 20
Parreñas, Rhacel Salazar, 64–65, 73–74
paternalism, 82–83, 149
pathology, 4–5, 8–9, 28–29, 32–34, 41–43, 45, 56–58, 63–64, 86, 94–95, 127
patriarchy, 28, 37–38, 54, 69–70, 84. *See also* heteropatriarchy
performance, 130–33, 145
Personal Responsibility and Work Opportunity Reconciliation Act (PWORA), 3, 9–10, 27–29, 31, 33–36, 41, 60, 84, 106
pesticides, 136–37

of, 24–25; survival and, 134; value and, 123–25; violence and, 50–51, 56–57, 134, 138–39; waste and, 61–62, 68, 72–73; welfare reform and, 7–8

racism, 15–16, 37–38, 62–63; environmental, 130; medical, 36, 133–34, 154–55

rationality, 39, 72, 126, 169n47

Reagan, Ronald, 3, 12–13, 28, 31–32, 44–45, 62–64, 129

Reaganomics, 30–31

realism, 39–40, 45, 83

reciprocity, 17–18, 24–25, 45, 55, 149; interspecies, 47–48. *See also* mutualism

refuse work, 61, 75–76. *See also* labor; sanitation; waste

relations, relationality, 16; of care, 55–57; contact, 66–68; kinship and, 87; queer, 88–89; of sexuality, 66–68; of support, 89–90, 119–20, 123–25; of waste management, 62–65, 68, 70–72, 76–78, 80–81, 86, 89–90; work ethic and, 61

representation, 19–20

reproduction: racialized, 29, 32–33, 47; social, 6–7, 11, 20, 32–33

resource distribution: dependency and, 8–9; disability and, 153–55; infrastructural violence and, 11–13, 48–49; labor and, 60–61, 75; migration and, 94–95; privatization of, 41–42, 107–11; state and, 5–6, 8–10, 23–24, 27–29, 32, 34–35, 60–61, 94–95, 129; uneven, 4–6, 10, 15–16, 19, 24, 27–29, 56–57. *See also* welfare reform

respectability, 74–76, 84

responsibility, personal, 35–36, 50, 55

rights, 5–6, 132

road narrative, 94–104, 106

Roane, J. T., 60

Robbins, Bruce, 120, 180n122

Roberts, Dorothy, 7–8, 31–32

Rodríguez, Juana María, 67

Roosevelt, Franklin Delano, 7

Rubenstein, Michael, 120, 180n122

Rubin, Gayle, 84–85

rupture, ruptural possibilities, 4–5

Rushin, Kate, "The Bridge Poem," 15

safety net, 7, 10–11, 23, 27–28, 32, 63, 107–8, 129–31, 134–36, 162

Salamanca, Omar Jabary, 10

Sanchez, Jesús Benito, 96–97, 181n130

Sandahl, Carrie, 19

Sandoval, Chela, 54–55

sanitation, 3–5, 59–62, 64–66, 71–77; privatization of, 74–75; strikes, 74–75, 174n66

SAP. *See* structural adjustment program

Sapphire, *Push*, 10, 28–30, 33–34, 36–43, 51–57, 87–88, 126, 162–63

Sapphire Sapphos, 13–14

Sassen, Saskia, 112–14

Savarese, Emily Thornton, 115

Savarese, Ralph James, 115

scarcity, 24, 39, 57, 139–40, 144–45

Schalk, Sami, 20, 108–9, 121–22, 177n10

school lunches, 10

Schram, Sanford F., 32

Scott, Darieck, 69–71

Second New Deal, 7

self-care, 12–13

settler colonialism, 96–97, 166n28

sex: care and, 60–61; waste and, 62–66

sex education, 36–37

sexism, 133–34

sexuality: abjection and, 69–70, 72–73, 78–79, 88; disability and, 66–68, 78–79, 86–87, 173n31; interdependency and, 81–82; kinship and, 54–55, 84–88; lesbian consciousness, 16–17; racialized, 19–20, 32, 63–64, 66–68; relations of, 66–68; state and, 19–20, 29, 32, 63–64; waste and, 72–73, 75–78

sex work, 11, 73–74, 76–77

shame, 70–72, 77–78, 86–87, 90, 134, 152–53, 158

Shange, Ntozake, *For Colored Girls Who Have Considered Suicide / When the Rainbow Is Enuf*, 149–50

Shaviro, Steven, 65, 89–90
sickness, 1–2, 108, 131, 136–37, 146, 148–51, 154, 158–59, 162
Simone, AbdouMaliq, 6
Singer, Linda, 32–33
Sins Invalid, 14–15, 20, 116–17, 132–33; "10 Principles of Disability Justice," 132, 151–52
slum clearance, 100–101
Smith, Neil, 39–40
Smith, Sidonie, 146–47, 183n18
social health, 137–38
socialism, 135–36, 153–54
social mobility, 38, 43, 55
social reproduction. *See under* reproduction
Social Security Act, 7–8
Social Security Disability Insurance (SSDI), 130, 134–36, 138–39, 141–42
social worker, 1, 37–38, 42–43, 51, 142, 159
solidarity, 14–17, 33, 56–57, 67–68, 107; trans-species, 47
Spade, Dean, 10, 166n28
speculative fiction, 24–25, 56, 65, 83, 144–45, 153
Spillers, Hortense, 31–32, 44–45
Spinoza, Baruch, 65, 89–90, 176n133
SSDI. *See* Social Security Disability Insurance
SSI. *See* Supplemental Security Income
Stallings, L. H., 63–64
state: capital and, 30; care and, 6–14, 43, 52, 57, 60, 131; dependency and, 3, 5–6, 8–10, 12, 15, 32, 41; disability and, 3–6, 8–9, 12–13, 19–20, 40–41, 56–57, 60, 63, 105–6, 116, 131, 135, 139–40, 142–44, 151–55; family and, 63–64, 69–70, 84; gender and, 19–20, 29; health/care and, 135–36, 138–40, 142–44, 153–54; infrastructure and, 4–5, 9–10, 34–42, 44–45, 51–52, 57, 63; race and, 4–5, 19–20, 32, 63–64; resource distribution and, 5–6, 8–10, 23–24, 27–29, 32, 34–35, 60–61, 94–95, 129; sexuality and, 19–20,

29, 32, 63–64; violence of, 3, 7–14, 19–20, 29, 34, 37–38, 50, 52, 55–57, 63, 138–39, 142–44; welfare reform and, 60, 63–64, 75, 108–9, 116; work ethic and, 73–77
State Children's Health Insurance Program (SCHIP), 106
structural adjustment program (SAP), 8–9, 94–95, 108–1
subjectivity: abjection and, 68–73, 173n32; borderless, 129; dependency and, 29, 125; disability and, 19–20; family and, 84, 88–89; infrastructural support of, 6, 114–15, 118–20; intersubjectivity and, 72, 118–20, 125; labor and, 76–77, 114; racialized, 6, 84, 88–89; sexuality and, 12, 68–73, 88–89
sublime, 117–20, 180n122
Supplemental Security Income (SSI), 3, 8–9, 79, 106, 130, 135–36, 138, 142
support, 2–3, 23–25, 56–57, 134–35, 144–46, 148–50; infrastructures of, 6, 63, 83, 92–93, 116, 118–20, 124, 126–27, 134, 149–52, 155; interspecies, 47–48; labor of, 6–7, 15–18, 49, 52–53, 61, 65–68, 73–74, 77–80; relations of, 89–90, 123–24, 125
surveillance, 7–8, 19–20, 30–33, 51
survival, 1–2, 6–7, 17, 44–45, 48–51, 55–57, 79–80, 83, 94–95, 101–2, 107–8, 115–16, 121–26, 130–32, 134–35, 139–40, 151, 162–63
Switzerland, Lukas Klinik, 141–42

TANF. *See* Temporary Assistance for Needy Families
Taylor, Linda, 129
Taylor, Sunaura, 79, 175n82
Tea, Michelle, 158
teaching, 55
Teish, Luisah, 49
Temporary Assistance for Needy Families (TANF), 9, 33, 106
testimony, 19–20; somatic, 137–38

www.ingramcontent.com/pod-product-compliance
Lightning Source LLC
Chambersburg PA
CBHW031057280326
41928CB00049B/781